Emerging Ecosystem-Centric Business Models for Sustainable Value Creation

Xenia Ziouvelou
National Centre for Scientific Research "Demokritos", Greece & University of Southampton, UK

Frank McGroarty
University of Southampton, UK

A volume in the Advances in Business Strategy and Competitive Advantage (ABSCA) Book Series

IGI Global
PUBLISHER of TIMELY KNOWLEDGE

Published in the United States of America by
IGI Global
Business Science Reference (an imprint of IGI Global)
701 E. Chocolate Avenue
Hershey PA, USA 17033
Tel: 717-533-8845
Fax: 717-533-8661
E-mail: cust@igi-global.com
Web site: http://www.igi-global.com

Library of Congress Cataloging-in-Publication Data

Names: Ziouvelou, Xenia, 1975- editor. | McGroarty, Frank (Francis Joseph Anthony), editor.
Title: Emerging ecosystem-centric business models for sustainable value creation / Xenia Ziouvelou and Frank McGroarty, editors.
Description: Hershey, PA : Business Science Reference, [2021] | Includes bibliographical references and index. | Summary: "This book explores emerging technology-enabled ecosystems and ecosystem-centric business models in theory and practice from a business and technological perspective"-- Provided by publisher.
Identifiers: LCCN 2020002787 (print) | LCCN 2020002788 (ebook) | ISBN 9781799848431 (hardcover) | ISBN 9781799853787 (paperback) | ISBN 9781799848448 (ebook)
Subjects: LCSH: Technological innovations--Management. | Sustainable development. | Embedded Internet devices.
Classification: LCC HD45 .E3645 2020 (print) | LCC HD45 (ebook) | DDC 658--dc23
LC record available at https://lccn.loc.gov/2020002787
LC ebook record available at https://lccn.loc.gov/2020002788

This book is published in the IGI Global book series Advances in Business Strategy and Competitive Advantage (ABSCA) (ISSN: 2327-3429; eISSN: 2327-3437)

British Cataloguing in Publication Data
A Cataloguing in Publication record for this book is available from the British Library.

Advances in Business Strategy and Competitive Advantage (ABSCA) Book Series

ISSN:2327-3429
EISSN:2327-3437

Editor-in-Chief: Patricia Ordóñez de Pablos, Universidad de Oviedo, Spain

MISSION

Business entities are constantly seeking new ways through which to gain advantage over their competitors and strengthen their position within the business environment. With competition at an all-time high due to technological advancements allowing for competition on a global scale, firms continue to seek new ways through which to improve and strengthen their business processes, procedures, and profitability.

The **Advances in Business Strategy and Competitive Advantage (ABSCA) Book Series** is a timely series responding to the high demand for state-of-the-art research on how business strategies are created, implemented and re-designed to meet the demands of globalized competitive markets. With a focus on local and global challenges, business opportunities and the needs of society, the **ABSCA** encourages scientific discourse on doing business and managing information technologies for the creation of sustainable competitive advantage.

COVERAGE

- Strategic Management
- Business Models
- Small and Medium Enterprises
- Tacit Knowledge
- Co-operative Strategies
- Economies of Scale
- Resource-Based Competition
- International Business Strategy
- Innovation Strategy
- Foreign Investment Decision Process

IGI Global is currently accepting manuscripts for publication within this series. To submit a proposal for a volume in this series, please contact our Acquisition Editors at Acquisitions@igi-global.com or visit: http://www.igi-global.com/publish/.

The Advances in Business Strategy and Competitive Advantage (ABSCA) Book Series (ISSN 2327-3429) is published by IGI Global, 701 E. Chocolate Avenue, Hershey, PA 17033-1240, USA, www.igi-global.com. This series is composed of titles available for purchase individually; each title is edited to be contextually exclusive from any other title within the series. For pricing and ordering information please visit http://www.igi-global.com/book-series/advances-business-strategy-competitive-advantage/73672. Postmaster: Send all address changes to above address.

Titles in this Series

For a list of additional titles in this series, please visit: http://www.igi-global.com/book-series/

ICT as Innovator Between Tourism and Culture
Célia M. Q. Ramos (University of Algarve, Portugal) Silvia Quinteiro (University of Algarve, Portugal) and Alexandra R. Gonçalves (University of Algarve, Portugal)
Business Science Reference • © 2022 • 330pp • H/C (ISBN: 9781799881650) • US $215.00

Impact of Disruptive Technologies on the Sharing Economy
Ford Lumban Gaol (Bina Nusantara University, Jakarta, Indonesia) Natalia Filimonova (Vladimir State University, Russia) and Chandan Acharya (College of Staten Island, City University of New York, USA)
Business Science Reference • © 2021 • 269pp • H/C (ISBN: 9781799803614) • US $245.00

Global Corporate Social Responsibility Initiatives for Reluctant Businesses
Syed Abdul Rehman Khan (School of Management and Engineering, Xuzhou University of Technology, Xuzhou, China & Department of Business Administration, ILMA University, Karachi, Pakistan & Beijing Key Laboratory of Urban Spatial Engineering, Beijing, China) Zhang Yu (Chang'an University, China) Mirela Panait (Petroleum-Gas University of Ploiesti, Romania & Institute of National Economy, Bucharest, Romania) Laeeq Razzak Janjua (Poznan University of Economics and Business, Poland) and Adeel Shah (Institute of Business Management, Pakistan)
Business Science Reference • © 2021 • 280pp • H/C (ISBN: 9781799839880) • US $195.00

Impacts and Implications for the Sports Industry in the Post-COVID-19 Era
Armand Faganel (University of Primorska, Slovenia) Igor Rižnar (University of Primorska, Slovenia) and Arne Baruca (Texas A&M University, USA)
Business Science Reference • © 2021 • 304pp • H/C (ISBN: 9781799867807) • US $215.00

Computational Thinking for Problem Solving and Managerial Mindset Training
Luisa Dall'Acqua (University of Bologna, Italy & LS TCO, Italy)
Business Science Reference • © 2021 • 293pp • H/C (ISBN: 9781799871262) • US $225.00

IGI Global
PUBLISHER of TIMELY KNOWLEDGE

701 East Chocolate Avenue, Hershey, PA 17033, USA
Tel: 717-533-8845 x100 • Fax: 717-533-8661
E-Mail: cust@igi-global.com • www.igi-global.com

Table of Contents

Detailed Table of Contents

Managing and measuring value co-creation in industrial services are emerging themes from the perspective of industry and scientific research. Thus, this chapter aims to review the literature in order to identify the criteria for value co-creation management and measuring used to measure value co-creation in the industrial service ecosystem. To achieve this goal, the authors conducted a systematic literature review and a content analysis of the portfolio resulting from the review. Based on the findings, eight criteria were listed for managing value co-creation in the B2B (business-to-business) services sector. In addition, they identified a lack of limited integration and interdependence between the criteria shown in the literature for cooperative service management among companies.

Considering the call for understanding the broader social and cultural context of value co-creation within emerging multilevel co-creative service systems, this research aims to explore the social and cultural processes along with psychological processes in terms of their influence on resource integration. It primarily adopts the customer perspective of resource integration. First, an integrative structure is developed and then the identified antecedents are positioned under relevant category proposing the multi-perspective VCC antecedent' framework. Further, the extant knowledge about VCC antecedents is used to set the agenda for future research. The study is based on an in-depth review of 85 key articles carefully extracted from a broad set of 1100 papers on VCC within the Scopus database. This review work provides a clear state of the art of VCC antecedents and has a direct implication for managers involved in designing the co-creation strategies for their customers.

One critical aspect of science is the ability to reproduce the same experiment by another researcher. In other to do so, the same ambient, variables, data, setup should be considered. The method tells how the original researcher planned and did their research, but how can others replicate or even advance the preview research? The scientific community has been focusing on efforts to increase transparency and reproducibility and develop a "culture of reproducibility." When researchers share their data, their workflow, and co-evolute a way of doing research, all the players win. The value co-creation is established in a business ecosystem. The actor who is part of the business platform by the co-creation can leverage the advantage of one or more partners that make up the platform. Thus, the knowledge created from the interaction between the different technological domains and knowledge shared on the platform can improve all the research and researchers. Stating that, this chapter proposes a business ecosystem model to ensure research repeatability.

Applying a business model approach, this chapter identifies various challenges in digital platform and platform-based business model development in the case of a physical port ecosystem. Using an empirical case, the chapter identifies the prerequisites and consequences of opportunities, value, and advantages for an existing ecosystem that aims to create a "digital twin." It contributes to academic discussions on the intersection of ecosystems, platforms, and business models by exploring the antecedents and controversies of configuring ecosystem boundaries in a digital context. Moreover, the chapter contributes to research by analyzing how a previously closed ecosystem seeks to open its boundaries and interfaces, both internally among the internal ecosystem members and externally to the outside business environment.

As latest advancements signify the fourth industrial revolution, artificial intelligence (AI) and internet of things (IoT) became the focal points for innovators. IoT-enabled technology can be used to gather and explore huge amounts of data from both virtual and physical environments, and AI provides the means for effectively processing and manipulating resulting information to optimize or automate processes. In this chapter, the related state of the art is presented, along with the characteristics that enable the creation of hybrid innovation ecosystems. An overview of IoT and AI platforms is included, which can be utilized even by non-experts to compose advanced cost-effective services. Also, related notions such as interoperability and engagement are also discussed. Although such components can be applied in a multitude of domains, to provide a concrete example of innovation enablement, the smart grid ecosystem is employed. Here, participants, either from the supply or the demand side, take advantage of IoT and AI technology to address new business requirements that arise.

The value chain of agri-food is radically changed due the fact that consumers, as well as various players in the agro-logistics chain, seek for increased and trustful food safety. Given the specific characteristics of the agri-food supply chain, having numerous origin points, several aggregations hubs at different levels and then again numerous points of sales, the need of a holistic approach in collecting, forwarding and interpreting data in an interoperable way is a dire need. In this chapter, the authors present the architecture of the traceability platform KalaΘosTM and its IoT management module called, GP CoreIoTTM. The KalaΘos infrastructure includes a network of sensors devices at farms, equipment, trucks, aggregation, processing, and logistics facilities, connected to a network of LoRa gateways. Its open architecture

Preface

A hyperconnected, constantly evolving world has emerged. A world where people (Internet of People), things (Internet of Things), and data (Internet of Data) are linked together, shaping the global economy while demanding new, innovative approaches for value creation. The era of hyper-connectivity is no longer characterized by centralized firm-centric business structures and traditional intra-firm and inter-firm processes (Ziouvelou and McGroarty, 2018). Open, distributed ecosystemic formations have started to emerge, utilizing cutting edge technologies such as Artificial Intelligence (AI), Internet of Things (IoT), Distributed Ledger Technologies, etc., aiming to harness the collective power, co-creation ability, and intelligence of the crowd, the data, and the environment in an open participatory value co-creation mode.

In this new ecosystemic formations, the question that emerges is how value is created/co-created among diverse stakeholders and value exchanges, and how it is captured in these dynamic digital ecosystems. In addition, one wonders whether the frameworks, models, and tools that organizations used to create value in the past will remain the same in this new physical, digital and phygital (physical and digital) business environment. Existing literature on ecosystems, business models, and business model innovation is starting to examine these aspects.

Emerging Digital Ecosystems and Ecosystem-Centric Business Models for Sustainable Value Creation explores emerging value creation and co-creation in emerging technology-enabled ecosystems and ecosystem-centric business models in theory and practice, from a business and technological perspective, and in a range of industrial settings (such as FinTech (Financial Technology) markets, Industrial services ecosystems, Ports and Digital Twins, Smart cities, Smart Farming and Agro-logistic, Scientific Publishing, PropTech (Real Estate Technology) markets) aiming to contribute to the existing knowledge of innovative technology-advanced ecosystems and business models, facilitating their design, implementation, and sustainable value creation and co-creation. It examines the dynamics of this technology-powered revolution and how it is influencing the foundations of value creation and business modeling in novel ecosystemic formations across the HMD triangle: Human, Machine, and Data.

ORGANIZATION OF THE BOOK

The book is organized into seven chapters. A brief description of each of the chapters follows:

Chapter 1 identifies the key factors for measuring value co-creation in the industrial service ecosystem. The chapter reviews existing research in the area and identify eight key criteria for managing value co-creation in the B2B (business to business) services sector while examining existing challenges.

Chapter 2 examines customer-centered antecedents of value co-creation ecosystems. The authors of this chapter, focus on understanding the broader social and cultural context of value co-creation within emerging multilevel co-creative service systems. As their research explores the social and cultural processes along with psychological processes and explore the implications in designing co-creation strategies for customers.

Chapter 3 takes a scientific community-driven ecosystem approach and debate about co-creation and co-evolution scientific practices. The authors examine value co-creation in a diverse context, namely scientific publishing, adopting a business ecosystem approach in order to jointly co-created shared value.

Chapter 4 adopts an ecosystem-centric and business model approach in a "digital twin" context. The authors of this chapter focus their discussion in the intersection of ecosystems, platforms, and business models by exploring the antecedents and controversies of configuring ecosystem boundaries in a digital context. They further analyse how a closed ecosystem seeks to open its boundaries and interfaces, both internally among the internal ecosystem members and externally to the outside business environment.

Chapter 5 presents the latest advancements that signify the 4th industrial revolution, namely Artificial Intelligence (AI) and Internet of Things (IoT) and the emerging ecosystems that are empowered by them. The author presents an overview of AI and IoT platforms that enable the creation of hybrid innovation ecosystems, that create share value and address new business requirements.

Chapter 6 examines IoT ecosystems in the context of smart-farming and agro-logistic. The authors of this chapter detail data-and device-driven IoT business models in ecosystems and value chains that are radically changed due to deman-driven forces. It is concluded that a systematic and holistic approach in such data-and device driven IoT ecosystems is needed.

Chapter 7 addresses the issue of financial technology (FinTech) ecosystems for consumers and business. The authors of this chapter propose a modeling framework that connects civil society and industrial community in order to promote social work activities that are financially rewarded through a FinTech as a platform. The study explores crowd-engagement in such a technology-driven and crowd-driven ecosystem in impacting the physical, social, and financial status of individual participant thus, promoting a healthy society.

Xenia Ziouvelou
National Centre for Scientific Research "Demokritos", Greece & University of Southampton, UK

Frank McGroarty
University of Southampton, UK

REFERENCES

Ziouvelou & McGroarty. (2018). A Business Model Framework for Crowd-Driven IoT Ecosystems. *International Journal of Social Ecology and Sustainable Development, 9*(3), 14-33.

Chapter 1
Key Factors for Measuring Value Co-Creation in the Industrial Service Ecosystem

Andrei Bonamigo
https://orcid.org/0000-0002-6670-9755
Fluminense Federal University, Brazil

Marcela Cohen Martelotte
Fluminense Federal University, Brazil

Julia Fonseca Mourão
Fluminense Federal University, Brazil

ABSTRACT

Managing and measuring value co-creation in industrial services are emerging themes from the perspective of industry and scientific research. Thus, this chapter aims to review the literature in order to identify the criteria for value co-creation management and measuring used to measure value co-creation in the industrial service ecosystem. To achieve this goal, the authors conducted a systematic literature review and a content analysis of the portfolio resulting from the review. Based on the findings, eight criteria were listed for managing value co-creation in the B2B (business-to-business) services sector. In addition, they identified a lack of limited integration and interdependence between the criteria shown in the literature for cooperative service management among companies.

DOI: 10.4018/978-1-7998-4843-1.ch001

1. INTRODUCTION

Value co-creation in the service industry has been revealed as a strategy for innovating, increasing economic gains and improving the business performance in economic, social and environmental aspects (Ekman, Raggio, & Thompson, 2016; Lacoste, 2016; Ma et al., 2019). Therefore, measuring value co-creation is meaningful to the decision makers in the industrial service ecosystem.

The value co-creation concept has been developed in different areas. In general, value co-creation refers to the joint collaborative actions among service providers and customers, resulting in products or services improvements (Bolton and Saxena-Iyer (2009). For Grönroos (2012), value co-creation can occur only through direct interactions. However, these interactions are not an automatic shortcut to value creation; instead, they form a platform for joint value co-creation.

Industrial services are studied from a variety of perspectives. Jackson and Cooper (1988) consider industrial services as the ones that are offered to industrial customers. Gitzel, Schmitz, Fromm, Isaksson, and Setzer (2016) defined industrial services as activities that directly support a customer's value creation by influencing positively their industrial production processes.

In this way, by creating value in industrial services in a Business-to-Business (B2B) environment, the authors define that industrial services comprise the offering of benefits between companies in a way that adds value to the business process.

In developed economies, many manufacturing companies of industrial goods obtain more than 50% of their profits through services. In this way, the value co-creation is considered as a strategy to maximize gains through new or better services that are offered (Huang, 2018; Strähle, Füllemann, & Bendig, 2012).

However, the uncertainty of the contracting company and the service provider about the effectiveness of the expectation, as well as the internal and/or external partners' contributions, have been identified as theoretical and practical gaps in the ecosystem of industrial services (Jaakkola & Hakanen, 2013; Janeschek, Hottum, Kicherer, & Bienzeisler, 2013; West, Gaiardelli, Resta, & Kujawski, 2018; Wu, 2017). In addition, the uncertainty of the contracting company, regarding the renewal or the creation of future contracts with the service provider, creates a wide range of relationship expectations, which have been shown to be subjective and intuitive from the client's point of view (Lin & Hsieh, 2011; Olya, Altinay, & De Vita, 2018; Steinbach, Wallenburg, & Selviaridis, 2018).

Thus, it is necessary to measure value co-creation in industrial services, so that contract risks can be managed (Van Poucke, Matthyssens, van Weele, & Van Bockhaven, 2018). Besides that, quantifying the joint collaboration impact in the business (Wikström & L'Espoir Decosta, 2018), and supporting managers' decisions, regarding the performance of their partners.

Although being relevant to measure value co-creation in industrial services, it is a challenge to quantify a subjective and multidimensional concept. As many experts have already highlighted before, what it is not measured cannot be managed. This famous quote is constantly attributed to the importance of performance indicators in organizations. Measuring what is being done, enables a better management to achieve the desired goals.

According to the European Commission (2003, apud Saltelli, Nardo, Saisana, and Tarantola (2005), "composite indicators are a way of distilling reality into a manageable form". They can be used to summarize complex or multidimensional issues in order to support decision-makers. Thus, the analysis of indicators is seen as an essential management tool in monitoring and evaluation activities, allowing the progress diagnosis, the quality improvements, the problems solving, besides warning about the need for change (Lin & Wu, 2011; S. Prakash, Soni, Rathore, & Singh, 2017; Smets et al., 2018).

The production of data that describes the impacts of a company's actions becomes a fundamental tool for evaluating, planning and giving support to the managers for a better decision-making. Thereby, several studies are being developed regarding the construction of value co-creation indicators in the industrial service sector (Malik et al., 2018; Ng & Priyono, 2018; Takenaka, Nishino, & Nishikori, 2018).

Based on the issues presented above, this chapter aims to review the literature in order to identify the criteria for value co-creation management and measuring used to measure value co-creation in the industrial service ecosystem.

2. METHODOLOGY

In this work, the researchers followed the method proposed by Helio Aisenberg Ferenhof and Fernandes (2016) called Systematic Search Flow (SSF) in order to conduct the literature review. The SSF method is composed by four phases as presented in Figure 1: (i) research protocol; (ii) analysis; (iii) synthesis; (iv) write.

Based on the SSF method, the researchers present the four phases, divided into eight sub-phases (steps) reproduced in the research process.

Research Protocol

In the first step, the researchers established a research plan containing the question to be answered: "*What are the indicators available in the literature to measure the value co-creation in industrial services?*". This also involved some keywords and a set of inclusion and exclusion criteria.

Figure 1. The phases of Systematic Search Flow method
Source: Ferenhof and Fernandes (2016)

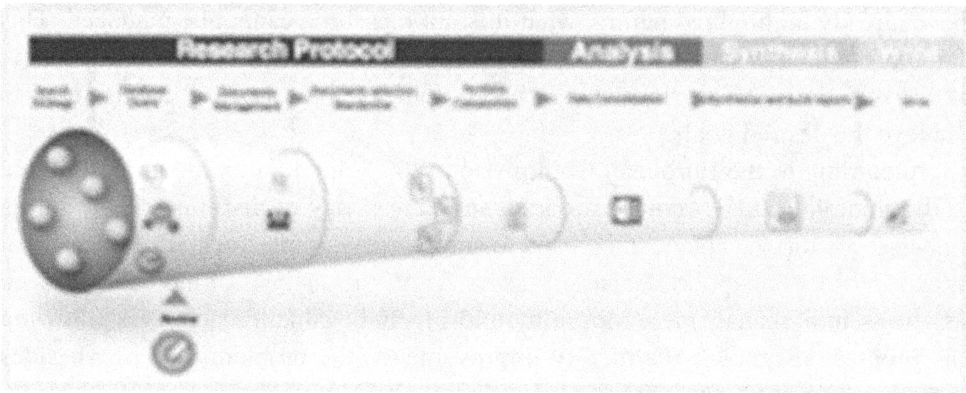

Then, the researchers defined the following research query: ((“industrial service” OR “service industr*”) AND (“indicators” OR “performance” OR “metric”) AND (“co-creation” OR “co-production” OR cocreation)). In this search, the inclusion criteria were: empirical papers, peer-reviewed, English, Spanish, Portuguese; and indexed in the following databases: Compendex, Ebesco, Emerald, ProQuest, Science Direct, Scopus and Web of Knowledge.

In the third step, the researchers looked for this combination based in the title, keywords and abstract. The search on the databases was made on June 27th of 2019 and returned 885 documents. Then, the researchers managed the documents by importing the references to a reference manager software. Later, the duplicate ones were deleted, resulting in 828 documents.

In the fourth step, the researchers scanned the documents’ abstracts and, when appropriate, read parts of the texts to make sure that they are within the scope of interest. This allowed a reduction to 798 documents, which fulfilled the research criteria. After this, the researchers composed the bibliographic portfolio for analysis, exporting the main information (author, year, title and journal name) from the reference manager software to a spreadsheet. Then, the researchers went through each data entry editing the content by coding it according to the listed criteria.

In the fifth step, the researchers also included the documents available with full-text access through Google®, Google Scholar®, Microsoft Academic Search®, Research Gate®, CAPES (Coordination of Improvement of Higher Education), or sent by email to the authors. It is worth mentioning that the researchers excluded gray literature such as reports, conference papers, non-academic researches and other languages.

Additionally, as recommended by the SSF method, the researchers produced a 'knowledge matrix' in a datasheet consisting of relevant criteria for establishing our understanding of measuring the value criterion in industrial services. Also, the researchers included other important information in the spreadsheet, such as findings, definition, gaps and citation in order to create the knowledge matrix.

In the sixth step, following the Synthesis phase, the data of each document were brought together in one spreadsheet. This revision enabled the researchers to categorize the findings under themes, which helped clarifying what it could be learned about indicators for measuring the value co-creation in industrial services.

In the seventh step, all authors worked jointly in order to identify themes for each individual entry. These discussion rounds also led to a further number of paper reductions, based in Figure 1, that showed the phases of the Systematic Search Flow method. At the end, 85 papers were included in the literature review. Finally, the last stage of our literature review process was devoted to the write-up of the findings. Table 1.

Table 1. Resulting bibliographic portfolio

Data base	Number of works found
Science Direct	480
Emerald	323
Scopus	16
Compendex	36
Web of Science	19
Ebesco	11
Total	**885**
Duplicates	**-57**
Total works for analysis	**828**

Source: Authors

(i) Analysis

Based on the resulting portfolio from the previous phase, the researchers conducted the content analysis of the documents. Content analysis was based on Bardin (2011). Consequently, the units of analysis were defined as the posteriori from the found contexts units in the literature review findings.

(ii) Synthesis

In this phase, the researcher synthesizes the most relevant research topics and build reports based on each analysis done on the previous phase.

(iii) Write

The final phase intends to consolidate the results by writing them up.

3. RESULTS AND DISCUSSION

The 85 papers were screened based on the full text using the criteria defined in Section two (i), resulting in 17 retained papers. Then, these 17 papers were completely read in order to define the units of analysis and context, according to Bardin (2010). This resulting portfolio of papers, which will be analyzed in this work, is presented in Table 2.

Table 2. Review portfolio

Code	Authors and Year	Title	Documents
A1	Ruiz-Alba, Soares, Rodríguez-Molina, and Frías-Jamilena (2019)	Servitization strategies from customers' perspective: the moderating role of co-creation	Journal of Business & Industrial Marketing
A2	Jääskeläinen and Thitz (2018)	Prerequisites for performance measurement supporting purchaser-supplier collaboration	Benchmarking: An International Journal
A3	Olya et al. (2018)	An exploratory study of value added services	Journal of Services Marketing
A4	Zhang, Tingting, Torres, and Chen (2018)	Engaging customers in value co-creation or co-destruction online	Journal of Services Marketing
A5	Braun, Pereira, Sellitto, and Borchardt (2017)	Value co-creation in maintenance services: case study in the mechanical industry	Business Process Management Journal
A6	Taghizadeh, Jayaraman, Ismail, and Rahman (2016)	Scale development and validation for DART model of value co-creation process on innovation strategy	Journal of Business & Industrial Marketing
A7	Ceric, D'Alessandro, Soutar, and Johnson (2016)	Using blueprinting and benchmarking to identify marketing resources that help co-create customer value	Journal of Business Research

continues on following page

Table 2. Continued

Code	Authors and Year	Title	Documents
A8	Santos-Vijande, López-Sánchez, and Rudd (2016)	Frontline employees' collaboration in industrial service innovation: routes of co-creation's effects on new service performance	Journal of the Academy of Marketing Science
A9	M. Kohtamäki and J. Partanen (2016)	Co-creating value from knowledge-intensive business services in manufacturing firms: The moderating role of relationship learning in supplier-customer interactions	Journal of Business Research
A10	Greer (2015)	Defective co-creation: Developing a typology of consumer dysfunction in professional services	European Journal of Marketing
A11	Kohtamäki and Helo (2015)	Industrial services – the solution provider's stairway to heaven or highway to hell?	Benchmarking: An International Journal
A12	J. Zhang and He (2014)	Key dimensions of brand value co-creation and its impacts upon customer perception and brand performance: An empirical research in the context of industrial service	Nankai Business Review International
A13	Rubalcaba, Michel, Sundbo, Brown, and Reynoso (2012)	Shaping, organizing, and rethinking service innovation: a multidimensional framework	Journal of Service Management
A14	Sofianti, Suryadi, Govindaraju, and Prihartono (2012)	Measuring the performance of customer knowledge co-creation	IEEE 6th International Conference on Management of Innovation and Technology
A15	Enz and Lambert (2012)	Using cross-functional, cross-firm teams to co-create value: The role of financial measures	Industrial Marketing Management
A16	Ngoc Thuy (2011)	Using service convenience to reduce perceived cost	Marketing Intelligence & Planning
A17	G. Prakash (2011)	Service quality in supply chain: empirical evidence from Indian automotive industry	Supply Chain Management: An International Journal

It is worth highlighting the diversity of countries where these studies were realized, such as Spain [A1], Malaysia [A6], Australia [A7, A10], China [A12], USA [A15], Vietnam [A16] and India [A17]. About the application areas, the authors can list the following: pharmaceutical sector [A1], telecommunication industry [A6, A7], health-care and financial services [A10], air transport services [A16], automobile manufacturing industry [A17].

Regarding the methodology used in the studies, some of them applied a qualitative approach [A2, A4, A5, A10, A12, A15], some conducted a survey [A1, A6, A7,

A8, A9, A12, A14, A16, A17] or used secondary data [A3]. Considering those who conducted a survey, some used Likert-type scale [A1, A6, A8, A9, A12, A14, A17]; and some listed the survey questions in their paper [A6, A7, A9, A12, A14, A17]. Finally, about the statistical methods used to analyze survey data, most of the studies performed structural equation modelling (SEM) [A1, A6, A8, A9, A12, A16, A17].

Next, eight units of analysis were defined, and the units of contexts were listed, resulting in 35 units of context, as can be seen in Table 3.

Table 3. Criteria for the management of value co-creation in industrial services

Record unit	Context unit	Frequency
Satisfaction & Quality	A4 – Value co-creation results when engagement leads to customer delight. A7 – Blueprinting used to assess service. A16 – Perceived service quality as consumer judgment of product excellence. A16 – Relationship between service convenience, service quality and customer satisfaction. A17 – Scale to measure service quality in the supply chain. A17 – Source of value for the organization, positively influencing the customer.	6
Performance indicator	A1 – The degree to which companies engage in the co-creation of service will influence their performance results. A2 –Performance measurement prerequisites to support strategic purchasing, aiming at value co-creation. A3 – Development of a model based on eight indicators of the prosperity for simulation of value added in service industries. A6 – DART model (dialogue, access, risk assessment, and transparency). A14 – Company performance with competitor. A14 – Level of customer visit.	6
Employees	A4 - Employee behavior influences customers' engagement in value co-creation, or co-destruction, in online channels. A8 – Employees actively contribute to innovation, and consequently to the co-creation of value. A8 – Employees play a key role in the success of service innovation. A8 – Co-creation seen as employee empowerment. A15 – Difference in value co-creation when a company is linked to key customers and suppliers through cross-functional team and when it is not.	5
Customer relationship	A4 – The duality of customer engagement-induced value co-creation/co-destruction in online channels. A9 – Relationship learning as a moderator of the relation between a supplier's knowledge-intensive business services offerings and a customer's sales performance. A10 – Customer's participation is critical to value co-creation. A12 – The branding process involves different kinds of value co-creation activities on interfaces between firm-employees, firm-customers, employees-customers, and firm-other stakeholders. A14 – Customer relationship management (CRM).	5

continues on following page

Table 3. Continued

Record unit	Context unit	Frequency
Value perception	A1 – Firms cannot create value individually. A5 – Emphasizes the value co-creation from outsourcing. A5 – companies outsource their non-core competencies, resulting in a joint value co-creation process. A11 – The offer of fuller market packages in order to add value to core products.	4
Customer confidence & trust	A4 – Value co-creation also results when customers feel that their feedback is important and/or valued/recognized. A6 – Company should expose the potential risk of using upcoming product/service, in order to gain customers' confidence. A7 – Benchmarking to identify best internal practices, and how they affect customers' trust. A7 – Consumers' trust is crucial for value co-creation.	4
Value co-destruction	A4 – Value co-creation and co-destruction can exist simultaneously. A10 – Previously co-created value destruction. A10 – Misbehavior can be directed at a company's employees, merchandise, financial assets, customers, and facilities.	3
Innovation	A6 – Companies are making efforts to create value with their consumers as part of the innovation process in order to gain competitive advantage. A13 – Employee-driven innovation.	2

Based on the content analysis, the authors discuss here each of the 35 units of context in order to identify the criteria for managing value co-creation in industrial services. The authors start with "satisfaction & quality".

Customer satisfaction is directly linked to the perceived quality of products and services provided by the organization (G. Prakash, 2011). Therefore, quality in customer perception is considered an important indicator of value co-creation (G. Prakash, 2011), and measuring customer satisfaction and perceived quality becomes relevant.

The literature is also concerned with the creation of a scale to measure the service quality in the manufacturing supply chain. G. Prakash (2011) presented a model and related set of propositions to demonstrate that the flow of service elements, embedded in the product flow, is a source of value addition for the organization and influences the supplier.

Some studies have investigated the relationship between customers' satisfaction, and service quality, along with other elements. Ngoc Thuy (2011) studied the relationship between service convenience, customer satisfaction, and perceived service quality of domestic airline services. The research results have shown that service convenience has a positive effect on customers' satisfaction, and on service quality.

Quality can also be understood as the consumers' judgment about a company (Ngoc Thuy, 2011). For this reason, one of the practices used in organizations, regarding service analysis, is the blueprinting. "Service blueprinting can be used to assess the value of the service and, consequently, to take appropriate action to improve service quality and overall service value" (Ceric et al., 2016). It provides a set of tools for identifying the essential inside-out (operand) and outside-in (operant) resources and capabilities to create and deliver customer value.

Finally, concerning online channels, Zhang et al. (2018) conducted a research where customers described their personal experiences with online engagement in value co-creation, and co-destruction, incidents. One of the findings of their research is that service speed and quality are important for stimulating value co-creation. Another finding is that value co-creation occurs when engagement leads to customer delight, for online customer engagement.

With regard to "performance indicator", Jääskeläinen and Thitz (2018) initially highlights the importance of performance indicators as a supporter of value creation. Thus, there is concern with the production of measurement scales and performance measurement that would contribute to the added value. In particular, prerequisites to support performance measurement stand out focus on measuring purchaser supplier collaboration. The literature provides parameters to measure the true value of purchaser-supplier collaboration, as responsiveness to customer, competencies and time to market. In this way, collaboration agents are actively working together sharing knowledge, information, risks and profits to achieve common goals (Jääskeläinen & Thitz, 2018).

Ruiz-Alba et al. (2019) investigate the impact of different levels of services on performance by using co-creation as a moderating factor. The performance indicator of their study is based on financial and market performance.

Focusing on the process of co-creation with the client, a study was proposed to validate the scale measurements of DART constructs under four dimensions of value co-creation (dialogue, access, risk assessment, and transparency). The results suggest a significant relationship between the value co-creation process, the client and innovation strategy, indicating that higher level of practicing innovation strategy leads to more market performance (Taghizadeh et al., 2016).

Other aspect of the performance indicator is related with measurement of customer knowledge management (CKM). It is argued that a good CKM brings benefits to company in term of customer loyalty, customer trust, customer satisfaction and quality and timing of customer relationship. The study also presents competitor company performance and customer visit level data (Sofianti et al., 2012).

Olya et al. (2018) uses eight indicators of the prosperity index to develop a value-added predictor in service industries. The prosperity index indicators are: economy; entrepreneurship and opportunity; governance; education; health; safety and security; personal freedom; social capita. Based on a sample of 104 countries, they conclude that not only the prosperous countries achieve a high level of valued added in service industries, but also some countries in which important conditions are not at the same level of prosperous countries. This result shows the complexity of interactions between these conditions, to the achievement of a high level of valued added.

In relation to employees' participation in value co-creation practices, studies bring new perspectives. One of them is co-creating value through frontline employees. About this, it can be said that the employees actively contribute to innovation and, consequently, to the co-creation of value (Santos-Vijande et al., 2016). Their research points out that there are three components of employee sentiment, which are important for service innovation, and confirm that frontline employee co-creation can enhance these components. As a result, motivation, commitment and satisfaction of frontline employees can be increased in the co-creation process. It also can be concluded that, by generating a sense of belonging, employees feel more motivated and committed and, consequently, more satisfied with their work (Santos-Vijande et al., 2016).

Therefore, it is clear that co-creation is a way to promote the empowerment of employees, generating visible changes in the organization. Co-creation programs can positively influence project decision makers, which will culminate in service innovations. Thus, employee satisfaction with co-creation, results in service innovations (Santos-Vijande et al., 2016).

About online channels, Zhang et al. (2018) points out key factors of employee behavior that can impact value co-creation, by positively influencing online customer engagement. These factors are: responsiveness, empathy, helpfulness and politeness.

Moreover, considering cross-functional teams, Enz and Lambert (2012) developed a method for measuring value co-creation in financial terms, exploring the differences when a company is linked to key customers and key suppliers through cross-functional teams and when it is not. The conclusion indicates that value co-creation was higher when cross-functional, cross-firm teams were involved.

Concerning "customer relationship", the literature considers it an important indicator for value creation, as the customer participates in the process of co-creation. Furthermore, there is duality of customer engagement that can both co-create and destroy value (Zhang et al., 2018), which can be related with the customers' level of participation in the co-creation process.

Greer (2015) mentions that there is an optimum level of customer participation, because participation, in quality or quantity, beyond this level will reduce the value of a service encounter. And although consumers may be unaware of this optimal participative behavior, the findings of Greer (2015) study provide empirical evidence that professional service providers delimit value co-creation with thresholds of engagement that consumers ideally not cross.

Customer relationship can be measured through the customer relationship management (CRM), which is responsible for measuring the productivity of customer knowledge co-creation. As a result, CRM brings benefits to company in term of customer loyalty; customer trust; customer satisfaction and quality; and timing of customer relationship (Sofianti et al., 2012).

About the relationship between firm-employees, firm-customers, employees-customers, and firm-other stakeholders, J. Zhang and He (2014) detected that the branding process involves different kinds of value co-creation activities on interfaces between these actors. To study this J. Zhang and He (2014) develop a conceptual model to explore the key components in the co-creation customer experience, involving as observations employees as stakeholders in the development of a strong brand.

Marko Kohtamäki and Jukka Partanen (2016) tested the effect of relationship learning on the relation between a supplier's knowledge-intensive business services offerings and a customer's sales performance, in the supplier-customer relationship. They found out that there is a positive moderating role of the relationship learning, enabling value co-creation.

Regarding "value perception", the studies claim that it comes from a variety of perspectives. It is noteworthy that companies cannot create value individually because it comes from collaboration between partners. In this sense, the concept of "servitization" emerges. Servitization can be understood as a strategy that contributes to the development of the customers' processes and capabilities in a B-to-B context, through close collaboration in the design of services that are jointly co-created. It also can be seen as a "value co-creation" process, systems and structure enabling value perception as resources from co-creation. Management systems integrated with value creation processes enable chain optimization and consequently generate a competitive advantage (Ruiz-Alba et al., 2019).

To investigate if the perception about the servitization strategies adopted by firms is affected by services' levels offered to their customers, Ruiz-Alba et al. (2019) performed a quantitative research creating measurable indicators. Ruiz-Alba et al. (2019) also investigated if co-creation moderates the impact of service types on servitization and on performance, and further, if co-creation moderates the impact of servitization on performance. It is worth mentioning that in their study, co-creation was defined as co-creation of design in services. Research findings suggest that when the co-creation level is high, the advanced services that were moderated by co-creation showed a significant impact on performance, through the mediating effect of servitization.

Still with respect to servitization, Kohtamaki and Helo (2015) listed three maturity levels of servitization in manufacturing companies: equipment providers; solution providers; performance providers. The last one refers to firms that instead of selling products or services, they "bill" the services on the value created, or performance. Here, the intention is enabling the customer to continuously increase the co-created value.

In this way, perception of value is responsible for indicating increased offer of more complete packages, focused on customer combination of goods, services, support and knowledge adds value to the core (Kohtamaki & Helo, 2015).

As well as servitization, outsourcing is a strategy for value co-creation. By focusing only on their core business, many companies have outsourced part of their processes to service providers, resulting in a joint value co-creation process (Enz & Lambert, 2012).

The next context units are about "value co-destruction". Value co-destruction can be defined as "a decline in an individual's or an organization's well-being, resulting from an interactional process between them." (Plé & Chumpitaz Cáceres, 2010). Customers are value co-creators, but they can also be value co-destructors destructors if they do not perform their functions properly (Zhang et al., 2018).

There are some circumstances in the interaction customer-organization that can cause value co-destruction. Misunderstandings or malfunctioning resources, for example, can result in angry customers, that may post, online, adverse comments about the company, reducing sales and leading to loss of customers.

Zhang et al. (2018) develop a theoretical model to understand value co-creation and co-destruction, through customer engagement in online channels. They point out that the co-destruction of value may occur at both accidental and intentional levels, and define three categories of customers' value co-destruction in online channels: people, organization, and technology. When customers feel unjustly treated, they tend to desire revenge to punish the company, and to retaliate the company on social media, by warning other customers. That is why the authors concluded that customer retaliation, and revenge, positively influence customer engagement in value co-destruction in online channels. Employees that show rudeness and lack of empathy in their behavior, long delays resulting from company's incompetency, the negative attitudes of the company, and technology failures, also positively influence customer engagement in value co-destruction.

It is interesting noticing that co-creation co-destruction are two aspects of the value co-creation process that can exist simultaneously. Zhang et al. (2018) highlights that the criticality of consumer participation in value co-creation presents both an opportunity and a threat to professional service organizations.

In her research, Greer (2015) addresses the concept of "defective co-creation behavior", which does not necessarily destroy value previously co-created, but obstructs value creation. The defective co-creation behavior occurs when consumers fail to provide sufficient quality or quantity inputs to facilitate value co-creation. To investigate this, Greer (2015) analyzed critical incidents of defective co-creation, collected from health-care and financial service providers. Previously studies had identified some types of dysfunctional behavior, which were confirmed in her study. They are: property abuse; fraudulence; verbal abuse; physical aggression.

In addition to these for forms of dysfunctional behavior, this study identified two new types: under participation and over participation, which empirically indicates that there is an optimum level of customer participation, in order to facilitate the value co-creation.

With regard to "confidence and trust", the authors found out that confidence can be understood as a specific resource for creating customer value. From a new direction in service management research, there is the benchmarking practice used for such findings. Benchmarking identifies the best internal practices defined by formalized accreditation processes, and how these practices impact on consumers' trust in the organization, which is crucial for value co-creation (Ceric et al., 2016).

Taghizadeh et al. (2016) says that in order to build trust and confidence with customers, and treat them as effective value co-creators, the company should show them the potential risk of using the product/service. Beyond this, the company must show transparency of information related to the product/service, regarding pricing and features.

For Zhang et al. (2018), when customers realize that their feedback is important or recognized by the company, they feel valued. It positively influences customer engagement in online channels, resulting in value co-creation.

Finally, the last context unit is about "innovation". An examined paper claims that the popularity of innovative product development among consumers is making companies to rely more on innovation activities, in order to meet their demands. As a result, companies have found, in the process of co-creating value with their consumers, the answers to gain competitive advantages (Taghizadeh et al., 2016). And besides this, by allowing consumer to personalize their products and services, the company customize consumer experiences. Therefore, value co-creation enables companies to deal with heterogeneous markets in order to meet consumer needs.

In this sense, the cooperation between multiple actors allows access to complementary resources, such as equipment, financial assets, knowledge, among others; so that innovation is jointly driven among the authors. Additionally, imitability is restricted by competitors as it incorporates resources from different areas limited to the competitor developing or replicating the products or services provided through cooperation between companies (Bonamigo, 2017).

Considering this approach, the changing role of consumer from an external element to a co-producer can be accomplished by a series of co-creation activities. The DART activities, named "dialogue, access, risk assessment, and transparency", as a meaningful co-creation with customers, is a systematically process that can transform consumer efforts, skills and knowledge into unique competitive advantages (Taghizadeh et al., 2016).

Taghizadeh et al. (2016) study the effect of the DART model of value co-creation on innovation strategy, and the influence of innovation strategy on companies' market performance. The research was applied in the telecommunication sector, and the results indicate a statistically significant relationship between the value co-creation process and the innovation strategy. In addition, it was concluded that the innovation strategy is directly related to companies' market performance.

More specifically, the findings concerning the DART model in their research indicate that the "Dialogue, Risk Assessment and Transparency" activities play an influential role in formulating innovation strategies for the telecommunication sector. The "dialogue" session with customers, make it easier to the company identifying future opportunities and threats to develop new services. Besides this, as consumers become co-creators of value, company should inform them about the potential risk related to the consumption of a particular service or product, in order to gain consumer confidence and treat them as effective value co-creators. Finally, to achieve value co-creation, companies must have "transparency" of information regarding their services or products (Taghizadeh et al., 2016).

According to Lai, Jackson, and Jiang (2017), information transparency, which is considered critical to these authors, can be mitigated through the Internet of Things (IoT) concept use, as it can move the flow of information with transparency, better control, and efficiency.

Rubalcaba et al. (2012) mention the researches that investigate the innovations that significantly changed how customers co-create value. In this way, some studies consider different co-creation roles: user, payer, and buyer. Depending on the context, the same customer might perform the three roles.

Along with customers, employees have participated in innovation processes and consequently in co-creation value. Even when the customer perspective is the focus, it is important to keep the employee perspective, because employees and customers appear complementary for service innovation. Communication between employees and customers is important and can enhance customers' perceptions of quality, while suggesting ideas that can lead to innovations (Rubalcaba et al., 2012). Employee-driven innovation is beneficial as it makes them part of the process and creates a sense of satisfaction. Likewise, when they actively contribute to innovation, and consequently to value creation, they play a key role in the success of service innovation.

Rubalcaba et al. (2012) conclude that service innovation must combine value creation for the service organization, customers, employees and society in a balanced way, to be successful in the long run. On the other hand, H. A. Ferenhof, Bonamigo, and Forcellini (2016) point out that innovation generated through cooperation between companies can jeopardize players' knowledge. In this sense, trust among players and the creation of confidentiality terms are applicable devices to mitigate innovation risks through cooperation between multiple companies (Grönroos & Helle, 2010; Hakanen & Jaakkola, 2012; Heim, Han, & Ghobadian, 2018).

However, Dolinska and d'Aquino (2016) mention that the co-evolution of innovation is a highly dynamic process, which demands management of tensions between the cooperating actors' interfaces, given that unexpected effects and interactions may occur in the co-evolutionary process of companies. And Somda, Kamuanga, and Tollens (2005), point out that the lack of technology can be a limiting factor for motivating cooperation between actors as well as limiting company productivity.

4 CONCLUSION

This chapter aims to review the literature in order to identify the criteria for value co-creation management and measuring used to measure value co-creation in the industrial service ecosystem. Eight criteria were listed for the co-creation management in industrial services. Among them: Satisfaction & Quality; Performance indicator; Employees; Customer relationship; Value perception; Customer confidence & trust; Value co-destruction and Innovation.

In the paper's portfolio, we note that some studies empirically investigate the impact of value co-creation on performance indices, such as sales performance, market performance, and innovation performance. However, we observed that the indicators adopted to manage value co-creation are poorly detailed on how the metrics are empirically operationalized. In addition, we identified that the indicators for the management of co-creation in industrial services are disintegrated, which is an aspect that hinders cooperation management.

Once the key elements for measuring value co-creation are pointed out in this study, we identify the theoretical and practical contributions. Regarding theory, it can be said that this study fills a theoretical gap regarding the recognition of key factors to measure value co-creation, as well as their weaknesses in existing control metrics. Considering the practical contributions, it is possible to recognize the basic elements for managing the cooperation between multiple companies, as well as to support the decision regarding the control variables for the value co-creation management in industrial services.

For future studies, the authors recommend the development of indicators that bring together the eight key elements presented in this study. A second study involves empirically testing these control elements, which were identified in theory by the authors.

As limitations of this study, the authors evidence that few studies present the detailing of how they empirically operationalized the metrics presented.

REFERENCES

Bardin, L. (2011). Análise de conteúdo. 3. reimp. Lisboa: Ediçoes, 70.

Bolton, R., & Saxena-Iyer, S. (2009). Interactive Services: A Framework, Synthesis and Research Directions. *Journal of Interactive Marketing*, *23*(1), 91–104. doi:10.1016/j.intmar.2008.11.002

Bonamigo, A. (2017). A management model for dairy production based on the ecosystem business concept (Doutorado). Universidade Federal de Santa Catarina, UFSC, Florianópolis.

Braun, E. L., Pereira, G. M., Sellitto, M. A., & Borchardt, M. (2017). Value co-creation in maintenance services: Case study in the mechanical industry. *Business Process Management Journal*, *23*(5), 984–999. doi:10.1108/BPMJ-09-2014-0090

Ceric, A., D'Alessandro, S., Soutar, G., & Johnson, L. (2016). Using blueprinting and benchmarking to identify marketing resources that help co-create customer value. *Journal of Business Research*, *69*(12), 5653–5661. doi:10.1016/j.jbusres.2016.03.073

Dolinska, A., & d'Aquino, P. (2016). Farmers as agents in innovation systems. Empowering farmers for innovation through communities of practice. *Agricultural Systems*, *142*, 122–130. doi:10.1016/j.agsy.2015.11.009

Ekman, P., Raggio, R. D., & Thompson, S. M. (2016). Service network value co-creation: Defining the roles of the generic actor. *Industrial Marketing Management*, *56*, 51–62. doi:10.1016/j.indmarman.2016.03.002

Enz, M. G., & Lambert, D. M. (2012). Using cross-functional, cross-firm teams to co-create value: The role of financial measures. *Industrial Marketing Management*, *41*(3), 495–507. doi:10.1016/j.indmarman.2011.06.041

Ferenhof, H. A., Bonamigo, A., & Forcellini, F. A. (2016). Ecossistema de negócios: o conhecimento pode estar em risco. In M. Macedo, C. S. Teixeira, & S. L. Jr (Eds.), *Gestão do conhecimento e capital intelectual em habitats de inovação* (Vol. 1). Novas Edições Acadêmicas.

Ferenhof, H. A., & Fernandes, R. F. (2016). Desmistificando a revisão de literatura como base para redação científica: Método SSF. *Revista ACB*, *21*(3), 550–563.

Gitzel, R., Schmitz, B., Fromm, H., Isaksson, A., & Setzer, T. (2016). Industrial services as a research discipline. Enterprise Modelling and Information Systems Architectures-An International Journal, 11(4).

Greer, D. A. (2015). Defective co-creation: Developing a typology of consumer dysfunction in professional services. *European Journal of Marketing*, *49*(1/2), 238–261. doi:10.1108/EJM-07-2012-0411

Grönroos, C. (2012). Conceptualising value co-creation: A journey to the 1970s and back to the future. *Journal of Marketing Management*, *28*(13-14), 1520–1534. doi:10.1080/0267257X.2012.737357

Grönroos, C., & Helle, P. (2010). Adopting a service logic in manufacturing: Conceptual foundation and metrics for mutual value creation. *Journal of Service Management*, *21*(5), 564–590. doi:10.1108/09564231011079057

Hakanen, T., & Jaakkola, E. (2012). Co-creating customer-focused solutions within business networks: A service perspective. *Journal of Service Management*, *23*(4), 593–611. doi:10.1108/09564231211260431

Heim, I., Han, T., & Ghobadian, A. (2018). Value Co-Creation in ICT Services Company: A Case Study of a Cross-Border Acquisition. *Journal of East-West Business*, *24*(4), 319–338. doi:10.1080/10669868.2018.1467841

Huang, L. (2018). Creating and Delivering Sustainable Customer Solutions: On Organizing Capabilities in the Era of Servitization. In Organizing Marketing and Sales: Mastering Contemporary B2B Challenges (pp. 223-239). Emerald Publishing Limited.

Jaakkola, E., & Hakanen, T. (2013). Value co-creation in solution networks. *Industrial Marketing Management*, *42*(1), 47–58. doi:10.1016/j.indmarman.2012.11.005

Jääskeläinen, A., & Thitz, O. (2018). Prerequisites for performance measurement supporting purchaser-supplier collaboration. *Benchmarking*, *25*(1), 120–137. doi:10.1108/BIJ-08-2016-0121

Jackson, R. W., & Cooper, P. D. (1988). Unique aspects of marketing industrial services. *Industrial Marketing Management*, *17*(2), 111–118. doi:10.1016/0019-8501(88)90013-2

Janeschek, S., Hottum, P., Kicherer, F., & Bienzeisler, B. (2013). The dynamics of service productivity and value creation: A service life cycle perspective. *Service Industries Journal*, *33*(3-4), 366–377. doi:10.1080/02642069.2013.747518

Kohtamaki, M., & Helo, P. (2015). Industrial services - the solution provider's stairway to heaven or highway to hell? *Benchmarking*, *22*(2), 170–185. doi:10.1108/BIJ-01-2015-0002

Kohtamäki, M., & Partanen, J. (2016). Co-creating value from knowledge-intensive business services in manufacturing firms: The moderating role of relationship learning in supplier-customer interactions. *Journal of Business Research*, *69*(7), 2498–2506. doi:10.1016/j.jbusres.2016.02.019

Lacoste, S. (2016). Sustainable value co-creation in business networks. *Industrial Marketing Management*, *52*, 151–162. doi:10.1016/j.indmarman.2015.05.018

Lai, C. T., Jackson, P. R., & Jiang, W. (2017). Shifting paradigm to service-dominant logic via Internet-of-Things with applications in the elevators industry. *Journal of Management Analytics*, *4*(1), 35–54. doi:10.1080/23270012.2016.1259967

Lin, J. S. C., & Hsieh, C. C. (2011). Modeling service friendship and customer compliance in high-contact service relationships. *Journal of Service Management*, *22*(5), 607–631. doi:10.1108/09564231111174979

Lin, J. S. C., & Wu, C. Y. (2011). The role of expected future use in relationship-based service retention. *Managing Service Quality*, *21*(5), 535–551. doi:10.1108/09604521111159816

Ma, Y., Rong, K., Luo, Y., Wang, Y., Mangalagiu, D., & Thornton, T. F. (2019). Value Co-creation for sustainable consumption and production in the sharing economy in China. *Journal of Cleaner Production*, *208*, 1148–1158. doi:10.1016/j.jclepro.2018.10.135

Malik, A., Setiawan, A., Suhandi, A., Permanasari, A., Dirgantara, Y., Yuniarti, H., . . . Hermita, N. (2018). *Enhancing communication skills of pre-service physics teacher through hot lab related to electric circuit.* Paper presented at the Journal of Physics: Conference Series. 10.1088/1742-6596/953/1/012017

Ng, M.-M., & Priyono, I. (2018). The Effect of Service Quality on Student Satisfaction and Student Loyalty: An Empirical Study. *Journal of Social Studies Education Research*, *9*(3), 109–131.

Ngoc Thuy, P. (2011). Using service convenience to reduce perceived cost. *Marketing Intelligence & Planning*, *29*(5), 473–487. doi:10.1108/02634501111153683

Olya, H., Altinay, L., & De Vita, G. (2018). An exploratory study of value added services. *Journal of Services Marketing*, *32*(3), 334–345. doi:10.1108/JSM-12-2016-0415

Plé, L., & Chumpitaz Cáceres, R. (2010). Not always co-creation: Introducing interactional co-destruction of value in service-dominant logic. *Journal of Services Marketing*, *24*(6), 430–437. doi:10.1108/08876041011072546

Prakash, G. (2011). Service quality in supply chain: Empirical evidence from Indian automotive industry. *Supply Chain Management*, *16*(5), 362–378. doi:10.1108/13598541111155866

Prakash, S., Soni, G., Rathore, A. P. S., & Singh, S. (2017). Risk analysis and mitigation for perishable food supply chain: A case of dairy industry. *Benchmarking*, *24*(1), 2–23. doi:10.1108/BIJ-07-2015-0070

Rubalcaba, L., Michel, S., Sundbo, J., Brown, S. W., & Reynoso, J. (2012). Shaping, organizing, and rethinking service innovation: A multidimensional framework. *Journal of Service Management*, *23*(5), 696–715. doi:10.1108/09564231211269847

Ruiz-Alba, J. L., Soares, A., Rodríguez-Molina, M. A., & Frías-Jamilena, D. M. (2019). Servitization strategies from customers' perspective: The moderating role of co-creation. *Journal of Business and Industrial Marketing*, *34*(3), 628–642. doi:10.1108/JBIM-02-2017-0028

Saltelli, A., Nardo, M., Saisana, M., & Tarantola, S. (2005). Composite indicators: the controversy and the way forward. *Statistics, Knowledge and Policy Key Indicators to Inform Decision Making: Key Indicators to Inform Decision Making*, 359-372.

Santos-Vijande, M. L., López-Sánchez, J. Á., & Rudd, J. (2016). Frontline employees' collaboration in industrial service innovation: Routes of co-creation's effects on new service performance. *Journal of the Academy of Marketing Science*, *44*(3), 350–375. doi:10.100711747-015-0447-4

Smets, M., Smeets, M., Van den Bulck, S., Janssens, S., Aertgeerts, B., & Vaes, B. (2018). Defining quality indicators for heart failure in general practice. *Acta Cardiologica*, 1–8. PMID:30261830

Sofianti, T. D., Suryadi, K., Govindaraju, R., & Prihartono, B. (2012). *Measuring the performance of customer knowledge co-creation.* Paper presented at the 2012 IEEE 6th International Conference on Management of Innovation and Technology, ICMIT 2012, June 11, 2012 - June 13, 2012, Bali, Indonesia. 10.1109/ICMIT.2012.6225819

Somda, J., Kamuanga, M., & Tollens, E. (2005). Characteristics and economic viability of milk production in the smallholder farming systems in The Gambia. *Agricultural Systems*, *85*(1), 42–58. doi:10.1016/j.agsy.2004.07.011

Steinbach, T., Wallenburg, C. M., & Selviaridis, K. (2018). Me, myself and I: Non-collaborative customer behavior in service outsourcing – the key role of outcome orientation and outcome attributability. *International Journal of Operations & Production Management*, *38*(7), 1519–1539. doi:10.1108/IJOPM-05-2017-0297

Strähle, O., Füllemann, M., & Bendig, O. (2012). *Service now! Time to wake up the sleeping giant*. Bain & Company.

Taghizadeh, S. K., Jayaraman, K., Ismail, I., & Rahman, S. A. (2016). Scale development and validation for DART model of value co-creation process on innovation strategy. *Journal of Business and Industrial Marketing*, *31*(1), 24–35. doi:10.1108/JBIM-02-2014-0033

Takenaka, T., Nishino, N., & Nishikori, H. (2018). Service benchmarking for the co-creation of service ecosystem. *Procedia CIRP*, *67*, 574–576. doi:10.1016/j.procir.2017.12.263

Van Poucke, E., Matthyssens, P., van Weele, A., & Van Bockhaven, W. (2018). The effects of purchasing proactivity on value creation and supply risk reduction in sourcing projects: Implications for marketers' capabilities. *Industrial Marketing Management*. Advance online publication. doi:10.1016/j.indmarman.2018.12.003

West, S., Gaiardelli, P., Resta, B., & Kujawski, D. (2018). Co-creation of value in Product-Service Systems through transforming data into knowledge. *IFAC-PapersOnLine*, *51*(11), 1323–1328. doi:10.1016/j.ifacol.2018.08.349

Wikström, S., & L'Espoir Decosta, P. (2018). How is value created? – Extending the value concept in the Swedish context. *Journal of Retailing and Consumer Services*, *40*, 249–260. doi:10.1016/j.jretconser.2017.10.010

Wu, L. W. (2017). The bright side and dark side of co-production: A dyadic analysis. *Management Decision*, *55*(3), 614–631. doi:10.1108/MD-11-2016-0789

Zhang, J., & He, Y. (2014). Key dimensions of brand value co-creation and its impacts upon customer perception and brand performance: An empirical research in the context of industrial service. *Nankai Business Review International*, *5*(1), 43–69. doi:10.1108/NBRI-09-2013-0033

Zhang, T., Lu, C., Torres, E., & Chen, P.-J. (2018). Engaging customers in value co-creation or co-destruction online. *Journal of Services Marketing*, *32*(1), 57–69. doi:10.1108/JSM-01-2017-0027

Chapter 2
Customer-Centered Antecedents of a Value Co-Creation Ecosystem:
Integrating Psychological, Social, and Cultural Processes

Sumit Saxena
Indian Institute of Technology, Ropar, India

Amritesh
Indian Institute of Technology, Ropar, India

ABSTRACT

Considering the call for understanding the broader social and cultural context of value co-creation within emerging multilevel co-creative service systems, this research aims to explore the social and cultural processes along with psychological processes in terms of their influence on resource integration. It primarily adopts the customer perspective of resource integration. First, an integrative structure is developed and then the identified antecedents are positioned under relevant category proposing the multi-perspective VCC antecedent' framework. Further, the extant knowledge about VCC antecedents is used to set the agenda for future research. The study is based on an in-depth review of 85 key articles carefully extracted from a broad set of 1100 papers on VCC within the Scopus database. This review work provides a clear state of the art of VCC antecedents and has a direct implication for managers involved in designing the co-creation strategies for their customers.

DOI: 10.4018/978-1-7998-4843-1.ch002

INTRODUCTION

The concept of "Value co-creation" (VCC) rooted in service-dominant logic has gained wider acceptance by the research community across multiple academic disciplines during the last decade (Ramaswamy, & Ozcan, 2018). C.K Prahlad & Venkat Ramaswamy proposed the idea of value co-creation as joint creation of value by the company and the customer (Prahalad, & Ramaswamy, 2004).The idea had shown an initial inclination towards business economics which had a latent assumption of involving customers to take part in co-producing firm's offerings that subsequently tend to reduce the cost of production. Later, Vargo & Lusch (2004) advanced the idea of value co-creation to resource based view and claimed that actors involved in co-creation integrate their operand (primarily tangible) and operant resources (like knowledge & skills) to create value for each-other. Resource integration has emerged as a key to co-creation which soon attracted attention of researchers to the extent that led to a more precise and comprehensive definition of value co-creation as McColl-Kennedy et al. (2012) proposed *''VCC could be understood as the benefit realized from integration of resources through activities and interactions with collaborators in the customer's service network''.* Vargo and Lusch (2017) also aligned their views on value co-creation as an ongoing interplay of reciprocal exchange driven by creation and application of resources. Resource integration has largely been seen as the central activity as well as drivers of co-creation. Payne et al. (2008) closely examined the process of co-creation and explained three interconnected processes, namely, customer processes, supplier processes, and, encounter processes. Part of those processes are executed in the provider's space, and the rest happens in the customer's space and their extended service network that is primarily customer dependent (Grönroos, & Gummerus, 2014). The resources and practices generated during customer and supplier processes interact in the encounter process, and thereby generate value.

Context of co-creation have been given more importance gradually and the researchers started looking at co-creation at a much broader levels, and their unit of analysis has shifted from dyadic interactions of customer and provider, to numerous multilevel interactions happening across multiple stakeholders (including suppliers, employees, customers, extended customer network, policy makers, citizen, etc.) of the ecosystem (Fyrberg Yngfalk, 2013; Alves, et al., 2016; Vargo & Lusch, 2017). There has been a growing concern of researchers to adopt an ecosystem view of value co-creation to identify the contextual factors that have substantial bearings on co-creation experiences. Prior studies are yet to identify such factors which have multi-level influences across different stakeholders focusing a co-creation ecosystem. The ecosystem trends in value co-creation in businesses are studied from three different perspectives, first, strategy perspective, where value is instrumental; second, service marketing perspective, where value is phenomenological; and third, information systems perspective, where value is functional in nature (Autio, & Thomas, 2020). From a practical standpoint, when the firm understand their customer's co-creation pre-requisites (especially at social & cultural level), then they could re-design their co-creation strategy in such a way that they may target not just the customers but also the broader interconnected network of customer's service ecosystem to create a better service experience. The ideas co-created by both customers and employees are found to result into increased performance by organizations (Taghizadeh, et al., 2019). Broadening the perspective may also help organizations to offer better value propositions and gain competitive advantage, thereby realizing the true business potential of value co-creation (Saarijärvi et al., 2013). Autio et al. (2016) further explained the different mechanism by which ecosystem context can enhance the co-creation potential of customer-provider dyad within the service ecosystem. An ecosystem view of value co-creation helps in creating integrated value offering (Betz & Jung, 2021).

The role of resource integration as a prerequisite (or a part of) value co-creation thus becomes more critical to examine as the complexities and dynamics of co-creation ecosystem grows. The different types of co-creation mechanisms offer unique customer resources thereby creating different value propositions such as economic, functional, symbolic, and emotional (Saarijärvi, 2012).The resources do not exist in isolation, instead, those are found in a given context of service network (Chandler, & Vargo, 2011). The emerging ecosystem view of value co-creation further mandates the need for research on resource integration in a broader multilevel service network (Helkkula et al., 2018) where customers integrate the resources and create value in their own perspective. It has been strongly argued that social and cultural context of the participating actors are supposed to supply much of the resources required for co-creation (Edvardsson et al., 2011; Devereux, & Gallarza, 2019). This article focuses towards enlarging the perspective towards macro level interactions and tries to identify the social and cultural processes in addition to already emphasized psychological processes of co-creation in terms of their influence on resource integration (Edvardson, 2011; Chandler & Vargo, 2011). The present study adopts the customer perspective of value co-creation where customers and their network are the key resource integrator who performs intended actions to achieve the desired co-created experience.

METHOD

The study mainly explores the antecedents of value co-creation through a systematic review process (Tranfield et al., 2003). A keyword search of three well thought prefix words 'co-crea*', cocrea*, and 'co crea*' is performed on Scopus for the period 2004-2019, which gave an initial pool of 1100 articles. The articles only from marketing area are retained while most of others pertaining to economics and public health are removed. Later, the working papers, commentaries and book chapters, were removed and abstracts were analyzed. Further, the studies focusing only from customer's perspective are retained in the final list. Thus, 85 articles[1] are systematically selected from an initial pool of 1100 articles from the social science domain for the review work after applying proper inclusion and exclusion criteria. The stages of article selection are summarized in figure 1. The descriptive information about the collected articles can be found in table 1.

Following a lens-directed review approach (Järvinen, 2008), an in-depth qualitative review of all 85 articles is performed to identify the key antecedents in terms of various types of customer resources which facilitates value co-creation process. The antecedents are conceptualized under a proposed integrative framework consisting of psychological, social and cultural focus. Detailed explanations of each of those identified antecedents and their potential influential role in a co-creation ecosystem are presented later.

THE CONCEPTUAL FRAMEWORK

In order to put our results in a conceptual framework, several theoretical frameworks are explored in literature. Two important theoretical frameworks are identified which aligns with our idea of psycho-social and cultural viewpoint. First is Arnould's "Resource Classification" framework focusing on three types of operant resources i.e., physical, social & cultural (Arnould et al., 2006). Findsrud et al.'s (2018) further complemented the idea by providing an in-depth theoretical discussion on motivation construct which connects the physical and psychological aspect of resources relevant to value co-creation. Second is the "Service System" framework within the VCC ecosystem (Vargo et al., 2008), where several systems interact with each other for mutual benefit. This framework identifies three interrelated systems which involves psychological, social and cultural systems. Our search for customer-centered resource integration framework essentially looks at the broader network on the customer side which creates a part of the larger value co-creation ecosystem. We assume that a customer system is composed of a 'self-system' (as proposed by Bandura, 1991) made up of both physical and psychological components along with social & cultural systems (Mangone, 2018) in which the customer is embedded. Building on the idea of embeddedness of an individual with its ecosystem we propose a resource integration framework by incorporating the divergent aspects into a typical landscape where the VCC antecedents are rooted (figure 2).

Figure 1. Article selection process

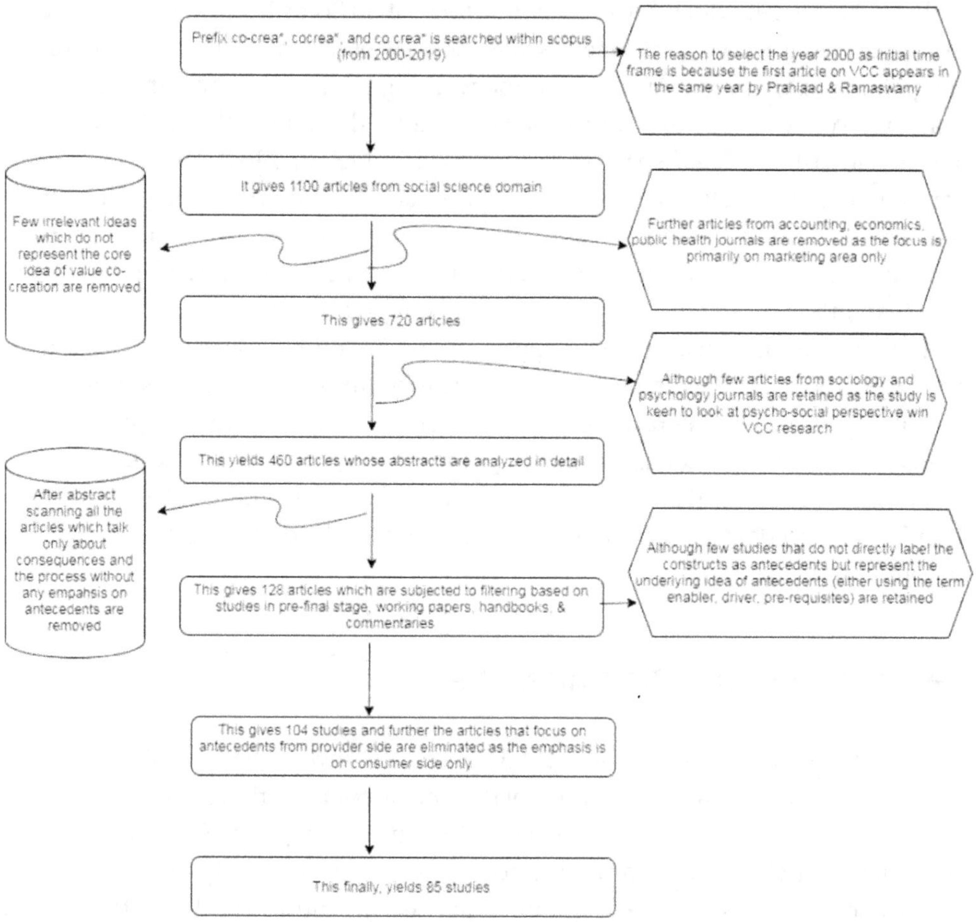

ANTECEDENTS OF RESOURCE INTEGRATION IN VALUE CO-CREATION

Psychological Antecedents

Motivation: Motivation has been identified as the missing driver of value co-creation in the marketing literature (Findsrud et al., 2018). Earlier researchers identified different types of internal and external consumer motives that facilitate value co-creation. Occhiocupo, & Friess (2013) explore self-expression, recognition, relationship building & skill development as key motivating factor towards value co-creation. Similarly, Neghina et al. (2015) identify three motivational needs, i.e., need for communication, need for relating, and need for knowing as important antecedents to co-creation. Other studies identify freedom of expression (Ind et al., 2019), affiliation, expression, experience, and recognition (Palma et al., 2019), need for empowerment (Anh, & Thuy, 2017) etc. as the motivational drivers of co-creation. Roberts et al. (2014) observe that consumers engage in co-creation activity due to self-centered reason which should have hedonic and economic value. Altruism/altruistic motive is observed as a key antecedent in Robert et al.'s study (2014) in context to community-level co-creation.

Figure 2. Customer centered resource integration processes in value co-creation

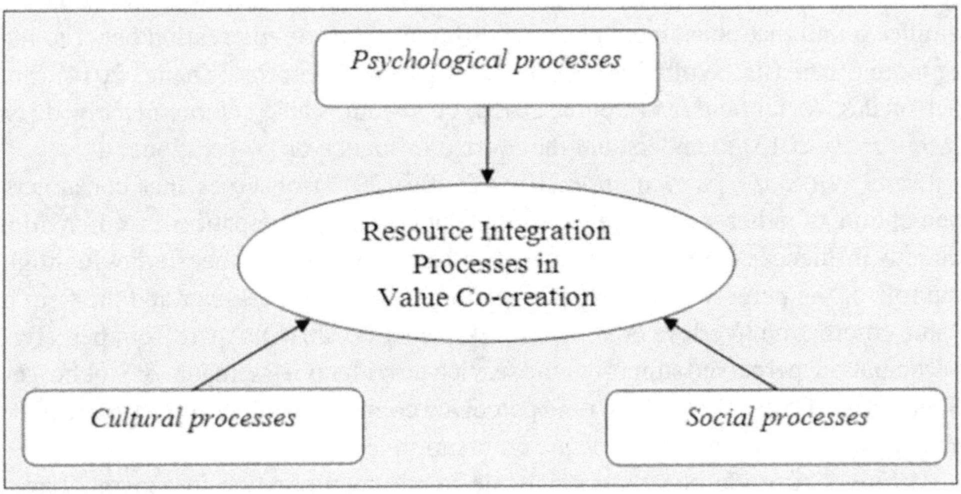

Ability: Consumer ability (also discussed as self-efficacy) is identified as one of the important psychological factors influencing value co-creation. It is often discussed in literature, along with motivation and opportunity. Zhang (2014) identifies consumer ability to co-create and resource integration capacity as an important dimension affecting value co-creation. Several studies are identified which focus on self-efficacy as an antecedent to VCC (Chen et al., 2015; Soltani et al., 2017). The ability could also be considered to be rooted in non-human resources, such as ICT capability (Polo Peña et al., 2014). Ability is also reflected in recent notion of interactive knowledge co-creation viewed from customer engagement and customer empowerment perspective (Shin et al., 2020).

Clarity: Value co-creation literature often mentions role clarity and goal clarity as key antecedents (Bharti et al., 2015). Role clarity could be understood as the degree to which the customer knows in advance what role he has to play. Customer readiness for co-creation assumes role clarity as one of the sub-dimensions, along with motivation and ability (Wang et al., 2011). Studies assert that self-efficacy alone cannot drive co-creation instead, customer role clarity is also required (Chen et al., 2015; Yousefian, 2015). Role clarity improves overall customer experience, which in turn influences value co-creation outcomes (Verleye, 2015). Some studies also discuss about role size, role awareness, and role-related resources in interactional value co-creation (Plé, 2016). The clarity in goal is another important psychological factor in co-creation which is primarily outcome oriented (Aggarwal, & Basu, 2014).

Perceived benefits: Damkuviene et al. (2012) divide the co-creation benefits into tangible (like economic benefits) and intangible categories (like psychological benefits). It is evident in studies that the way a consumer perceives the benefits of co-creation; it will affect their actual co-creation ability, intention, and behavior. Studies found that consumers perceive different types of co-creation benefits like economic benefits, symbolic benefits, and psychic benefits (Zhang, 2014); and personal & social benefits (Ophof, 2013). Few studies also explore perceived risk (Merz et al., 2013) to understand the reverse influence on co-creation.

Perceived actor participation: Kasnakoglu (2016) observes that consumers' perception of other actors' (e.g., service provider) participation in co-creation directly influences the consumer level of co-creation. Several other studies highlight the role of the perceived active participation of both the customer and the firm in value co-creation (Verleye et al., 2017; Ekman et al., 2016). Apart from perceived participation, perceived support of the service provider (Grissemann, & Stokburger-Sauer, 2012; Choi & Lotz, 2016) and perceived community support (Liu et al., 2020) also influences the customer's value co-creation level.

Attitude: Attitude plays a critical role in value co-creation in general (Lee et al. (2019) and customer-to-customer value co-creation in particular (Zadeh et.al, 2019). Consumer's attitude towards co-creation affects consumers' participation in co-creation (Lorenzo-Romero et al., 2014). Shamim et al., (2017) constructed a scale measuring customer value co-creation attitude, which is made up of three crucial attitude dimensions, i.e., responsive attitude, interaction attitude, and knowledge sharing attitude.

Trust: Different forms of trust constructs are found in the literature that influences value co-creation. Some of those mentions trust & personal innovativeness (Sarmah & Rahman, 2018); integrity trust &benevolence trust (Zhao et al., 2015); and trust & connection (Neghina et al., 2015). Trust drives the customer's willingness to share the information for value co-creation (Bharti et al., 2015; Yi & Gong, 2013). See-To & Ho (2014) noted that consumers' trust in the product influences their co-creation efforts. More recently, Roy et.al (2020) observes trust within fair service environment (within hotel industry) as key antecedent to co-creation. Trust can also be seen at multiple levels, such as 'brand level' and 'service personnel level' (Luk et al., 2018).

Past co-creation/perceived experience: Literature reveals that customer's prior experience with co-creation directly affects the future value co-creation (Merrilees, 2016). Verleye (2015) observes that customer role readiness influences co-creation experiences, and this influence varies with customer's expected co-creation benefits. Adding further, Bolton, et al. (2018) proposes a conceptual framework to understand customer's experience at three different realms i.e., digital, physical, and social. Apart from past experience, a consumer's perceived experience during the process of value co-creation affects a consumer's future co-creation behavior. The perceived experience is intrinsic in nature and often discussed along with other intrinsic elements such as hedonism, altruism etc. (Hernăndez-López, & Del Barrio-García, 2018; Zare et al. (2018).

Actor engagement: Actor engagement is identified as an important antecedent in the literature (Qazi, & Ali, 2017; Zhang et al., 2017). In this line, the most popular study of Jaakkola & Alexander (2014) gives a detailed explanation (along with new propositions) about the connection between customer engagement and value co-creation. Few studies, aligned towards customer participation and involvement are also positioned under engagement theme within this review work because many scholars admitted that engagement is a higher-order construct including participation and involvement as its sub-dimensions (Brodie et al., 2011).

Personality traits: Personality has emerged as the key antecedent to VCC in the recent literature. One of the frequently occurring personality traits in co-creation studies is 'innovativeness' (Sarmah, & Rahman, 2018). Zare et al. (2018) observe that consumer segments (referred to as innovators) with innovative traits are favorably inclined towards co-creation. Information seeking tendency represents another crucial aspect of personality trait within co-creation literature (Dahl et al., 2018). Information seeking helps the customer solve uncertainty and mastering the co-creation process (Yi & Gong, 2013).

Social Antecedents

Social interactions: Consumer's social interaction influences value co-creation. Consumers who enjoy social interactions share more knowledge with other stakeholders and result in higher co-creation levels (McDonald, & Karg, 2014 and Romero, 2017). Social interactions affect the co-creation experiences which in turn influence the involvement in value co-creation(Johnson, & Neuhofer, 2017). Osei-Frimpong et al. (2015) observe the effect of social interactions at a dyadic level. Buhalis et al. (2019) explain how social interactions mediated by ICT makes its impact at the co-creative ecosystem.

Social identity: Several studies observe the impact of social identity on value co-creation. Zhao et al. (2015) explore a link between social identity and value co-creation in the context of online health communities. Lan et al. (2017) observes an association between C2C identification and value co-creation behavior. Consumers actually extend their self-identity based on social identification. Few studies found social identity as a mediator between perceived value & co-creative participation behavior (Dholakia et al., 2004). Another study founds how social identity moderate customer's participation behavior and customer citizenship behavior (Yi & Gong, 2013).

Sense of community: Sense of community is reported as a key antecedent to value co-creation. It could be understood as 'when customers feel socially identified and develop a sense of association with other customers having the same preferences for goods or services' (Yang & Li, 2016). Qazi & Ali (2017) empirically verify the relationship between a sense of community and customer co-creation behavior.

Recently, Nadeem et.al (2020) position social emotional support (representing sense of belonging) as key antecedent to value co-creation. Chou et al. (2016) observe the mediating influence of sense of virtual community while exploring the relationship between perceived online justice and virtual value co-creation behavior. On the same line, a study reported that co-creation experience does not directly influence the co-creation, instead, it is mediated by a sense of community and perceived fairness (Gebauer et al., 2013).

Social expertise: Social expertise affects value co-creation indirectly through consumer expertise. Although consumer expertise is a psychological construct, and social expertise is conceptualized distinctly as a social construct that represents the knowledge available in the customer's social surroundings (Barrutia et al., 2016). Along a similar line of thought, Eletxigerra et al., (2018) attempted to examine the influence of consumer's social operant resources on the different measures of value co-creation.

Social trust: Social trust could be simply understood as mutual trust among the members of the community. Chow & Chan, (2008) have interpreted this construct as "the degree of one's willingness to be vulnerable to the actions of other people". Social trust has been reported as an antecedent to knowledge sharing attitude and knowledge sharing intention (Chow & Chan, 2008). Pappas et al. (2017) conceptualize trust through three dimensions i.e., trusting beliefs, institutional trust, and disposition to trust and supported a significant relationship between trust and value co-creation.

Social network: Consumer' social (and/or service) network has a key impact on value co-creation. Literature asserts strong and weak ties among members of the network. These ties could be characterized through strong emotional connection, intimacy, and reciprocal services among actors in the network (Granovetter, 1983). All three dimensions of network i.e., network size, network density & centrality are reported to influence value co-creation (Black & Gallan, 2015). The balanced and dense social network actually triggers consumer motivation to share information and co-create further (Tóth et al., 2018). Recently,

Social *(Institutional) norms:* Some studies observed the impact of social institutions or norms on customer's value co-creation behavior (Wang et al., 2014). Social norms represent the socially shared guidelines both for expected and accepted behavior (Birenham, & Sagarin, 1976). Zadeh et al. (2019) explore the effect of social norms on consumers value co-creation intention using the theory of planned behavior (Ajzen, 1991). Lee et al. (2019) have studied the influence of subjective norms on value co-creation. Understanding social norms may inform a researcher as how an institution influences customer centricity and value co-creation at both individual and collective levels.

Actor embeddedness: Researchers identify actor embeddedness as one of the key antecedents of value co-creation behavior (Laud, & Karpen, 2017). Laud, & Karpen, (2017) empirically argue how different dimensions of customer's social embeddedness influences the value co-creation behavior. Moving one step further, Wajid et al. (2019) examines how actor embeddedness influences actor engagement levels and their co-creation behavior at the micro-level in a service ecosystem.

Collective social/societal value: The collective societal value is the social value possessed by multiple actors collectively in a particular co-creation environment (Tregua et al., 2015). Tregua et al., (2015) suggests that consumers' societal value affects value co-creation more often than individual values. Societal/Social values represent 'morally' correct behavior practiced in the society. Such social values enhance the customer's awareness of their role in a value co-creation process.

Cultural Antecedents

Shared practices: Researchers have started realizing the importance of cultural factors in value co-creation since the last few years (Vargo et al., 2016). Shared co-creation practices are found to influence value co-creation through structures and systems (Arnould & Thompson, 2005). Practices are considered both at the individual and market-level in literature. Different types of resource integration practices are evident in studies that may affect co-creation (Vargo & Akaka, 2012). For example, Chandler & Vargo, 2011) have examined interactional practices in a service context; Pop et al., (2018) have focused on communication practices and ethical business practices.

Symbolic resources: Symbolic resources are important element of a shared culture. Literature suggests that consumers draw their own meanings in the value propositions offered by the service provider (Arnould, 2007). This meaning is rooted in the cultural context of the consumer. Thus consumers, while using the available resources, generate symbolic meaning through both inward (using emotions) and outward (social connections) orientation (Zittoun, 2007). Many researchers link consumers' symbolic resources with value co-creation that have their role at the level of co-creation ecosystem (Venkatesh & Penaloza, 2014; Meynhardt et al., 2016; Baron, & Warnaby, 2011).

Cultural norms: Apart from practices and resources, cultural norms or rules are found to influence value co-creation (Belk et al., 2013). Researchers assert that consumers get influenced by the norms rooted in their cultural context while co-creating value with stakeholders (Engeström, 2015; Hepi et al., 2017). Hepi et.al's (2017) model itself mentions that cultural norms along with other elements influence consumer engagement and subsequent value co-creation in a social service ecosystem. Few researchers also believe that consumer current practices re-construct the existing norms and accordingly affect value co-creation (Akaka et al., 2013).

Although social & cultural norms look similar, it is argued that there are cultural differences around social norms in a particular macro environment (Gelfand, 2019). Researchers asserted that consumers living in collectivist culture are more inclined towards co-creation than an individualistic culture. On the related line, Shamim, & Ghazali (2015) proposed that customers with interdependent self-construal nature will positively contribute towards value co-creation behavior. Collectivistic culture enhances the consumer's pro-activeness and encourages them to engage in co-creation (Csaba, 2017; Voyer et al. 2017).

Specialized knowledge: Arnould (2005) conceptualized specialized knowledge and skills as one of the forms of cultural resources. Specialized knowledge rooted in culture is considered a key factor influencing co-creation. In this line recently, Davey, & Grönroos (2019) asserts that consumer's health literacy (a form of specialized knowledge) played an important role in health care value co-creation. Baron, & Warnaby (2011) further confirm the role of specialized knowledge (along with other elements like consumer skills, history, and imagination) in context to British library services.

Above discussions elaborated on how the various antecedents are positioned differently on the basis of their key characteristics and theoretical alignment. Interestingly, within each category (psycho-social-cultural) some of the antecedents behave in a multifaceted way i.e., the construct act at the multiple levels, i.e., from a customer-provide dyad, to a service ecosystem. For example, any actor's participation in resource integration process depends on other actors' participation, which implies that all the actors determine the participation of each other in the ecosystem. Those antecedents can be summarized in the following figure (figure 3). Tables 2(a), 2(b), & 2(c) in the appendix provide a brief description of above discussed antecedents along with the key contributing researchers.

Figure 3. Multi-perspective VCC antecedent framework representing the psychological, social & cultural orientation

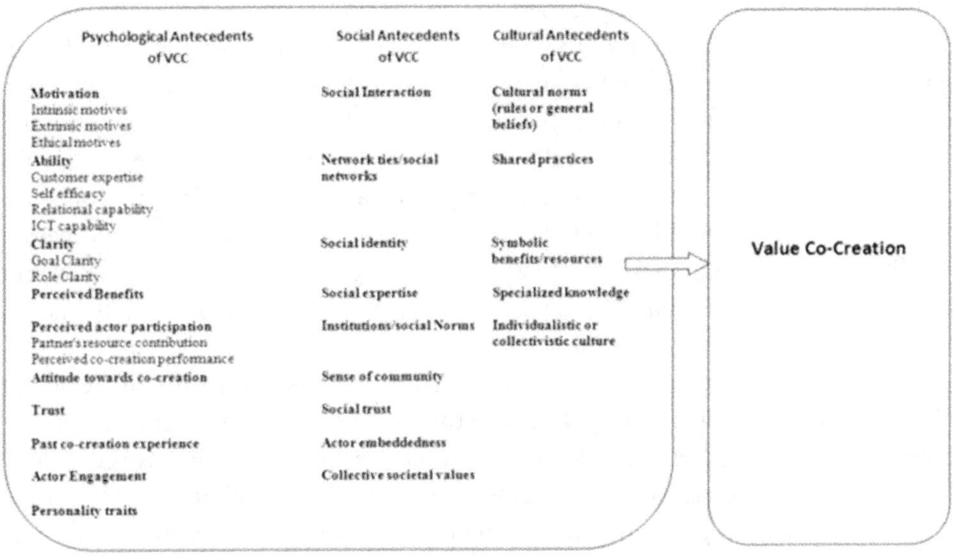

AGENDA FOR FUTURE RESEARCH

The study provides relevant descriptive information and analytical interpretation of antecedents and their role in co-creation, which could be used for developing new frameworks, models, and mid range theories. Study observes several connections between psychological, social and cultural antecedents, on the basis of which important propositions are offered. These propositions (see below) reflect the multi-level VCC antecedents i.e. co-creation antecedent encompassing both micro-psychological and macro-social perspectives.

First of all, the motivation mostly explored at actor's psychological level is observed to have strong connection with social factors like social identity and social reputation (Bettiga et.al, 2018; Haslam et.al, 1996). If the consumer identify himself as a good co-creator within his community, his intrinsic motivation to co-create enhances. Also, if consumer is more concerned about his social reputation while enacting the role of co-creator, he will strengthen his intrinsic motives and resources to co-create further. This shows that customer action (to co-create) is socially motivated. It also aligns with the notion that actors (within social network) enjoy social interactions through congruent goals (co-creation goal). Thus, it is proposed that *"Consumer intrinsic motivation towards co-creation is influenced by social motivations (induced by social reputation & social identity) and thus psychological-social motivation jointly influences the value co-creation process".*

Secondly, trust as VCC antecedent which is mostly analyzed at interpersonal level (between service provider and service recipient) is actually a multilevel concept (Fulmer, & Dirks, 2018). The interpersonal trust which represents the faith at dyadic level (service provider and service recipient) is transitioned by faith within the service ecosystem (comprised of several dyads in service environment). In simple words, if the social institutions infuse the feeling of security in actor's mind, then actors will feel confident and develops more trust (Spadaro, 2020) thereby sharing resources to reciprocate trust. Thus, it is implied that consumer's interpersonal trust (on co-creation stakeholders) which influences the overall co-creation process, is conditioned by actor's social trust (within the co-creative ecosystem). Therefore, it is proposed that *"Consumer's multilevel trust (i.e. interpersonal trust + social trust) affects the value co-creation process"*.

Third, it is found that the consumer ability/efficacy is not merely the reflection of his own co-creation capacity, but is a combination of skill set acquired through multiple interactions (for example: 'C2C co-creative interaction ' Rihova et.al, 2013) in the co-creation ecosystem. Consumers often co-learn, and co-develop various abilities by mobilizing and integrating other's (suppliers, other consumers, citizens, policy makers, service providers, apomediary etc) resources (Caridà, Edvardsson, & Colurcio, 2019) in service ecosystem, thereby using this ability (collective ability/efficacy) in the co-creation process. This aligns with the emerging idea of collective intelligence (Wise, Paton, & Gegenhuber, 2012). Overall, it is proposed that *"Consumer's collective ability/efficacy influences the value co-creation process"*.

Fourth, it is observed that consumer's (personal) experiences gained during co-creation (with multiple actors) are not static, instead dynamic in nature. These experiences are subjective in nature and continuously re-shaped by emerging social norms and cultural practices (Jaakkola et al, 2015). It means the same experience which boosts the consumer's co-creation activity earlier, may inhibit the co-creation now, due to restrictive norms developed in the society or due to misuse of symbolic resources by actors. Thus, social experiences (Ponsignon, & Derbaix, 2020) may indirectly affect the co-creation by transforming the personal (psychological) experiences. Finally, it is proposed that *"Consumer personal-social experiences jointly affect the co-creation efforts by actor in the co-creation ecosystem"*.

Fifth, it is observed that resources are optimally integrated within multicultural (Benet-Martínez, 2012) environment. Multicultural co-creation space could be understood as service context where actors are cosmopolitan and posses the specialized knowledge (traditional knowhow of culture) required to co-create. Multicultural consumers have a large pool of resources (due to access to different cultures) that could be used freely (as they are less restricted by social norms) to co-create (Akaka et.al, 2013). Also, the symbolic resources imbibed by consumers living in multicultural environment transforms his personality traits (like creativity, pro-social orientation, & information seeking tendency) required for effective resource sharing. Therefore, it is proposed that *"multiculturalism favorably influences the value co-creation process by providing better resource conditions for value co-creation in the service ecosystem"*.

The study also put forward a set of future research questions based on the psychological, social, and cultural processes and the underlying antecedents identified in this article. (refer to Table-3 in the appendix for details).

CONCLUSION AND LIMITATIONS

This study has explored the antecedents of resources integration in value co-creation research and placed them under an integrative framework. Through systematic review, this study presented a comprehensive picture of all the customer centered antecedents of value co-creation identified so far, with their brief conceptualizations, their theoretical orientations, and their potential relationships with the value co-creation outcomes. Several important social and cultural antecedents are reported that further enrich the sociological viewpoint to value co-creation research, which was otherwise dominated by a psychological viewpoint only. Although, without psychological process an effective co-creation is not feasible, the social and cultural antecedents are supposed to play a pivotal role as the focus of analysis broadens from dyadic level to ecosystem level. Overall, the knowledge pool of identified antecedents provides rich information regarding value in social and cultural context without ignoring the importance of psychological processes. Socio-cultural processes especially explain how the customer's surrounding ecosystem plays an important role in co-creating value for himself and the other involved stakeholders. For example, consumers' intrinsic motivation, interest to co-create, and role clarity, which directly affects his co-creative functions, are affected by social norms, culturally driven meanings, and the sense of community. Several actors in the ecosystem access and apply the resources through their practices embedded in socio-cultural processes to successfully perform their co-creation roles. The review also hints at the growing dynamics of VCC antecedents at multiple levels of the service ecosystem, i.e., individual, dyadic, and macro-social levels. For example, 'goal clarity' as an antecedent indicates an actor's cognitive state which is relatively free from other actors' behavior in the ecosystem. However, 'goal congruence' in a co-creative service interaction represents the condition where the actor's psychological conviction is dependent on the psycho-social state of another partner's in the ecosystem. Further, depicting the connections between psycho-social & cultural antecedents, few important propositions are also offered. These propositions reflect the multi-level VCC antecedents (psycho-social motivation, multilevel trust, collective efficacy, personal-social experiences, and multiculturalism) by highlighting the link between actor's micro-psychological and macro-social co-creation antecedents.

There are certain limitations to this study as well. First, the study does not use papers published in non-English language. Second, the study looks from consumer side and future research could explore the VCC antecedents from the provider's perspective also. Despite these limitations, it is expected that this review work may help researchers as a good comprehensive reference for further research.

ACKNOWLEDGMENT

This research received no specific grant from any funding agency in the public, commercial, or not-for-profit sectors.

REFERENCES

Aggarwal, P., & Basu, A. K. (2014). Value co-creation: Factors affecting discretionary effort exertion. *Services Marketing Quarterly*, *35*(4), 321–336. doi:10.1080/15332969.2014.946876

Ajzen, I. (1991). The theory of planned behavior. *Organizational Behavior and Human Decision Processes*, *50*(2), 179–211. doi:10.1016/0749-5978(91)90020-T

Akaka, M. A., Schau, H. J., & Vargo, S. L. (2013). The Co-Creation of Value-in-Cultural-Context. In Consumer Culture Theory. Emerald Group Publishing Limited.

Alves, H., Fernandes, C., & Raposo, M. (2016). Value co-creation: Concept and contexts of application and study. *Journal of Business Research*, *69*(5), 1626–1633. doi:10.1016/j.jbusres.2015.10.029

Anh, P. N. T., & Thuy, P. N. (2017). The effects of interaction behaviors of service frontliners on customer participation in the value co-creation: A study of health care service. *Service Business*, *11*(2), 253–277. doi:10.100711628-016-0307-4

Arnould, Price, & Malshe. (2006). Toward a Cultural Resource-Based Theory of the Customer. *The Service-Dominant Logic of Marketing: Dialog, Debate, and Directions*, 91-104.

Arnould, E. (2005). Animating the big middle. *Journal of Retailing*, *81*(2), 89–96. doi:10.1016/j.jretai.2005.03.001

Arnould, E. J. (2007). Service-dominant logic and consumer culture theory: Natural allies in an emerging paradigm. In *Consumer culture theory* (pp. 57–76). Emerald Group Publishing Limited.

Arnould, E. J., & Thompson, C. J. (2005). Consumer culture theory (CCT): Twenty years of research. *The Journal of Consumer Research, 31*(4), 868–882. doi:10.1086/426626

Autio, E., Thomas, L., & Gann, D. (2016). *Ecosystem value co-creation*. Innovation & Entrepreneurship Department Working Papers: 28. London, UK: Imperial College Business School.

Autio, E., & Thomas, L. D. (2020). Value co-creation in ecosystems: Insights and research promise from three disciplinary perspectives. In *Handbook of Digital Innovation*. Edward Elgar Publishing. doi:10.4337/9781788119986.00017

Bandura, A. (1991). Social cognitive theory of self-regulation. *Organizational Behavior and Human Decision Processes, 50*(2), 248–287. doi:10.1016/0749-5978(91)90022-L

Baron, S., & Warnaby, G. (2011). Individual customers' use and integration of resources: Empirical findings and organizational implications in the context of value co-creation. *Industrial Marketing Management, 40*(2), 211–218. doi:10.1016/j.indmarman.2010.06.033

Barrutia, J. M., Paredes, M. R., & Echebarria, C. (2016). Value co-creation in e-commerce contexts: Does product type matter? *European Journal of Marketing, 50*(3–4), 442–463. doi:10.1108/EJM-10-2014-0603

Belk, R. W., Price, L., & Peñaloza, L. (Eds.). (2013). *Consumer culture theory*. Emerald Group Publishing. doi:10.1108/S0885-2111(2013)15

Benet-Martínez, V. (2012). Multiculturalism: Cultural, social, and personality processes. In K. Deaux & M. Snyder (Eds.), *Handbook of personality and social psychology*. Oxford University Press.

Bettiga, D., Lamberti, L., & Noci, G. (2018). Investigating social motivations, opportunity and ability to participate in communities of virtual co-creation. *International Journal of Consumer Studies, 42*(1), 155–163. doi:10.1111/ijcs.12409

Betz, C., & Jung, R. (2021). Conceptualizing and Analyzing Business Ecosystem Service Offerings. *Proceedings of the 54th Hawaii International Conference on System Sciences*, 1-10.

Bharti, K., Agrawal, R., & Sharma, V. (2015). Literature review and proposed conceptual framework. *International Journal of Market Research, 57*(4), 571–604. doi:10.2501/IJMR-2015-012

Birenham, A., & Sagarin, E. (1976). *Norms and human behavior*. Praeger.

Black, H. G., & Gallan, A. S. (2015). Transformative service networks: Cocreated value as well-being. *Service Industries Journal, 35*(15-16), 826–845. doi:10.1080/02642069.2015.1090978

Bolton, R. N., McColl-Kennedy, J. R., Cheung, L., Gallan, A., Orsingher, C., Witell, L., & Zaki, M. (2018). Customer experience challenges: Bringing together digital, physical and social realms. *Journal of Service Management, 29*(5), 776–808. Advance online publication. doi:10.1108/JOSM-04-2018-0113

Brodie, R. J., Hollebeek, L. D., Jurić, B., & Ilić, A. (2011). Customer engagement: Conceptual domain, fundamental propositions, and implications for research. *Journal of Service Research, 14*(3), 252–271. doi:10.1177/1094670511411703

Buhalis, D., Harwood, T., Bogicevic, V., Viglia, G., Beldona, S., & Hofacker, C. (2019). Technological disruptions in services: Lessons from tourism and hospitality. *Journal of Service Management, 30*(4), 484–506. Advance online publication. doi:10.1108/JOSM-12-2018-0398

Caridà, A., Edvardsson, B., & Colurcio, M. (2019). Conceptualizing resource integration as an embedded process: Matching, resourcing and valuing. *Marketing Theory, 19*(1), 65–84. doi:10.1177/1470593118772215

Chandler, J. D., & Vargo, S. L. (2011). Contextualization and value-in-context: How context frames exchange. *Marketing Theory, 11*(1), 35–49. doi:10.1177/1470593110393713

Chen, S. C., Raab, C., & Tanford, S. (2015). Antecedents of mandatory customer participation in service encounters: An empirical study. *International Journal of Hospitality Management, 46*, 65–75. doi:10.1016/j.ijhm.2015.01.012

Choi, L., & Lotz, S. (2016). Motivations leading to customer citizenship behavior in services: Scale development and validation. *Journal of Consumer Marketing, 33*(7), 539–551. doi:10.1108/JCM-01-2016-1683

Chou, E. Y., Lin, C. Y., & Huang, H. C. (2016). Fairness and devotion go far: Integrating online justice and value co-creation in virtual communities. *International Journal of Information Management, 36*(1), 60–72. doi:10.1016/j.ijinfomgt.2015.09.009

Chow, W. S., & Chan, L. S. (2008). Social network, social trust and shared goals in organizational knowledge sharing. *Information & Management*, *45*(7), 458–465. doi:10.1016/j.im.2008.06.007

Csaba, F. F. (2017). Commentary on "Co-creating stakeholder and brand identities: A cross-cultural consumer perspective". *Journal of Business Research*, *70*, 411–413. doi:10.1016/j.jbusres.2016.06.018

Dahl, A. J., Peltier, J. W., & Milne, G. R. (2018). Development of a value Co-creation wellness model: The role of physicians and digital information seeking on health behaviors and health outcomes. *The Journal of Consumer Affairs*, *52*(3), 562–594. doi:10.1111/joca.12176

Damkuviene, M., Tijunaitiene, R., Petukiene, E., & Bersenaite, J. (2012). Customer perceived co-creation value: Synthesis of the extant literature. *Social Research*, *4*(29), 59–68.

Davey, J., & Grönroos, C. (2019). Health service literacy: Complementary actor roles for transformative value co-creation. *Journal of Services Marketing*, *33*(6), 687–701. doi:10.1108/JSM-09-2018-0272

Devereux, M. T., & Gallarza, M. G. G. (2019). Social value co-creation: Insights from consumers, employees, and managers. In *Corporate social responsibility: Concepts, methodologies, tools, and applications* (pp. 55–79). IGI Global. doi:10.4018/978-1-5225-6192-7.ch004

Dholakia, U. M., Bagozzi, R. P., & Pearo, L. K. (2004). A social influence model of consumer participation in network-and small-group-based virtual communities. *International Journal of Research in Marketing*, *21*(3), 241–263. doi:10.1016/j.ijresmar.2003.12.004

Edvardsson, B., Tronvoll, B., & Gruber, T. (2011). Expanding understanding of service exchange and value co-creation: A social construction approach. *Journal of the Academy of Marketing Science*, *39*(2), 327–339. doi:10.100711747-010-0200-y

Ekman, P., Raggio, R. D., & Thompson, S. M. (2016). Service network value co-creation: Defining the roles of the generic actor. *Industrial Marketing Management*, *56*, 51–62. doi:10.1016/j.indmarman.2016.03.002

Eletxigerra, A., Barrutia, J. M., & Echebarria, C. (2018). Place marketing examined through a service-dominant logic lens: A review. *Journal of Destination Marketing & Management*, *9*, 72–84. doi:10.1016/j.jdmm.2017.11.002

Engeström, Y. (2015). *Learning by Expanding*. Cambridge University Press.

Findsrud, R., Tronvoll, B., & Edvardsson, B. (2018). Motivation: The missing driver for theorizing about resource integration. *Marketing Theory*, *18*(4), 493–519. doi:10.1177/1470593118764590

Fulmer, A., & Dirks, K. (2018). Multilevel trust: A theoretical and practical imperative. *Journal of Trust Research*, *8*(2), 137–141. doi:10.1080/21515581.2018.1531657

Fyrberg Yngfalk, A. (2013). 'It's not us, it's them!'–Rethinking value co-creation among multiple actors. *Journal of Marketing Management*, *29*(9-10), 1163–1181. doi:10.1080/0267257X.2013.796318

Gebauer, J., Füller, J., & Pezzei, R. (2013). The dark and the bright side of co-creation: Triggers of member behavior in online innovation communities. *Journal of Business Research*, *66*(9), 1516–1527. doi:10.1016/j.jbusres.2012.09.013

Gelfand, M. (2019, Sep 9). *Understanding Cultural Differences Around Social Norms*. Retrieved from https://behavioralscientist.org/understanding-cultural-differences-around-social-norms/

Granovetter, M. (1983). The strength of weak ties: A network theory revisited. *Sociological Theory*, *1*, 201–233. doi:10.2307/202051

Grissemann, U. S., & Stokburger-Sauer, N. E. (2012). Customer co-creation of travel services: The role of company support and customer satisfaction with the co-creation performance. *Tourism Management*, *33*(6), 1483–1492. doi:10.1016/j.tourman.2012.02.002

Grönroos, C., & Gummerus, J. (2014). The service revolution and its marketing implications: Service logic vs service-dominant logic. *Managing Service Quality*, *24*(3), 206–229. doi:10.1108/MSQ-03-2014-0042

Haslam, S. A., Oakes, P. J., Turner, J. C., & McGarty, C. (1996). Social identity, self-categorization and the perceived homogeneity of in groups and outgroups: The interaction between social motivation and cognition. In R. M. Sorrentino & E. T. Higgins (Eds.), *Handbook ofmotivation and cognition* (Vol. 3, pp. 182–222). Guilford.

Helkkula, A., Dube, A., & Arnould, E. (2018). The contextual nature of value and value co-creation. The SAGE handbook of service-dominant logic, 118-132.

Hepi, M., Foote, J., Finsterwalder, J., Carswell, S., & Baker, V. (2017). An integrative transformative service framework to improve engagement in a social service ecosystem: The case of He Waka Tapu. *Journal of Services Marketing*, *31*(4/5), 423–437. doi:10.1108/JSM-06-2016-0222

Hernández-López, L., & Del Barrio-García, S. (2018). Value Co-Creation in Ecotourism: Finding Solutions in a Digital Era. Journal of Business. *Universidad del Pacífico (Lima, Peru)*, *10*(1), 38–51.

Ind, N., Coates, N., & Lerman, K. (2019). The gift of co-creation: What motivates customers to participate. *Journal of Brand Management*. Advance online publication. doi:10.105741262-019-00173-7

Jaakkola, E., & Alexander, M. (2014). The role of customer engagement behavior in value co-creation: A service system perspective. *Journal of Service Research*, *17*(3), 247–261. doi:10.1177/1094670514529187

Jaakkola, E., Helkkula, A., & Aarikka-Stenroos, L. (2015). Service experience co-creation: Conceptualization, implications, and future research directions. *Journal of Service Management*, *26*(2), 182–205. doi:10.1108/JOSM-12-2014-0323

Järvinen, P. (2008). On developing and evaluating of the literature review. *The 31st Information Systems Research Seminar*.

Johnson, A. G., & Neuhofer, B. (2017). Airbnb–an exploration of value co-creation experiences in Jamaica. *International Journal of Contemporary Hospitality Management*, *29*(9), 2361–2376. doi:10.1108/IJCHM-08-2016-0482

Kasnakoglu, B. T. (2016). Antecedents and consequences of cocreation in credence-based service contexts. *Service Industries Journal*, *36*(1-2), 1–20. doi:10.1080/02642069.2016.1138472

Laamanen, M., & Skålén, P. (2015). Collective–conflictual value co-creation: A strategic action field approach. *Marketing Theory*, *15*(3), 381–400. doi:10.1177/1470593114564905

Lan, J., Ma, Y., Zhu, D., Mangalagiu, D., & Thornton, T. (2017). Enabling value co-creation in the sharing economy: The case of mobike. *Sustainability*, *9*(9), 1504. doi:10.3390u9091504

Laud, G., & Karpen, I. O. (2017). Value co-creation behaviour–Role of embeddedness and outcome considerations. *Journal of Service Theory and Practice*, *27*(4), 778–807. doi:10.1108/JSTP-04-2016-0069

Lee, Y. L., Pan, L. Y., Hsu, C. H., & Lee, D. C. (2019). Exploring the sustainability correlation of value Co-creation and customer loyalty-A case study of fitness clubs. *Sustainability*, *11*(1), 97. doi:10.3390u11010097

Lin, X., Sarker, S., & Featherman, M. (2019). Users' psychological perceptions of information sharing in the context of social media: A comprehensive model. *International Journal of Electronic Commerce*, *23*(4), 453–491. doi:10.1080/10864415.2019.1655210

Liu, W., Fan, X., Ji, R., & Jiang, Y. (2020). Perceived Community Support, Users' Interactions, and Value Co-Creation in Online Health Community: The Moderating Effect of Social Exclusion. *International Journal of Environmental Research and Public Health*, *17*(1), 204. doi:10.3390/ijerph17010204 PMID:31892188

Lorenzo-Romero, C., Constantinides, E., & Brünink, L. A. (2014). Co-creation: Customer integration in social media based product and service development. *Procedia: Social and Behavioral Sciences*, *148*, 383–396. doi:10.1016/j.sbspro.2014.07.057

Luk, S. T., Liu, B. S., & Li, E. L. (2018). Effect of multilevel trust on effort-in-use and service co-design behaviour. *Journal of Services Marketing*, *32*(4), 505519. doi:10.1108/JSM-08-2015-0261

Mangone, E. (2018). The Cultural System and the Social Problems. In *Social and Cultural Dynamics* (pp. 53–62). Springer. doi:10.1007/978-3-319-68309-6_5

McColl-Kennedy, J. R., Vargo, S. L., Dagger, T. S., Sweeney, J. C., & Kasteren, Y. V. (2012). Health care customer value cocreation practice styles. *Journal of Service Research*, *15*(4), 370–389. doi:10.1177/1094670512442806

McDonald, H., & Karg, A. J. (2014). Managing co-creation in professional sports: The antecedents and consequences of ritualized spectator behavior. *Sport Management Review*, *17*(3), 292–309. doi:10.1016/j.smr.2013.07.004

Merrilees, B. (2016). Interactive brand experience pathways to customer-brand engagement and value co-creation. *Journal of Product and Brand Management*, *25*(5), 402–408. doi:10.1108/JPBM-04-2016-1151

Merz, M. Y., Czerwinski, D., & Merz, M. A. (2013). Exploring the antecedents for value co-creation during healthcare service provision. *Journal of Business and Behavioral Sciences*, *25*(2), 152.

Meynhardt, T., Chandler, J. D., & Strathoff, P. (2016). Systemic principles of value co-creation: Synergetics of value and service ecosystems. *Journal of Business Research*, *69*(8), 2981–2989. doi:10.1016/j.jbusres.2016.02.031

Nadeem, W., Juntunen, M., Shirazi, F., & Hajli, N. (2020). Consumers' value co-creation in sharing economy: The role of social support, consumers' ethical perceptions and relationship quality. *Technological Forecasting and Social Change*, *151*, 119786. doi:10.1016/j.techfore.2019.119786

Neghina, C., Caniëls, M. C., Bloemer, J. M., & van Birgelen, M. J. (2015). Value cocreation in service interactions: Dimensions and antecedents. *Marketing Theory*, *15*(2), 221–242. doi:10.1177/1470593114552580

Occhiocupo, N., & Friess, M. (2013, June). Exploring what motivates consumers to co-create value in virtual fashion communities. In Lucrare prezentată la Forumul Naples Forum on Service, Ischia (Vol. 13). Academic Press.

Ophof, S. (2013). *Motives for customers to engage in co-creation activities* (Bachelor's thesis). University of Twente.

Osei-Frimpong, K., Wilson, A., & Owusu-Frimpong, N. (2015). Service experiences and dyadic value co-creation in healthcare service delivery: A CIT approach. *Journal of Service Theory and Practice*, *25*(4), 443–462. doi:10.1108/JSTP-03-2014-0062

Palma, F. C., Trimi, S., & Hong, S. G. (2019). Motivation triggers for customer participation in value co-creation. *Service Business*, *13*(3), 557–580. doi:10.100711628-018-00395-w

Pappas, I. O., Mikalef, P., Giannakos, M. N., & Pavlou, P. A. (2017). Value co-creation and trust in social commerce: An fsQCA approach. *Proceedings of the 25th European Conference on Information Systems (ECIS)*, 2153–2168.

Payne, A. F., Storbacka, K., & Frow, P. (2008). Managing the co-creation of value. *Journal of the Academy of Marketing Science*, *36*(1), 83–96. doi:10.100711747-007-0070-0

Plé, L. (2016). Studying customers' resource integration by service employees in interactional value co-creation. *Journal of Services Marketing*, *30*(2), 152–164. doi:10.1108/JSM-02-2015-0065

Polo Peña, A. I., Frías Jamilena, D. M., & Rodríguez Molina, M. Á. (2014). Value co-creation via information and communications technology. *Service Industries Journal*, *34*(13), 1043–1059. doi:10.1080/02642069.2014.939641

Ponsignon, F., & Derbaix, M. (2020). The impact of interactive technologies on the social experience: An empirical study in a cultural tourism context. *Tourism Management Perspectives*, *35*, 100723. doi:10.1016/j.tmp.2020.100723

Pop, O. M., Leroi-Werelds, S., Roijakkers, N., & Andreassen, T. W. (2018). Institutional types and institutional change in healthcare ecosystems. *Journal of Service Management, 29*(4), 593–614. doi:10.1108/JOSM-02-2017-0041

Prahalad, C. K., & Ramaswamy, V. (2004). *The future of competition: Co-creating unique value with customers*. Harvard Business Press.

Qazi, A. A., & Ali, F. (2017). The antecedents and consequents of customer value co-creation among small and medium enterprises. *Pakistan Journal of Commerce and Social Sciences, 11*(3), 934–958.

Ramaswamy, V., & Ozcan, K. (2018). What is co-creation? An interactional creation framework and its implications for value creation. *Journal of Business Research, 84*, 196–205. doi:10.1016/j.jbusres.2017.11.027

Rihova, I., Buhalis, D., Moital, M., & Gouthro, M. B. (2013). Social layers of customer-to-customer value co-creation. *Journal of Service Management, 24*(5), 553–566. doi:10.1108/JOSM-04-2013-0092

Roberts, D., Hughes, M., & Kertbo, K. (2014). Exploring consumers' motivations to engage in innovation through co-creation activities. *European Journal of Marketing, 48*(1/2), 147–169. doi:10.1108/EJM-12-2010-0637

Romero, J. (2017). Customer engagement behaviors in hospitality: Customer-based antecedents. *Journal of Hospitality Marketing & Management, 26*(6), 565–584. doi:10.1080/19368623.2017.1288192

Roy, S. K., Balaji, M. S., Soutar, G., & Jiang, Y. (2020). The antecedents and consequences of value co-creation behaviors in a hotel setting: A two-country study. *Cornell Hospitality Quarterly, 61*(3), 353–368. doi:10.1177/1938965519890572

Saarijärvi, H. (2012). The mechanisms of value co-creation. *Journal of Strategic Marketing, 20*(5), 381–391. doi:10.1080/0965254X.2012.671339

Saarijärvi, H., Kannan, P. K., & Kuusela, H. (2013). Value co-creation: Theoretical approaches and practical implications. *European Business Review, 25*(1), 6–19. doi:10.1108/09555341311287718

Sarmah, B., & Rahman, Z. (2018). Antecedents of co-creation intention and their role in developing technology-based new services via customer involvement: A conceptual analysis. *International Journal of Business Excellence, 15*(2), 239–255. doi:10.1504/IJBEX.2018.091921

See-To, E. W., & Ho, K. K. (2014). Value co-creation and purchase intention in social network sites: The role of electronic Word-of-Mouth and trust–A theoretical analysis. *Computers in Human Behavior*, *31*, 182–189. doi:10.1016/j.chb.2013.10.013

Shamim, A., & Ghazali, Z. (2015). The role of self-construals in developing customer value co-creation behavior. *Global Business and Management Research*, *7*(2), 19–27.

Shamim, A., Ghazali, Z., & Albinsson, P. A. (2017). Construction and validation of customer value co-creation attitude scale. *Journal of Consumer Marketing*, *34*(7), 591–602. doi:10.1108/JCM-01-2016-1664

Shin, H., Perdue, R. R., & Pandelaere, M. (2020). Managing customer reviews for value co-creation: An empowerment theory perspective. *Journal of Travel Research*, *59*(5), 792–810. doi:10.1177/0047287519867138

Soltani, M., Jandaghi, G., & Forouzandeh Shahraki, P. (2017). Co-Creation Intention; Presenting a Model of Antecedents and its Impact on Attitude Toward the Product (Case Study in Shatel Company). *Iranian Journal of Management Studies*, *10*(1), 143–174.

Spadaro, G., Gangl, K., Van Prooijen, J. W., Van Lange, P. A., & Mosso, C. O. (2020). Enhancing feelings of security: How institutional trust promotes interpersonal trust. *PLoS One*, *15*(9), e0237934. doi:10.1371/journal.pone.0237934 PMID:32916694

Taghizadeh, S. K., Rahman, S. A., & Marimuthu, M. (2019). Idea generation leveraged from value co-creation process enhances new service development performance. *Journal of Strategic Marketing*, *27*(6), 483–504. doi:10.1080/0965254X.2018.1430052

Tóth, Z., Peters, L. D., Pressey, A., & Johnston, W. J. (2018). Tension in a value co-creation context: A network case study. *Industrial Marketing Management*, *70*, 34–45. doi:10.1016/j.indmarman.2017.08.015

Tranfield, D., Denyer, D., & Smart, P. (2003). Towards a methodology for developing evidence-informed management knowledge by means of systematic review. *British Journal of Management*, *14*(3), 207–222. doi:10.1111/1467-8551.00375

Tregua, M., Russo-Spena, T., & Casbarra, C. (2015). Being social for social: A co-creation perspective. *Journal of Service Theory and Practice*, *25*(2), 198–219. doi:10.1108/JSTP-09-2013-0183

Vargo, S. L., & Akaka, M. A. (2012). Value cocreation and service systems (re) formation: A service ecosystems view. *Service Science*, *4*(3), 207–217. doi:10.1287erv.1120.0019

Vargo, S. L., & Lusch, R. F. (2004). Evolving To a New Dominant Logic For Marketing. *Journal of Marketing*, *68*(1), 1–17. doi:10.1509/jmkg.68.1.1.24036

Vargo, S. L., & Lusch, R. F. (2016). Service-dominant logic. Marketing Theory: A Student Text. Sage Publications.

Vargo, S. L., & Lusch, R. F. (2017). Service-dominant logic 2025. *International Journal of Research in Marketing*, *34*(1), 46–67. doi:10.1016/j.ijresmar.2016.11.001

Vargo, S. L., Maglio, P. P., & Akaka, M. A. (2008). On value and value co-creation: A service systems and service logic perspective. *European Management Journal*, *26*(3), 145–152. doi:10.1016/j.emj.2008.04.003

Venkatesh, A., & Penaloza, L. (2014). The value of value in CCT. *Marketing Theory*, *14*(1), 135–138. doi:10.1177/1470593113500386

Verleye, K. (2015). The co-creation experience from the customer perspective: Its measurement and determinants. *Journal of Service Management*, *26*(2), 321–342. doi:10.1108/JOSM-09-2014-0254

Verleye, K., Jaakkola, E., Hodgkinson, I. R., Jun, G. T., Odekerken-Schröder, G., & Quist, J. (2017). What causes imbalance in complex service networks? Evidence from a public health service. *Journal of Service Management*, *28*(1), 34–56. doi:10.1108/JOSM-03-2016-0077

Voyer, B. G., Kastanakis, M. N., & Rhode, A. K. (2017). Co-creating stakeholder and brand identities: A cross-cultural consumer perspective. *Journal of Business Research*, *70*, 399–410. doi:10.1016/j.jbusres.2016.07.010

Wajid, A., Raziq, M. M., Malik, O. F., Malik, S. A., & Khurshid, N. (2019). Value co-creation through actor embeddedness and actor engagement. *Marketing Intelligence & Planning*, *37*(3), 271–283. doi:10.1108/MIP-07-2018-0241

Wang, H. K., Tseng, J. F., & Yen, Y. F. (2014). How do institutional norms and trust influence knowledge sharing? An institutional theory. *Innovation*, *16*(3), 374–391. doi:10.1080/14479338.2014.11081994

Wang, W., Hsieh, P., & Yen, H. R. (2011, May). Engaging customers in value co-creation: The emergence of customer readiness. In *2011 International Joint Conference on Service Sciences* (pp. 135-139). IEEE. 10.1109/IJCSS.2011.34

Wise, S., Paton, R. A., & Gegenhuber, T. (2012). Value co-creation through collective intelligence in the public sector: A review of US and European initiatives. *VINE Journal of Information and Knowledge Management Systems*, *42*(2), 251–276.

Yang, X., & Li, G. (2016). Factors influencing the popularity of customer-generated content in a company-hosted online co-creation community: A social capital perspective. *Computers in Human Behavior*, *64*, 760–768. doi:10.1016/j.chb.2016.08.002

Yi, Y., & Gong, T. (2013). Customer value co-creation behavior: Scale development and validation. *Journal of Business Research*, *66*(9), 1279–1284. doi:10.1016/j.jbusres.2012.02.026

Yousefian, J. (2015). *The Effect of Self-efficacy, Role Clarity, and Trust on Customer Well-being and Loyalty Through Value Co-creation: The Case of Fitness Centres* (Doctoral dissertation). University of Hull.

Zadeh, A. H., Zolfagharian, M., & Hofacker, C. F. (2019). Customer–customer value co-creation in social media: Conceptualization and antecedents. *Journal of Strategic Marketing*, *27*(4), 283–302. doi:10.1080/0965254X.2017.1344289

Zare, S., Bettiga, D., & Lamberti, L. (2018). Does one design fit them all? Study of drivers of co-creation interest along different consumer segments. *Journal of Strategic Marketing*, 1–21. doi:10.1080/0965254X.2018.1464051

Zhang, J. (2014, June). Customer resource integration: Antecedents and its impact on intent to co-create value. In *2014 11th International Conference on Service Systems and Service Management (ICSSSM)* (pp. 1-5). IEEE.

Zhang, M., Guo, L., Hu, M., & Liu, W. (2017). Influence of customer engagement with company social networks on stickiness: Mediating effect of customer value creation. *International Journal of Information Management*, *37*(3), 229–240. doi:10.1016/j.ijinfomgt.2016.04.010

Zhao, J., Wang, T., & Fan, X. (2015). Patient value co-creation in online health communities: Social identity effects on customer knowledge contributions and membership continuance intentions in online health communities. *Journal of Service Management*, *26*(1), 72–96. doi:10.1108/JOSM-12-2013-0344

Zittoun, T. (2007). Symbolic resources and responsibility in transitions. *Young*, *15*(2), 193–211. doi:10.1177/110330880701500205

KEY TERMS AND DEFINITIONS

Co-Creation Ecosystem: Represents the network of actors accessing, mobilizing, combining and re-combining the available resources (physical, social, and cultural), thereby creating value for each other and shaping the ecosystem of shared value.

Value Co-Creation: A synergistic process of creating, delivering, and exchanging value with key actors involved in service/goods consumption for mutual benefits through symbiotic relationship.

Value Co-Creation Antecedents: Represents the pre-conditions of effective co-creation of value by multiple stakeholders.

Value in Cultural Context: Value-creating practices in the market influenced by surrounding cultural norms and the symbolic resources form the cultural context of value.

Value in Social Context: Value creating practices in the market influenced by surrounding social structures forms the social context of value.

ENDNOTE

1 For the details regarding the final set of 85 articles mentioning the key antecedent variable, context, key authors, methodology, theory, and bibliographic details, refer to table A (i.e., supplementary material) available on request.

APPENDIX

Table 1. Key descriptive information about VCC antecedent articles (author generated based on Scopus advanced analytic features)

Top 10 journals publishing on antecedents of VCC	*Top 10 authors writing frequently on the related topic i.e. VCC antecedents*	*Top 10 countries (on the basis of frequency of documents and citations)*
1. Journal of Service Management (7)	1. L. Choi (6)	1. United States (27)
2. Journal of Services Marketing (4)	2. F.J. Cossío-silva (5)	2. United Kingdom (13)
3. Journal of strategic marketing (4)	3. C. France (5)	3. China (9)
4. Tourism management (4)	4. S.T.K. Luk (4)	4. Australia (8)
5. European Journal of Marketing (3)	5. B. Merrilees (4)	5. India (7)
6. International Journal of Contemporary Hospitality Management (3)	6. D. Miller (3)	6. Spain (5)
7. Journal of Business Research (3)	7. Z. Rahman (3)	7. Taiwan (5)
8. Journal of Service Theory and Practice (3)	8. M.A. Revilla-camacho (3)	8. Germany (4)
9. Sustainability (3)	9. B. Sarmah (2)	9. Hong Kong (4)
10. The Service Industries Journal (3)	10. M. Vega-vázquez (2)	10. New Zealand (3)

Note: Number in bracket represents the documents on value co-creation antecedents

Table 2a. Key psychological antecedents and authors (author generated)

Psychological antecedents	Key authors
Motivation Intrinsic motives (self esteem, self expression, learning, altruism, hedonism) Extrinsic motives (social recognition, identity construction, financial rewards) Ethical motives: (social welfare, helping others, morality)	Roberts, et.al, 2014; Palma, et.al, 2019; Zare, et.al, 2018; Neghina, et.al, 2015.
Ability Customer expertise Self efficacy Relational capability ICT capability	Zhang, 2014; Chen, et.al, 2015; Soltani, et.al, 2017.
Clarity Goal Clarity Role Clarity	Bharti, et.al, 2015; Chen,et.al, 2015; Yousefian, 2015; Plé, 2016; Aggarwal, & Basu, 2014.
Perceived Benefits Psychological benefits Emotional benefits Social benefits Economic benefits	Zhang, 2014; Ophof, 2013; Damkuviene, et.al, 2012.
Perceived actor participation Partner's resource contribution (fair or unfair) Perceived co-creation performance (own or other actor)	Kasnakoglu, 2016; Verleye, et.al, 2017; Ekman, et al., 2016.
Attitude towards co-creation	Zadeh, et.al, 2019; Lorenzo-Romero, et.al, 2014; Shamim, et.al, 2017; Lee, et.al, 2019.
Trust	Zhao, et.al, 2015; Sarmah & Rahman, 2018; Neghina, et.al, 2015; Bharti et.al 2015; Luk,et. al, 2018.
Past co-creation experience	Hernández-López, et.al, 2018; Palma et.al, 2019; Zare, et.al, 2018; Merrilees, 2016.
Actor Engagement Participation & Involvement	Zhang, et.al, 2017; Jaakkola & Alexander, 2014.
Personality traits Innovativeness Creativity Information seeking trait	Sarmah, & Rahman, 2018; Zare, et.al, 2018; Dahl, et.al, 2018.

Table 2b. Key social antecedents and authors (author generated)

Social antecedents	Key authors
Social Interaction	McDonald, & Karg, 2014; Romero, 2017; Johnson, & Neuhofer, 2017; Buhalis, et.al, 2019.
Network ties/social networks	Black & Gallan, 2015; Lin, et.al, 2019; Tóth,et.al, 2018.
Social identity	Zhao, et.al, 2015; Lan, et.al, 2017; Dholakia, et.al, 2004; Yi & Gong, 2013.
Social expertise	Barrutia, et.al, 2016; Eletxigerra,et.al, 2018.
Institutions/social Norms	Wang, et.al, 2014; Zadeh, et.al, 2019.
Sense of community	Qazi & Ali, 2017; Chou, et.al, 2016; Gebauer, et.al, 2013.
Social trust	Chow & Chan, 2008; Pappas, et.al, 2017.
Actor embeddedness	Laud, & Karpen, 2017; Wajid, et.al, 2019.
Collective societal values	Tregua,et.al, 2015; Laamanen, & Skålén, 2015.

Table 2c. Key cultural antecedents and authors (author generated)

Major Cultural antecedents	Key authors
Cultural norms (rules or general beliefs)	Belk, et.al, 2013; Engeström, 2015; Hepi,et.al, 2017;Csaba, 2017; Shamim, & Ghazali, 2015; Voyer, et.al, 2017.
Shared practices	Vargo, et.al, 2016; Arnould & Thompson, 2005; Nadeem,et.al, 2020.
Symbolic benefits/resources	Arnould, 2005; Zittoun, 2007; Meynhardt,et.al, 2016; Venkatesh & Penaloza, 2014.
Specialized knowledge	Davey & Gronroos, 2019; Baron, & Warnaby, 2011; Arnould, 2005.

Table 3. Future research questions under each of the explained categories

Research questions related to psychological processes: How do consumers' ability & motivation influence each other and affect resource access for value co-creation? How consumer motivations vary across different (individualistic or collectivist) cultures? How does interpersonal trust (between customer & provider) affect value co-creation through the actor's perceived fairness/perceived honesty? Does a lower level of goal congruence results in misalignment or disintegration of resources? How consumer's personal experiences affect shared co-creation experiences in context to co-creative interactions? How customer engagement and role clarity are associated with each-other in context to value co-creation intention/behavior? Is it true that consumers with independent self-construal are usually less interested to co-create with the service provider as compared to consumers with inter-dependent self-construal?	**Supporting References:** Roberts, et.al, 2014; Palma, et.al, 2019; Zare, et.al, 2018; Neghina, et.al, 2015; Zhang, 2014; Soltani, et.al, 2017; Bharti et.al, 2015; Plé, 2016; Aggarwal, & Basu, 2014; Zhang, 2014; Damkuviene, et.al, 2012; Kasnakoglu, 2016; Zadeh, et.al, 2019; Lorenzo-Romero, et.al, 2014; Shamim, et.al, 2017; Lee, et.al, 2019; Zhao, et.al, 2015; Sarmah & Rahman, 2018; Luk,et.al, 2018; Roy, et.al, 2020; Hernández-López, et.al, 2018; Merrilees, 2016; Jaakkola & Alexander, 2014.
Research questions related to Social processes: How social servicescape changes consumer expectations/perceived benefits in context to co-creation and affects overall VCC behavior? What is the influence of sense of community on the customer citizenship behavior component of co-creation behavior? How individual goals (like self-identity and experientialism) contradict a collective goal like a sense of community and group identity? What is the joint effect of social expertise and consumer expertise on value co-creation behavior? How C2C value interactions boost B2C consumer resource integration? How consumer's personal experiences affect shared social experiences in context to value co-creation and social innovation? How does shared language and shared vision influence social identity, which in turn influences co-creation behavior?	**Supporting References:** Romero, 2017; Johnson, & Neuhofer, 2017; Buhalis, et.al, 2019; Black & Gallan, 2015; Lan, et.al, 2017; Dholakia, et.al, 2004; Yi & Gong, 2013; Barrutia, et.al, 2016; Eletxigerra,et.al, 2018; Wang, et.al, 2014; Zadeh, et.al, 2019; Qazi & Ali, 2017; Chou, et.al, 2016; Gebauer, et.al, 2013; Pappas, et.al, 2017; Laud, & Karpen, 2017; Wajid, et.al, 2019; Tregua,et.al, 2015;Laamanen, & Skålén, 2015.
Research questions related to Cultural processes: How symbolic resources in a given customer ecosystem influence the collective efficacy of actors for co-creation? What are the dynamics of Collective–Conflictual practices within value co-creation? How unequal power relations affect the collective enactment practices of an actor? How consumers make sense of co-creative relationships with other actors in a service ecosystem using their knowledge of cultural context? Is it true that acculturated customer is usually more motivated to engage in co-creative activities?	**Supporting References:** Hepi,et.al, 2017; Vargo, et.al, 2016; Arnould & Thompson, 2005; Nadeem,et.al, 2020; Meynhardt,et.al, 2016; Venkatesh & Penaloza, 2014; Davey & Gronroos, 2019; Baron, & Warnaby, 2011; Csaba, 2017; Shamim, & Ghazali, 2015; Voyer, et.al, 2017.

Chapter 3
Scientific Community-Driven Ecosystem as a Supporter to Co-Create and Co-Evolute Science

Helio Aisenberg Ferenhof
https://orcid.org/0000-0001-5167-0838
Universidade Federal de Santa Catarina, Brazil

Marcos Paulo Alves de Sousa
https://orcid.org/0000-0002-3379-4754
Museu Paraense Emílio Goeldi, Brazil

ABSTRACT

One critical aspect of science is the ability to reproduce the same experiment by another researcher. In other to do so, the same ambient, variables, data, setup should be considered. The method tells how the original researcher planned and did their research, but how can others replicate or even advance the preview research? The scientific community has been focusing on efforts to increase transparency and reproducibility and develop a "culture of reproducibility." When researchers share their data, their workflow, and co-evolute a way of doing research, all the players win. The value co-creation is established in a business ecosystem. The actor who is part of the business platform by the co-creation can leverage the advantage of one or more partners that make up the platform. Thus, the knowledge created from the interaction between the different technological domains and knowledge shared on the platform can improve all the research and researchers. Stating that, this chapter proposes a business ecosystem model to ensure research repeatability.

DOI: 10.4018/978-1-7998-4843-1.ch003

INTRODUCTION

This chapter promotes the use of a business ecosystem to co-create and co-evolute science. According to Ziouvelou and McGroarty (2017, p. 1), "business success in this complex and constantly evolving system is determined by the ecosystem's ability to bring together a variety of strategic business elements in order to jointly co-created shared value". One critical aspect of science is the ability to reproduce the same experiment by another researcher. In order to do so, the same ambient, variables, data, setup should be considered. The method tells how the original researcher plan and did their research, but how can others have the same environment to check the consistency, replicate, or even advance the preview research? In computer science is not different; the same issues appear; how can other researchers repeat the experiment? Think, many different variables are not considered when describing the methodology, which should be — hardware, Software, Operational System, Database, Indexes, among others. So, the ability to reproduce the results of other researchers is a core tenet of the scientific method, and computational science has driven scientific development in many knowledge areas (Peng, 2011).

Nonetheless, many authors have drawn attention to the rise of purely computational experiments that are not reproducible (Cohen-Boulakia et al., 2017). Studies show that scientific work generally does not show all the essential experimental details for reproduction (Nekrutenko, 2012), and have difficulty replicating published experimental results (Loannidis et al., 2009). In recent years, the scientific community has been focusing on efforts to increase transparency and reproducibility and develop a "culture of reproducibility" for computer science. Research is considered reproducible when all data used are available, and the exploited computational analysis workflow is clearly described (Kulkarni et al., 2018). Workflow is a well-established way to capture the scientific method, and it can generate a graph abstract revealing the interrelated processing tasks. Workflows have become a valuable mechanism for specifying and automating scientific experiments running on distributed computing infrastructure. Researchers in different disciplines have embraced them to conduct a wide range of analyses and scientific pipelines (Deelman et al., 2009), mainly because a workflow can be considered as a model defining the structure of the computational and/or data processing tasks necessary for the management of a scientific process (Liu et al., 2012). The challenges in workflow reproducibility can be summarized as an insufficient and non-portable description of a workflow including missing details of the processing tools and execution environment, unavailable execution environments, missing third party resources and data, and reliance on external dependencies, such as external web services, which add difficulty to reproducibility at a later time (Qasha et al., 2016). Workflows are not only useful in representing and managing the computation but also as a way of sharing knowledge and experimental methods. When shared, they can help users to understand the overall experiment, or they can become an essential building block in their new experiments. Lastly, workflows can also be used to repeat or reproduce the experiment and replicate the original results (Qasha et al., 2016). As scientific workflows grow in complexity and importance, the designers of workflow management systems need a deeper and broader understanding of what workflows require and how they behave in order to drive improvements in algorithms for provisioning resources, scheduling computational jobs, and managing data. The community has lacked detailed knowledge of a range of scientific workflows because few workflow applications have been available for general use since many workflow users are reluctant to release their code and data (Juve et al., 2013). When researchers share their data, their workflow, and co-evolute a way of doing research, all the players win. It is a win-win situation. The value co-creation is established in a business ecosystem and, science and market can trust even more in the experiment and results. We identified that co-creation and co-evolution are typically missing when designing a workflow. We highlight that a business ecosystem is an emerging concept analogized to biology. Business ecosystems move beyond market positioning and industrial structure by having three major characteristics: symbiosis, platform, and co-evolution (Li, 2009). The actor who is part of the business platform by the co-creation can leverage the advantage of one or more partners that make up the platform (Galateanu and Avasilcai, 2013). Thus, the knowledge created from the interaction between the different technological domains and knowledge shared on the platform can improve all the research and researchers. Stating that, one of the significant challenges in achieving workflow reproducibility, however, is the heterogeneity of workflow components that demand different, sometimes conflicting sets of dependencies. Ensuring successful reproducibility of workflows requires more than merely sharing their specifications. It also depends on the ability to isolate necessary and sufficient computational artifacts and preserve them with adequate descriptions for future reuse (Qasha et al., 2016). The business ecosystem model can be a key to the success of sharing data, workflow, and methods.

This chapter discusses the scientific credibility crisis in reproducible computational research. Also, present that the act of only making the coding and data available does not guarantee reproducibility, even more, the current workflow systems for computational experiments still fail reproducibility. Because they usually do not present all the steps that were done (method) and do not share how they co-create and co-evolute the research. Furthermore, it presents the business ecosystem use as a model to ensure researches repeatability, the ability to co-create, co-evolute, showing different tools and techniques to guarantee that the computer data ambient can be shared with others to repeat the same experiment, having the same results. Once the computational environment can be easily shared, the research toughness can be established, and the advance will come from different business ecosystem actors, that can take advantage of the shared validated research environment to continue evolving, creating new knowledge supported by the previous ones.

THE SCIENTIFIC CREDIBILITY CRISIS IN REPRODUCIBLE COMPUTATIONAL RESEARCH

Computing is increasingly present in the advances of science, permeating all areas of knowledge in its various forms of scientific research, such as modeling, monitoring, simulation, and measurement. Recent significant scientific discoveries are the result of multidisciplinary teams' work involving computer scientists. According to a 2014 UK (417 respondents) survey, 92% of academics' scientists use some software in their research, 69% say that their research would not be practical without it, and 56% develop their software (Hettrick, 2014). In a similar survey targeting US National Postdoctoral Association members, 95% of the 209 respondents said they use research software, and 63% stated that it would not be practical to conduct their work without software (Nangia and Katz, 2017).

With these advances, the scientific community recognizes the importance of the reproducibility of computational methods to provide greater transparency and more efficient research review processes, which had been a significant challenge for computer science (Stodden et al., 2016). Computational reproducibility is the ability to replicate the same or similar computational results from the availability of primary data and computational experimentation used to generate the findings (Peng, 2011). Despite its importance, reproducibility is not yet standard and not trivial when it involves computational experiments, and this has led to a crisis of scientific credibility (Donoho et al., 2009). Researchers have been challenging to reproduce previously published analyze in several scientific papers. In a survey of over 1,500 scientists, more than 70 percent of them reported having been unable to reproduce other scientists' findings, and half of the surveyed scientists ran into problems trying to reproduce their results (Baker, 2016). Loannidis et al. (2009) evaluated 18 published research studies that used computational methods to evaluate gene expression data, but they were able to reproduce only two of those studies. Something is missing! How can other researchers repeat the studies? Even with the data available, it is difficult or impossible to reproduce it!

Make Data and Code Available does not Guarantee Reproducibility

Given these concerns, there is a movement between funding agencies, governmental institutions, journal editors, and individual researchers to adopt the "culture of reproducibility" for computational science (Peng, 2011). Currently, high impact journals increasingly consider reproducibility when evaluating and publishing manuscripts (Perkel, 2018). Some journals have adopted open data policy and advised researchers to publish data and code in open access repositories. Open digital repositories such as Zenodo.org and figshare.com provide permanent digital object identifiers (DOI) that can be linked to software code and other data used in publications. Although data policy in the open in journals has contributed to increasing availability of scientific data, open data alone does not guarantee reproducibility. Hardwicke and colleagues tried to reuse data and replicate the findings reported in 35 papers. Only in 22 papers, all results were reproduced; 11 of these papers were reproduced with the assistance of the original authors. 13 of the 35 papers did not fully reproduce the results, even with the author's assistance (Hardwicke et al., 2018). For data to have utility, they must be structured and sufficiently well documented, it must be accompanied by software, workflow and explanations, all of which need to be captured during the research cycle and with consistent and available results (Munafò et al., 2017). Just sharing the code does not reveal the details of the computational steps taken that were necessary to process data and generate the new discovery analysis (Beaulieu-Jones; Greene, 2017), and the reporting of these steps performed in research is not routine in the academic literature (Stodden et al., 2016).

Reproducibility is incredibly complicated because neither software nor data is static (Perkel, 2018). In times of big data, the massive volumes of data are produced at all times from a variety of sources, such as automatic sensor measurements, social network interactions, and data repository mining to build data compilations all produce data continuously updated and are being used in scientific discoveries. Frequently updated data pose significant challenges for reproducibility as they require continuous data management, traceability, and control (Yenni et al., 2019). Research software also evolves, whether to meet research itself new demands or because of the need for new operating environment updates. Any new software updates or their dependencies (libraries, packages, etc.) should be reported, including information about the new software version, its new features and their parameters, and on which operating system the stable version of the software will run (Piccolo; Frampton, 2016).

Current Systems to Support Scientific Workflows Still Fail Reproducibility

In general, computational experiments consist of a set of software-executed tasks that are chained. So that the output of one task is consumed as the input of the next task in the flow, this task chain interacts with many applications, which have dependencies and can manipulate large amounts of data, making it difficult to manage and control computational experiments. Due to the complexity of computational experiments, the scientific workflow approach has been widely used by scientists to integrate, structure, and orchestrate a wide range of various services and software tools into complex scientific processes to support scientific discoveries (Deelman et al., 2009) (Lin et al., 2009). The concept of workflows has been in use in a wide variety of domains, such as business processes, scientific research, and computing (Börger, 2011; Albrecht et al., 2012; Juve et al., 2013). A scientific workflow is an abstraction that formalizes the composition of several activities through data set production and consumption. Each activity corresponds to a computational application, and the dependencies between them represent the execution data flow, in which the output of one activity is input to another (Deelman et al., 2009).

In addition to being an essential tool for representing and managing computational resources, scientific workflows are useful for sharing knowledge and experimental methods and helping the user understand an experience, and have been used for reproducibility of experiments (Juve et al., 2013; Qasha et al., 2016). However, significant studies have shown several reproducibility problems in the scientific workflow, highlighting (Zhao et al., 2012; Qasha et al., 2016). In the vision of Banati et al. (2015), insufficient and non-portable description of a workflow including missing details of the processing tools and execution environment, unavailable execution environments, missing third party resources and data, and reliance on external dependencies, such as external web services, which add difficulty to reproducibility at a later time.

Faced with the scientific workflow reproducibility challenges, numerous systems to support scientific workflows have been proposed (Maechling et al., 2006; Chirigati et al., 2013; Wolstencroft et al., 2013; Deelman et al., 2015), two systems have seen widespread adoption: Jupyter Notebook (Kluyver et al., 2016) and Galaxy (Goecks et al., 2010). The first, Jupyter notebook, is an open-source, browser-based tool functioning as a virtual lab notebook to support workflows, code, data, and visualizations detailing the research process (Randles et al., 2017). Jupyter is an extremely efficient "literate programming" (Knuth, 1984) tool for online interactive analysis, which is used mainly in the scientific community to perform in a computational experiment and can combine executable code and descriptive text into a single document. There were more than 3 million Jupyter Notebooks shared publicly on GitHub (Rule et al., 2019). Interactively running and editing code in notebooks can delete key steps or introduce a "hidden state" that confounds analyses and confuses readers. Analyses documented in notebooks cannot be easily rerun if users do not first freeze their dependencies, share their data, and adequately describe their computing environment. Furthermore, many notebooks lack sufficient descriptive text to guide readers in using them (Rule et al., 2019).

The second, Galaxy is a popular web-based scientific workbench. It provides a framework for integrating computational tools and an environment for interactive data analysis, reuse, and sharing. The system automatically tracks and manages data provenance and provides support for capturing the context and intent of computational methods (Goecks et al., 2010). The most prominent workflow environment and with more than a decade of continuous development and use (Afgan et al., 2016). Despite Galaxy's success, it still falls short of achieving full reproducibility (Grüning et al., 2018). Currently, Galaxy focuses on the automation of scientific process analysis, which does not address all research steps involving the co-creation of knowledge. There is a growing need for workflow systems that promote researcher engagement to build knowledge collaboratively, and workflow environments should enable users to build communities, invite other users, and easily share workflows and results. The system should include techniques to allow users to comment, discuss, and rate not only workflows but also results, ideas, and techniques (Kanterakis et al., 2018).

Those tools/workflows assist on developing new research findings, also on delimiting roles and responsibilities on the project, but the tool by the tool, the workflow by the workflow *per se* still miss the stakeholder's interaction, with each other, with the tool, with the data, and even the systemic perspective of the research. What is proposed is the use of the business ecosystem concept to guide a way to ensure reproducibility.

Methodological Procedures

In order to incorporate a way of doing research, which all the players can co-evolute, a narrative literature review was conducted. According to Ferenhof and Fernandes (2016), narrative revision is also known as exploratory revision and is considered the traditional way of doing a literature review. For this kind of review, there is not the need for defining an explicit inclusion and exclusion criteria. The documents selection is made arbitrarily by the researchers, meaning the documents can be included according to their bias. It does not need to follow a systematic. Furthermore, there is no concern to exhaust the sources of information.

This chapter, authors decided to explore the scientific databases: Scopus, Web of Science, and Compendex seeking for constructs (business ecosystems, digital business ecosystems, knowledge ecosystems, crowd-driven ecosystems, among others), also computational systems and frameworks that could assist science reproducibility by the co-evolution and researcher's co-creation. One of the literature analyses aims were to identify the scientific ecosystem actors/players and also the drivers or key factors that could assist in ensuring science reproducibility and also having co-evolution and co-creation among the researchers. The synthesis of the analysis resulted in the proposed framework.

Business Ecosystem Framework to Ensure Science Reproducibility

Faraj et al. (2012, p. 788) stated that "both people and technology need to be connected in order to achieve a form of 'knowledge ecosystem' and 'collective intelligence' that is far more effective than any individual or singular group of people and computers". So, understand research as an ecosystem could assist with co-creation and co-evolution and, the players' identification is one critical aspect. Furthermore, the framework is also based on Ziouvelou and McGroarty (2017) crowd-driven ecosystem concept. The framework prescribes to change in the research logic, from researcher-centric to ecosystem-centric, in order to facilitate the research development, analysis, implementation, and replication. They are reinforcing the players' participation by the support of technology.

Based on a narrative literature review, it was possible to identify that several actors/players interact with each other to produce science. Those players comprise the science ecosystem. To expose our framework, we named seventeen, being: researcher, editor, reviewer, journals, retail, producer, manufacturer machinery/equipment, consumer, financial institution, supplier, legislator, government, cooperative, university, research institute, industry, the customer. Nevertheless, according to the literature exists some key factors that can improve scientific reproducibility, namely: open access, open data, technological capacity, workflow, traceability, actors' interaction, and the scientific method. To ensure science reproducibility, first, those players must understand the need for interaction. Second, based on this need, establish a direction. Third, identify which key factor should occur for the iteration to booster science reproducibility. The iteration should result in improvements inside and outside the research ecosystem. Figure 1 represents the proposed Scientific Research Key-Factors booster Theoretical Framework to ensure science reproducibility.

The framework works by the engagement and interaction with two or more actors of the research business ecosystem so that they can co-create value and enhance each essential element (Moore, 1996; Peltoniemi and Vuori, 2004; Li, 2009; Yu, Li, and Zhao, 2011; Galateanu and Avasilcai, 2013; Ziouvelou and McGroarty, 2017). The way the framework was built was rooted in the construct digital ecosystem, because "there is no permanent need for centralized or distributed control or single-role behavior. In a Digital Ecosystem, a leadership structure may be formed (and dissolved) in response to the dynamic needs of the environment" (Boley; Chang, 2007, p. 2). By those interactions, the players establish proceedings to plan, collect, register, and share all data, information, and knowledge needed to generate the research, and by doing that, ensure science reproducibility. The role idea is to generate the step by step with the procedures and data exposed in an open-access environment. For instance, in computer science, generate a virtual machine image with all the parameters set up, including data, source code, executable. It is expected that the ecosystem created by iterative player's interactions can ensure the traceability culture sharing all the environment need for reproducibility.

Figure 1. Scientific Research Key-Factors booster Theoretical Framework for ensuring science reproducibility
Source: Authors.

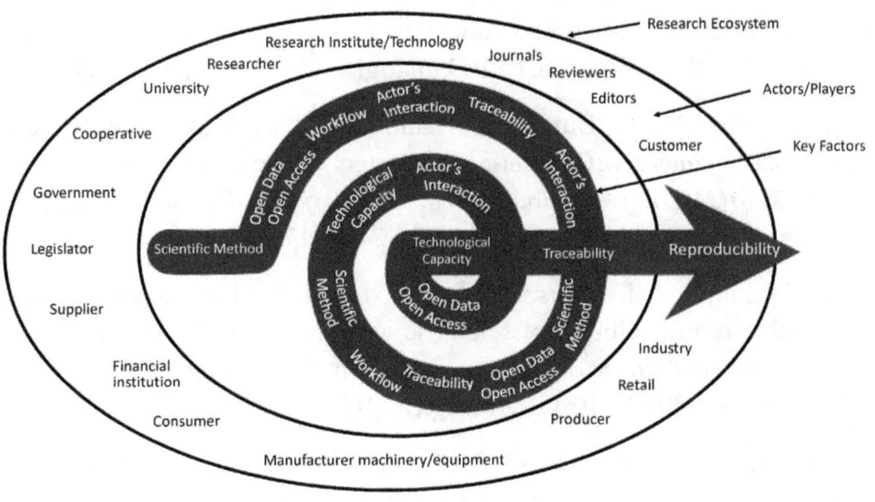

FINAL THOUGHTS

This chapter exposed the difficulty of reproducing the same experiment by another researcher. Also exposed even if the "original" researcher provides the data *per se* do not ensure the reproducibility. One possible solution is the use of a business ecosystem to co-create and co-evolute science. As recommended by the literature, a set of actions and interactions should be done in order to ensure scientific reproducibility. The proposed theoretical business ecosystem framework is one way to support it. For instance, computer science researches can generate a virtual machine image with all the parameters set up, including data, source code, executable. By opening the whole environment, the reproducibility and traceability are ensured. Furthermore, it is possible to create new researches using the same environment and generate a scientific community-driven ecosystem where researchers can exchange data, information, and knowledge. Further research should implement the theoretical framework and structure a method or systematic on how to create the proceedings to ensure reproducibility.

REFERENCES

Afgan, E., Baker, D., van den Beek, M., Blankenberg, D., Bouvier, D., Čech, M., Chilton, J., Clements, D., Coraor, N., Eberhard, C., Grüning, B., Guerler, A., Hillman-Jackson, J., Von Kuster, G., Rasche, E., Soranzo, N., Turaga, N., Taylor, J., Nekrutenko, A., & Goecks, J. (2016). The Galaxy platform for accessible, reproducible and collaborative biomedical analyses: 2016 update. *Nucleic Acids Research*, *44*(W1), W3–W10. doi:10.1093/nar/gkw343 PMID:27137889

Albrecht, M., Donnelly, P., Bui, P., & Thain, D. (2012). Makeflow: A Portable Abstraction for Data Intensive Computing on Clusters, Clouds, and Grids. *Proceedings of the 1st ACM SIGMOD Workshop on Scalable Workflow Execution Engines and Technologies - SWEET '12*. 10.1145/2443416.2443417

Banati, A., Kacsuk, P., & Kozlovszky, M. (2015). Four level provenance support to achieve portable reproducibility of scientific workflows. *2015 38th International Convention on Information and Communication Technology, Electronics and Microelectronics (MIPRO)*. 10.1109/MIPRO.2015.7160272

Beaulieu-Jones, B. K., & Greene, C. S. (2017). Reproducibility of computational workflows is automated using continuous analysis. *Nature Biotechnology*, *35*(4), 342–346. doi:10.1038/nbt.3780 PMID:28288103

Boley, H. & Chang, E. (2007). *Digital Ecosystems: Principles and Semantics*. Academic Press.

Börger, E. (2011). Approaches to modeling business processes: A critical analysis of BPMN, workflow patterns and YAWL. *Software & Systems Modeling*, *11*(3), 305–318. doi:10.100710270-011-0214-z

Carvalho, L. A. M. C., Essawy, B. T., & Garijo, D. (2017). Requirements for supporting the iterative exploration of scientific workflow variants. *Proceedings of the Workshop on Capturing Scientific Knowledge (SciKnow)*.

Chirigati, C. F., Shasha, D., & Freire, J. (2013). ReproZip: using provenance to support computational reproducibility. *Proceedings of the 5th USENIX Workshop on the Theory and Practice of Provenance.*

Deelman, E., Gannon, D., Shields, M., & Taylor, I. (2009). Workflows and e-Science: An overview of workflow system features and capabilities. *Future Generation Computer Systems, 25*(5), 528–540. doi:10.1016/j.future.2008.06.012

Deelman, E., Vahi, K., Juve, G., Rynge, M., Callaghan, S., Maechling, P. J., Mayani, R., Chen, W., Ferreira da Silva, R., Livny, M., & Wenger, K. (2015). Pegasus, a workflow management system for science automation. *Future Generation Computer Systems, 46*, 17–35. doi:10.1016/j.future.2014.10.008

Donoho, D. L., Maleki, A., Rahman, I. U., Shahram, M., & Stodden, V. (2009). Reproducible Research in Computational Harmonic Analysis. *Computing in Science & Engineering, 11*(1), 8–18. doi:10.1109/MCSE.2009.15

Faraj, S. A., Kolker, E., Bevilacqua, L., & Özdemir, V. (2012). Collective theranostics and postgenomics entrepreneurship: Rethinking innovations as knowledge ecosystems built by complex collaboration. *Expert Review of Molecular Diagnostics, 12*(8), 787–790. doi:10.1586/erm.12.124 PMID:23249193

Ferenhof, H. A., & Fernandes, R. F. (2016). Demystifying the Literature Review as basis for Scientific Writing: SSF Method. *Revista ACB, 21*(3), 550–563.

Galateanu, E., & Avasilcai, S. (2013). Business ecosystems architecture. *Annals of the Oradea University, 22*(1), 79–84.

Goecks, J., Nekrutenko, A., Taylor, J., & Galaxy Team, T. (2010). Galaxy: A comprehensive approach for supporting accessible, reproducible, and transparent computational research in the life sciences. *Genome Biology, 11*(8), R86. doi:10.1186/gb-2010-11-8-r86 PMID:20738864

Grüning, B., Chilton, J., Köster, J., Dale, R., Soranzo, N., van den Beek, M., Goecks, J., Backofen, R., Nekrutenko, A., & Taylor, J. (2018). Practical Computational Reproducibility in the Life Sciences. *Cell Systems, 6*(6), 631–635. doi:10.1016/j.cels.2018.03.014 PMID:29953862

Hardwicke, T. E., Mathur, M. B., MacDonald, K., Nilsonne, G., Banks, G. C., Kidwell, M. C., Hofelich Mohr, A., Clayton, E., Yoon, E. J., Henry Tessler, M., Lenne, R. L., Altman, S., Long, B., & Frank, M. C. (2018). Data availability, reusability, and analytic reproducibility: Evaluating the impact of a mandatory open data policy at the journalCognition. *Royal Society Open Science, 5*(8), 180448. doi:10.1098/rsos.180448 PMID:30225032

Hettrick, S. J. (2014). UK Research Software Survey 2014 [Data set]. doi:10.5281/zenodo.14809

Hothorn, T., & Leisch, F. (2011). Case studies in reproducibility. [PubMed]. *Briefings in Bioinformatics*, *12*(3), 288–300. doi:10.1093/bib/bbq084

Juve, G., Chervenak, A., Deelman, E., Bharathi, S., Mehta, G., & Vahi, K. (2013). Characterizing and profiling scientific workflows. *Future Generation Computer Systems*, *29*(3), 682–692. doi:10.1016/j.future.2012.08.015

Kanterakis, A., Potamias, G., Swertz, M. A., & Patrinos, G. P. (2018). Creating Transparent and Reproducible Pipelines: Best Practices for Tools, Data, and Workflow Management Systems. *Human Genome Informatics*, 15–43. doi:10.1016/B978-0-12-809414-3.00002-4

Karim, M., Michel, A., Zappa, A., Baranov, P., Sahay, R., & Rebholz-Schuhmann, D. (2017). *Improving data workflow systems with cloud services and use of open data for bioinformatics research.* Briefings Bioinf.

Kluyver, T., Ragan-Kelley, B., Perez, F., Granger, B., & Bussonnier. (2016). Jupyter Notebooks-A Publishing Format for Reproducible Computational Workflows (ELPUB). Academic Press.

Knuth, D. E. (1984). Literate programming. *The Computer Journal*, *27*(2), 97–111. doi:10.1093/comjnl/27.2.97

Leipzig, J. (2016). A review of bioinformatic pipeline frameworks. *Brief. Bioinf.* . doi:10.1093/bib/bbw020

Li, Y.-R. (2009). The technological roadmap of Cisco's business ecosystem. *Technovation*, *29*(5), 379–386. doi:10.1016/j.technovation.2009.01.007

Lin, C., Lu, S., Fei, X., & Chebotko, A. (2009). A Reference Architecture for Scientific Workflow Management Systems and the VIEW SOA Solution. *IEEE Transactions on Services Computing*, *2*(1), 79–92. doi:10.1109/TSC.2009.4

Loannidis, J. P. A. (2009). Repeatability of published microarray gene expression analyses. *Nature Genetics*, *41*(2), 149–155. doi:10.1038/ng.295 PMID:19174838

Maechling, P. (2006). SCEC CyberShake workflows—automating probabilistic seismic hazard analysis calculations. In E. D. I. Taylor, D. Gannon, & M. Shields (Eds.), *Workflows for e-Science*. Springer.

Moore, J. F. (1996). *The Death of Competition: Leadership and Strategy in the Age of Business Ecosystems*. Harper Collins Publishers.

Munafò, M. R., Nosek, B. A., Bishop, D. V. M., & Button, K. S. (2017). A manifesto for reproducible science. *Nature Human Behaviour, 1*(1), 21. . doi:10.103841562-016-0021

NangiaU.KatzD. S. (2017). *Track 1 Paper: Surveying the US National Postdoctoral Association Regarding Software Use and Training in Research.* doi:10.6084/m9.figshare.5328442.v3

Nekrutenko, A., & Taylor, J. (2012). Next-generation sequencing data interpretation: Enhancing reproducibility and accessibility. *Nature Reviews. Genetics, 13*(9), 667–672. doi:10.1038/nrg3305 PMID:22898652

Peltoniemi, M., & Vuori, E. (2004). Business ecosystem as the new approach to complex adaptive business environments. *Proceedings of eBusiness Research Forum*, 18, 267-281.

Peng, R. D. (2011). Reproducible research in computational science. *Science, 334*(6060), 1226–1227. doi:10.1126cience.1213847 PMID:22144613

Perkel, J. M. (2018). A toolkit for data transparency takes shape. *Nature, 560*(7719), 513–515. doi:10.1038/d41586-018-05990-5 PMID:30127481

Piccolo, S. R., & Frampton, M. B. (2016). Tools and techniques for computational reproducibility. *GigaScience, 5*(1), 30. Advance online publication. doi:10.118613742-016-0135-4 PMID:27401684

Qasha, R., Cala, J., & Watson, P. (2016). A framework for scientific workflow reproducibility in the cloud. *2016 IEEE 12th International Conference on e-Science (e-Science).* 10.1109/eScience.2016.7870888

Randles, B. M., Pasquetto, I. V., Golshan, M. S., & Borgman, C. L. (2017). Using the Jupyter Notebook as a Tool for Open Science: An Empirical Study. *2017 ACM/IEEE Joint Conference on Digital Libraries (JCDL).* 10.1109/JCDL.2017.7991618

Rule, A., Birmingham, A., Zuniga, C., Altintas, I., Huang, S.-C., Knight, R., Moshiri, N., Nguyen, M. H., Rosenthal, S. B., Pérez, F., & Rose, P. W. (2019). Ten simple rules for writing and sharing computational analyses in Jupyter Notebooks. *PLoS Computational Biology, 15*(7), e1007007. doi:10.1371/journal.pcbi.1007007 PMID:31344036

Stodden, V., McNutt, M., Bailey, D. H., Deelman, E., Gil, Y., Hanson, B., Heroux, M. A., Ioannidis, J. P. A., & Taufer, M. (2016). Enhancing reproducibility for computational methods. *Science, 354*(6317), 1240–1241. doi:10.1126cience.aah6168 PMID:27940837

Wolstencroft, K., Haines, R., Fellows, D., Williams, A., Withers, D., Owen, S., Soiland-Reyes, S., Dunlop, I., Nenadic, A., Fisher, P., Bhagat, J., Belhajjame, K., Bacall, F., Hardisty, A., Nieva de la Hidalga, A., Balcazar Vargas, M. P., Sufi, S., & Goble, C. (2013). The Taverna workflow suite: Designing and executing workflows of Web Services on the desktop, web or in the cloud. *Nucleic Acids Research*, *41*(W1), W557–W561. doi:10.1093/nar/gkt328 PMID:23640334

Yenni, G. M., Christensen, E. M., Bledsoe, E. K., Supp, S. R., Diaz, R. M., White, E. P., & Ernest, S. K. M. (2019). Developing a modern data workflow for regularly updated data. *PLoS Biology*, *17*(1), e3000125. doi:10.1371/journal.pbio.3000125 PMID:30695030

Yu, J., Li, Y., & Zhao, C. (2011). Analysis on structure and complexity characteristics of electronic business ecosystem. *Procedia Engineering*, *15*, 1400–1404. doi:10.1016/j.proeng.2011.08.259

Zhao, J., Gomez-Perez, J. M., Belhajjame, K., & Klyne, G. (2012). Why workflows break — Understanding and combating decay in Taverna workflows. *2012 IEEE 8th International Conference on E-Science*. 10.1109/eScience.2012.6404482

Ziouvelou, X., & McGroarty, F. (2017). Business Models for Crowd-driven IoT Ecosystems: A Review. *International Journal of Computer & Software Engineering*, *2*(2), 121. doi:10.15344/2456-4451/2017/121

Chapter 4
Opening Closed Business Ecosystem Boundaries With Digital Platforms:
Empirical Case of a Port

Marika Iivari
University of Oulu, Finland

Petri Ahokangas
University of Oulu, Finland

Marja Matinmikko-Blue
University of Oulu, Finland

Seppo Yrjölä
Nokia, Finland

ABSTRACT

Applying a business model approach, this chapter identifies various challenges in digital platform and platform-based business model development in the case of a physical port ecosystem. Using an empirical case, the chapter identifies the prerequisites and consequences of opportunities, value, and advantages for an existing ecosystem that aims to create a "digital twin." It contributes to academic discussions on the intersection of ecosystems, platforms, and business models by exploring the antecedents and controversies of configuring ecosystem boundaries in a digital context. Moreover, the chapter contributes to research by analyzing how a previously closed ecosystem seeks to open its boundaries and interfaces, both internally among the internal ecosystem members and externally to the outside business environment.

DOI: 10.4018/978-1-7998-4843-1.ch004

INTRODUCTION

Ecosystem as a concept has gained momentum within a wide array of research topics. Ecosystems are characterized as highly complex, interdependent, cooperative, competitive, and co-evolutional in pursuit of new innovations (Iansiti & Richards, 2006). Several types of ecosystems have been identified in previous studies (Ahokangas et al. 2018), such as business ecosystems (Moore, 1993; Iansiti & Levien, 2004), innovation ecosystems (Adner, 2006; Adner & Kapoor, 2010), industrial ecosystems (Frosch & Gallopoulos, 1989) entrepreneurial ecosystems (Isenberg 2010), and knowledge ecosystems (van der Borgh, Cloodt, & Romme, 2012). Common to all these typologies is the fact that they stress constant innovation and the joint creation and capture of value (Ahokangas, Boter, & Iivari, 2018).

Recent research on ecosystems has addressed such issues as the types of complementarity and interdependence (Jacobides, Cennamo, & Gawer, 2018), the roles of actors (Dedehayir, Mäkinen, & Ortt, 2018), orchestration (e.g. Pikkarainen, Ervasti, Hurmelinna-Laukkanen, & Nätti, 2017), interfaces of collaboration (Davis, 2016), and strategies for aligning actors and value proposition (Walrave, Talmar, Podoynitsyna, Romme, & Verbong, 2018). Moreover, extensive literature reviews have been conducted on ecosystems (see, e.g. Scaringella & Radziwon 2018; Tsujimoto, Kajikawa, Tomita, & Matsumoto, 2018). Academics have also proposed methodological frameworks for the study of ecosystems (e.g. Phillips & Ritala, 2019) and developed more practical tools for mapping, analyzing, and designing ecosystems (e.g. Talmar, Walrave, Podoynitsyna, Holmström, & Romme, 2018). Ecosystems can be studied based on context, how they are configured, and how organizations within them co-operate and relate to each other (Scaringella & Radziwon 2018).

Digital business ecosystems, digital platform operated ecosystems (Gawer & Cusumano, 2014; Phillips & Ritala, 2019), or technology ecosystems (Thomas & Autio, 2019) have been identified as distinct types of a business ecosystem. Digital business ecosystems are based to a large extent on open-source thinking, meaning that services and applications, together with software components and business models alike, interact, reproduce, and evolve (Pilinkienė & Maciulis, 2014). Digital business ecosystems can self-organize, adapt, and sustain themselves under different circumstances within the physical business ecosystem (Galateanu & Avasilcai, 2013). Digital business ecosystems can therefore be considered a partial digital representation of a physical business ecosystem (Nachira, Dini, & Nicolai, 2007). A so-called "digital twin" may be critical for the competitiveness and existence of an ecosystem, since digitalization can help physical ecosystems broaden the avenues of innovation as they span organizational and industry boundaries, foster new forms of collaboration among firms, and enable the creation of new kinds of services (Lanzolla, Pesce, & Tucci, 2020; Zott, Amit, & Massa, 2011). Hence, digital business ecosystems should not be viewed as just mediating interfaces, but as sociotechnical systems of their own, equally open, shared, heterogenous, unbounded, and evolving (Thomas & Autio, 2019).

Parallel to recent discussions on ecosystems in the digital context, platforms have emerged as a topic with a close relationship to ecosystems; platforms "grow" an ecosystem around them. According to McIntyre and Srinivasan (2017, p. 143), "platforms can be conceptualized as interfaces—often embodied in products, services, or technologies—that can serve to mediate transactions between two or more sides." An ecosystem's platform architecture can be defined as a conceptual blueprint that describes how the ecosystem is partitioned into a relatively stable platform, that is, a complementary set of varying modules and the design rules binding them together (Baldwin & Woodard, 2009; Cusumano & Gawer, 2002). Platform research has an intrinsically dualistic perspective to business (Gawer, 2014), as it comprises quite separate economic and engineering streams of literature. Within economics, platforms are treated as two-sided or multi-sided markets connecting supply and demand, while within engineering they serve as modular technological designs for facilitating innovation. Indeed, platforms and ecosystems are intertwined, consisting of a complex networked/layered system of modular components and interfaces, the scope and scale of which go beyond the immediate platform actors (Teece, 2018). Platform-based digital markets can alter the way companies generate and deliver value to end customers (Cennamo, 2019). Drawing a clear distinction in extant research between digital ecosystems and platforms is not always easy, though.

The emergence of varying theoretical streams, multiple definitions, and conceptualizations underscore the significance of ecosystems as a research phenomenon (Tsujimoto et al. 2018). This diversity has also resulted in criticism concerning "the ambiguous and metaphorical usage of the ecosystem concept, which limits the progression and accumulation of scholarly knowledge" (Phillips & Ritala, 2019, p. 1). The inconsistency regarding ecosystem terminology relates especially to two key dimensions, identified by Thomas and Autio (2019): what is the unit of analysis and what is the type of ecosystem service, referring to the type of innovative output collectively generated.

This chapter argues that the complexity surrounding ecosystems and platforms can be clarified via the *business model approach*. Business models are a concept that originated with the rise of the Internet (Wirtz, Schilke, & Ullrich, 2010; Weill & Woerner, 2015), the backbone of digital ecosystems. Business models define the requirements for how different internal and external inputs and ideas are turned into architectures, systems, and platforms (Chesbrough, 2012). Hence, the business model emerged as a solution to deal with the economics-engineering duality of perspectives in a context where the increased platformization and ecosystemization of businesses is prevalent. The purpose of business models is to describe *how* an entity, whether a single organization or a whole ecosystem, explores and exploits opportunities, creates and captures value, and explores and exploits advantages (Yrjölä, Ahokangas, & Matinmikko-Blue, 2019b). Business models can be identified as a boundary-spanning unit of analysis (Zott & Amit, 2010; Zott et al., 2011) that address especially the strategic decisions made regarding open organizational boundaries and the expected outcomes of openness (Iivari, 2015; Paulus-Rohmer, Schatton, & Bauernhansl, 2016; Casadesus-Masanell & Llanes, 2011). Therefore, business models can be seen as vehicles for—or tools to improve—ecosystemic interaction (Gomes, Iivari, Pikkarainen, & Ahokangas, 2018), and as a unit of analysis they also help define the business ecosystem's joint value proposition (Iivari, Ahokangas, Komi, Tihinen, & Valtanen, 2016).

The focus of this chapter is to explore how a digital platform can contribute to opening a closed ecosystem. The empirical case is a port that seeks to enhance ecosystemic interaction outside its boundaries, while improving efficiency and safety inside its boundaries via the introduction of a partly open digital platform. The framework of the chapter derives from business model literature. The research question is, "*how can we deal with the controversies stemming from bringing openness to closed ecosystems via digital platforms?*" Using an empirical study, this chapter primarily contributes to scientific discussions on resolving the metaphorical use of the ecosystem concept in management research. It also contributes to discussions on the antecedents of digitalization of physical business ecosystems and the choices and consequences related to ecosystem boundary conditions and the strategic level of openness. Thus, the study also contributes to business model literature. For the analysis, the study adopts a research approach that combines a qualitative case study and integrative anticipatory action research.

The rest of the chapter is organized as follows. First, the theoretical underpinnings are addressed in the following section. Then, the next section presents the research approach, empirical data collection process, and an analysis of the findings. The research conclusions are discussed in the final section, linking the empirics back to theory. Avenues for future research are addressed as the last part of the chapter.

CONNECTING ECOSYSTEMS, PLATFORMS, AND BUSINESS MODELS

There are characteristics that make an *ecosystem* distinctive as a concept. Ecosystems describe collectives that differ from other collectives, such as networks, clusters, or value chains, in terms of "participant heterogeneity, the nature of ecosystem outputs, the forms and characteristics of participant interdependence, and the modes of ecosystem governance" (Thomas & Autio, 2019, p. 2). Despite the diversity and challenges in ecosystems research (Scaringella & Radziwon, 2018; Phillips & Ritala, 2019; Thomas & Autio, 2019), five common notions can be identified (see Tsujimoto et al., 2018). First, ecosystems analyze both positive and negative aspects of organic networks. Second, the differing purposes and principles of individual actors may lead to unintended results at the ecosystem level. Third, the analytical borders of the ecosystem reflect the system surrounding a product or a service, including non-business actors. Fourth, analyzing ecosystem dynamism requires a longitudinal approach, and fifth, ecosystem research ought to "find patterns of decision-making and behavioral chains that strongly affect the growth and decline of the ecosystem under specific boundary conditions" (Tsujimoto et al., 2018).

Although ecosystem research has deep roots as a separate stream of literature, platform researchers have claimed that platforms "grow" an ecosystem around them. This has in part led to a rejuvenation of ecosystem literature, while it has also led researchers to focus on platform business models. The authors argue that business models as an approach can be used as a boundary condition to bridge ecosystem and platform discussions.

Business Models and Ecosystems

Although lacking a generally accepted definition, contents, or underlying assumptions (Doganova & Eyquem-Renault, 2009), the business model has become the tool for conducting boundary-spanning analyses in contemporary business research (Zott et al., 2011, Lanzolla et al., 2020). Two definitions of a business model can be used to bridge ecosystem and platform discussions in the digital context. First, Onetti, Zucchella, Jones, and McDougal-Covin (2012, p. 360) wrote that "we define the business model as the way a company structures its own activities in determining the focus, locus and modus of its business." Second, according to Amit and Zott (2001, p. 493), "a business model depicts the design of transaction content, structure, and governance so as to create value through the exploitation of business opportunities." The former of the two definitions assumes a focal company, while the latter does not. Both see business models from an action/activity perspective.

The extant literature provides three antecedent concepts for business models relevant to ecosystems and platforms: *opportunities* to be explored/exploited, *value* to be created/captured, and *advantages* to be explored and exploited (Morris, Schindehutte, & Allen, 2005; Teece, 2010; McGrath, 2010; Zott et al., 2011). If exploring and exploiting opportunities and advantages explain the motivation for action within an ecosystem (Gomes et al., 2018), then value creation, delivery, and capture (Osterwalder & Pigneur, 2010; Paulus-Rohmer et al., 2016), value co-creation and co-capture (Bengtsson & Kock, 2000), or value sharing (Verstraete & Jouison-Laffitte, 2011) can be seen as key elements of a functioning business model.

In addition, extant research offers three relevant neighboring outcome concepts for a business model: *scalability* (Stampfl, Prügl, & Osterloh, 2013; Nielsen & Lund, 2018), *replicability* (Aspara, Hietanen, & Tikkanen, 2010; Martins, Grindova, & Greenbaum, 2015), and *sustainability* (Bocken, Short, Rana, & Evans, 2014; Schaltegger, Hansen, & Lüdeke-Freund, 2016). Since scalability refers to a business model's internal growth potential and flexibility, replicability implies its external flexibility to adapt to various contextual requirements. Sustainability, in turn, is reflected in a business model's feasibility, viability, and environmental or societal impact. In this chapter, these six concepts comprise the core of the business model approach.

The concepts of opportunity, value, advantage, scalability, replicability, and sustainability have also been addressed in ecosystem and platform discussions, albeit with varying emphasis. In the ecosystem discussions (Autio, Nambisan, Thomas, & Wright, 2018), the focus has been more on shared opportunities and value creation and the creation of competitive advantages and sustainability (Gomes et al., 2018), whereas in platform-related discussions more space has been given to issues of scalability and replicability (Nielsen & Lund, 2018). Schaltegger et al. (2016, p. 6) argue that "a business model for sustainability helps describing, analyzing, managing and communicating 1) a company's sustainable value proposition to its customers, and all other stakeholders, 2) how it creates and delivers this value, 3) and how it captures economic value while maintaining or regenerating natural, social, and economic capital beyond its organizational boundaries." Similarly, Nielsen and Lund (2018, p. 4) discuss scalable business models as "a business model that is agile and which provides exponentially increasing returns to scale in terms of growth from additional resources applied." Also, business model replicability has been referred to as "the innovator firm's learning about and refining its (new) business model, by choosing the necessary components to replicate that model in suitable geographical locations, by developing capabilities to routinize knowledge transfer, and by maintaining the model in operation once it has been replicated" (Aspara et al., 2010, p. 43). Indeed, according to Jansson, Ahokangas, Iivari, Perälä-Heape, and Salo (2014, p. 5), a business ecosystem can be seen as a "bundle of interlinked business models," where value co-creation, co-capture, coopetition, and coevolution are visible.

Digital Platforms and Ecosystems

Platforms come in many forms and assume many definitions. The authors identify four key elements of digital platforms: components, interfaces, data, and algorithms (Yrjölä et al., 2019b). *Components* are add-on elements that connect to the platform to add functionality to it (Baldwin & Clark, 2000; Sanchez & Mahoney, 1996). Katz and Shapiro (1994) have discussed *interfaces* as specifications and design rules that describe how the platform and components interact and exchange information using well-documented and predefined standards, like application programming interfaces (APIs). The engineering tradition has placed components and interfaces either at the core or periphery of the system. Baldwin (2008) found that modularity decreases coordination and transaction costs across the module boundary, while interface standardization decreases the asset specificity of modules (Schilling, 2000). The increasing volume of *data* has transformed contemporary business practices (McAfee, Brynjolfsson, Davenport, Patil, & Barton, 2012; Bharadwaj, El Sawy, Pavlou, & Venkatamaran, 2013; Jeble, Kumari, & Patil, 2018), while the *algorithm* revolution and cloud computing have given rise to a platform economy. Computing power is converted into economic tools using algorithms operating on the raw material of data.

Gawer (2014) has divided platforms into three categories: 1) a company and its internal units, that is, the internal platforms; 2) a network of company and its suppliers, that is, the supply chain platforms; and 3) an ecosystem keystone actor and its supplement actors in a technology or business ecosystem, that is, the ecosystem platform. Gawer and Cusumano (2014, p. 417) identify internal (company or product) platforms "as a set of assets organized in a common structure from which a company can efficiently develop and produce a stream of derivative products," and which "define external (industry) platforms as products, services, or technologies that act as a foundation upon which external innovators, organized as an innovative business ecosystem, can develop their own complementary products, technologies, or services." Weil and Woerner (2015) propose four types of business models for digitalized context: 1) a supplier model that works in a value chain of another company, 2) a multichannel model that causes firms to restructure across several digital and physical touchpoints to serve their customers, 3) a modular model that builds on plug-and-play interfaces to complement their offerings, and 4) an ecosystem model that builds a customer-centric platform to facilitate ecosystemic interaction among customers.

As mentioned above, platforms have ecosystemic characteristics and the business model approach provides insights into ecosystemic interactions on platforms. These concepts partly overlap and lack widely accepted definitions in extant research. When combining the economic and engineering viewpoints with (digital) platforms, attention needs to be paid to *technical platform modularity and architecture* as well as to *service modularity and architecture* (Yrjölä, Ahokangas, & Matinmikko-Blue, 2019a; Yrjölä et al., 2019b).

Wirtz et al. (2010) have proposed a typological 4C business model framework for the Internet age. Each of the four types of business models have varying value propositions and revenue models: *connection* (e.g., wireless connectivity or a fiber) that enables interaction, *content* (e.g., data or information) that can be transferred over the available connections, *context* (e.g., search or location) that provides situational awareness of the activity in question, and *commerce* (e.g., marketplace and platforms) for data, information, or context over the available connectivity. From the ecosystem perspective, the typology can be interpreted as a set of nested layers, where lower layer business models are required as enablers and value levers for the higher layers to exist (Yrjölä, Ahokangas, & Matinmikko, 2015). In the IoT (Internet-of-Things) context, Iivari et al. (2016) have also noted the roles that infrastructure and hardware, platforms and data, devices and equipment, and applications and user interfaces play for the provisioning of digital services. This discussion has contributed to the development of three ecosystem-embedded, "platformic" business models: vertically structured (use-case specific), horizontally structured (service specific), and oblique (customer specific), which mix both horizontal and vertical structures (Ahokangas et al., 2019). We present the following themes for understanding ecosystems and platforms from the perspective of business model thinking:

- *Platform conceptualization.* Data access and ownership have become central for platforms. The role of data may involve corporations, governments, or customers. In addition, artificial intelligence and machine learning (i.e., algorithms) have emerged as crucial elements for managing platforms and utilizing the data on future platforms (Yrjölä et al., 2019a, 2019b).
- *Platformic interaction.* In recent literature, demand-side business models have come to complement supply-side business models (Priem, Wenzel, & Koch, 2018), and open and oblique business models have come to challenge traditional closed business models (Casadesus-Masanell & Llanes, 2011; Chan, 2015). Ecosystemic business models (Demil, Lecocq, & Warnier, 2018; Iivari et al., 2016) have emerged as a way to observe interaction between business models.
- *Innovation and managing complexity.* The engineering approach to platforms highlights innovation, as modularity makes managing the complexities of innovation easier and incremental. Profiting from innovation requires enabling and general-purpose technologies in the wireless world (Gawer, 2014; Teece, 2018).
- *Complementarity and configuration.* Complementarity relates to production, customers, asset prices, inputs, technologies, or innovation. With platforms, a focus on dynamic and integrative capabilities is important. This is important because platforms— whether internal, supply-chain, or industry—may differ and have different levels (lightly or loosely coupled) of complementarity (Gawer, 2014; Teece, 2018).

- *Openness and transparency.* Openness of business models starts from closed and extends towards open-edge, open-core, and open-source models (Casadesus-Masanell & Lanes, 2011). The openness and transparency of business models has to do with discussions about open innovation (Frankenberger, Weiblen, & Gassmann, 2014).
- *Organization and governance.* Governance of the platform may be based on ownership (managerial authority), contractual relationships, or ecosystem governance. The role of data is increasing on platforms, but challenges to data ownership and access prevail (Gawer, 2014; de Reuver, Sørensen, & Basole, 2017; Teece, 2018).
- *Competition and cooperation.* Competition may appear between platforms, between a platform and its partners, and between complementors (Teece, 2018). Inter-platform competition results in winner-take-all outcomes but also increased openness.
- *Economies of scale and scope.* Engineering discussions has been about economies of scale in service provisioning (Teece, 2018), while in business model discussions attention has been paid to business model scalability (Nielsen & Lund, 2018). The network effects (Gawer, 2014) of the platforms increase their value, but economies of scope pertain not only to service provisioning, but also to innovation.

The above list also relates to the choices and consequences that organizations need to consider in digital, ecosystemic, or platformic contexts. In the digital context, ecosystem stakeholder roles can also be classified as vertically structured, market-specific roles; as horizontally structured, non-domain specific roles; and as local, geographically bound roles (Krčo, Kranenburg, Lončar, Ziouvelou, & McGroarty, 2019), with the existence and role of the focal company in an ecosystem being an issue. Zahra and Nambisan (2012) maintain that strategic thinking, in terms of foresight and insight, plays an influential role in ecosystems, while they have also highlighted the role and existence of a central player in their classification of different types of ecosystems. Iansiti and Levien (2004) has termed these central players "keystones." Additionally, Van Alstyne, Parker, and Choudary (2016) have identified four key roles in the platform context: platform owner and providers, and platform consumers and producers. In this categorization, the platform owner has the focal role because it defines the rules and interfaces for interaction—thus defining the internal and external boundaries of the ecosystem. A business model as a tool in this context results in the active change of the organization's role in the ecosystem, where digitization offers opportunities for implementation (Paulus-Rohmer et al., 2016). The business model links the opening of ecosystems as a purposeful, strategic, boundary spanning activity.

RESEARCH APPROACH AND DATA ANALYSIS

This section briefly discusses the research approach and the context of the case, a digitalizing port ecosystem, providing a description and analysis of data and the key findings.

Case-based Anticipatory Action Research Methodology

This research applies an integrative anticipatory action learning methodology (Stevenson, 2002; Reason & Bradbury, 2008; Voros, 2008) combined with an interpretive case study (Andrade, 2009; Bhattacharya, 2012) to analyze the port case in the first stage—and anticipatory action research to (re)construct the theoretical framework in the second stage. The anticipatory action learning methodology facilitates learning within a social system (Stevenson, 2006) through a representative and collaborative action process that connects inquiry, anticipation, and learning. The integrative approach highlights the importance of integrating different worldviews and data that is well suited to the context (Voros, 2008). The method allows multiple levels of understanding to merge openly and progressively during the process. Action research is an interactive process (Stevenson, 2002) that underlines the necessity of experimenting, reflecting, and learning from exercises (Reason & Bradbury, 2008). The authors follow a research-oriented action research cycle (Eden & Huxham, 2006), where foreknowledge influences work for emergent theory, action for data generation, reflection, and theory exploration and development. Action learning is best utilized through collaborative workshops for data and content generation actions, where the participation of various stakeholders and the representation of multiple perspectives becomes possible. Thus, the methodology helps to integrate research with decision-making and action (Stevenson, 2002). As anticipatory action research presents a unique, participatory style for transforming an organization and society (Inayatullah, 2006), it can be utilized to validate empirical findings directly with ecosystem members. This enables the discovery of decision-making patterns and behavioral chains that have a direct impact on both the ecosystem's development and its boundary conditions (Tsujimoto et al., 2018).

The empirical study for this chapter was conducted using facilitated workshops with port ecosystem members in 2019. Two workshops were held in June 2019 and August 2019 to describe, explore, and analyze the port ecosystem, its digitalization via digital platform development, and the potential antecedents and outcomes of digitalizing the port ecosystem as a whole. A total of 30 people from various stakeholders attended each of the workshops representing the port itself, the companies working within the boundaries of the port, the current and future digital platform providers and users, the regulators influencing port activities, and representatives of the public and municipal-level authorities, as well as the researchers who facilitated the workshops. Participants from various types of organizations permanently located within the port (e.g., customs, construction companies, local vessels, warehousing and security facilities) and non-permanent clients (visiting vessels, customs customers, business organizations) comprised the ecosystem and jointly sought to address the development of a digital, platform-based business model.

Data collection in the workshops was facilitated by following the principles presented by Mackewn (2008) and using a predefined framework that began with a discussion about the role of the port (30 mins) and identifying all the stakeholders in the port ecosystem (1 hour). This part of the discussion was carried out in one group comprising all the workshop participants. To provide common grounds, the discussion was preceded by a presentation on the port platform. Next, the participants were divided into smaller groups of four to five people that continued to discuss the stakeholders' 1) key activities, goals and resources, competences, and contribution to the ecosystem; 2) key expectations, needs, benefits, challenges, and hassles to be solved via digitalization; 3) key partners (and their relationships within the port) and their customers' and competitors' efforts to map their position in the port ecosystem; and 4) key barriers, constraints, and objections to collaboration (4 hours). The results of the group work were presented to and shared with all participants in the workshop, and along with the notes of the workshop organizers, the results were combined into a dataset that was sent to the participants for comments, corrections, and potential additions. The first of the organized workshops focused on the whole ecosystem, and the latter on the digital platform of the ecosystem. The second workshop followed the same logic as the first one.

The findings of the first workshop include the mapping of the port ecosystem's stakeholders and their roles based on the topics discussed. The findings were organized first according to the connectivity, content, context, and commerce business models they represent, and second, according to the entire platform by looking at the platform components, interfaces, data, and algorithms. Figure 1 and table 1 present the key data and findings based on the theoretical framework. Regarding research quality, Floyd (2012) advises paying attention to the constructs (i.e., the ecosystem and platform frameworks used), contents (i.e., data collected and used), capacities (i.e., representativeness of stakeholders), and conditions (i.e., the contextual focus) of the research. The findings and conclusions were presented to the port ecosystem representatives to ascertain whether the conclusions were shared by all and considered trustworthy, that is to say, credible, transferable, dependable, and confirmable (Miles & Huberman, 1994; Lincoln & Guba, 1995).

Port Context

A port ecosystem is a transport hub through which goods are shipped. A physical port represents the characteristics of industrial ecosystems (Frosch & Gallopoulos, 1989) based on efficiency, optimization, and sustainability. A port is often dependent on the industry in the region. The port is a multi-stakeholder environment with conflicting interests of the different stakeholders, as studied by De Langen (2006). Traditionally, conflicting views have emerged from transport firms interested in limited costs, the local industries ensuring their operations, employees wanting to maintain existing benefits, and local governments and municipalities seeking economic benefits. Digitalization is entering the port ecosystem, similar to all other sectors, and because of digitalization the port is developing into a true business ecosystem instead of a local network of stakeholders.

The port studied in this case study is the Port of Oulu, owned by the City of Oulu and located in northern Finland. The port is a closed area where several organizations are located. Only organizations whose operations are related to shipping/logistics are allowed inside the closed port area. Most of the shipping is cargo from industries located in the region. The port is open for any vessel to access if it follows given rules. In addition to the ships arriving and departing, there is a significant amount of traffic in the harbor, including trucks and trains transporting the goods to be shipped.

The port ecosystem considered in the case study consists of several stakeholders, which are identified in figure 1. Goods owned by different cargo owners are transported through the port using a transport chain consisting of other logistics service providers, transport/railway companies, stevedoring and shipping companies. The port is a fenced area that includes physical and digital infrastructures. The port's operations are governed by several authorities, which highlights the role of security and safety operations in the area. Other port stakeholders identified in the case port include various support service providers, such as piloting, ice-breaking (wintertime), and towing. Specific regulations govern the operations of ports and make the port responsible for security and safety in the area, which has led to the port being a highly closed ecosystem. In its current state, the operations of the different port stakeholders are rather isolated, each keeping control of their own operations with very little information sharing. Currently, while vehicles accessing the harbor area are identified, the identity of people is not known.

The key challenge currently in the case port is the limited information sharing in the existing multi-stakeholder environment, where data is kept in isolation by the different stakeholders. This significantly restricts the efficient operations of the port and leads to extra work that could be avoided if up-to-date knowledge about port operations was available to the relevant stakeholders. The target state for the case port is to achieve more efficient, secure, and safe operations for the port stakeholders through situational awareness made available for the stakeholders. Situational awareness will be created by combining information from the different stakeholders with the help of a digital platform. Different data sources are envisaged for collecting information on the surroundings, including various types of cameras and sensors. The data is collected on a digital platform—in the form of a digital twin—run by the port and visualized and made available to the port stakeholders.

Figure 1. Stakeholders in the case port

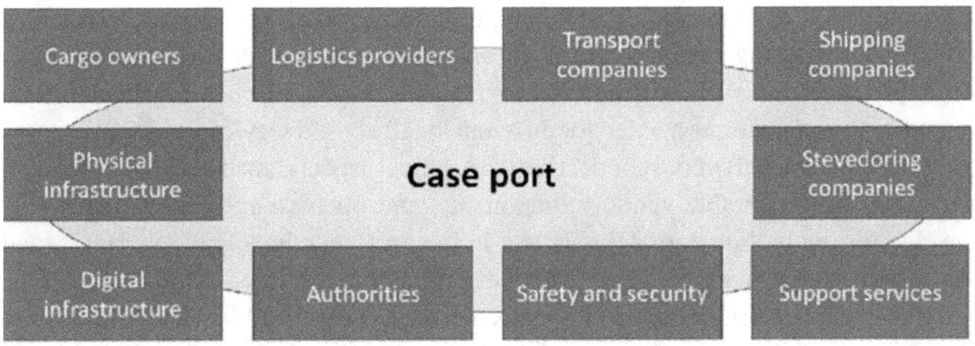

The port is owned by the local municipality, and the company established to manage the port is the focal, impartial player in the port ecosystem, which is planning to introduce a novel digital platform to the port to enable, in the long run, full-blown connectivity, content, context, and commerce business models.

Analysis of Findings

This section presents and analyzes the findings of the workshops. The raw data—in the form of post-it notes, notes and figures written and drawn on table cloths, flipcharts, PowerPoint slides, and Word documents created by the workshop participants and researchers facilitating the workshops—has been collected, arranged, categorized, and analyzed based on the theoretical framework.

As described in the theory section, this chapter looks at the digital business ecosystem through the lens of business models. The 4C business model framework by Wirtz et al. (2010), and extended by Yrjölä et al. (2015), was applied in the analysis of empirical findings together with the platform component classification presented by Yrjölä et al. (2019b). This integrated framework was employed to discover in detail how the port makes sense of itself in a digital context before creating a platform-based business model around its ecosystem. The mapping of digital platform-based business model enablers in the Port of Oulu ecosystem are shown in table 1. The 4C layers of the business model are placed in the vertical direction, while the four major elements of platform architecture are aligned in the horizontal direction. To help maintain technical correctness, the following discussion starts from the connectivity/computing layer and end with the commerce layer.

The port has invested in a private, closed mobile network (4G) and is expected to introduce a 5G network soon. Also, public mobile networks (4G) and private WiFi networks are available and used in the port area, used by the different ecosystem players for various purposes but in a siloed manner. For the port, the private and integrated 4G/5G connectivity and computing layer of the port builds on the idea of providing heterogeneous connectivity and computing service for various users—from machines to people with hand-held end devices—and the heterogeneous cloud computing architectures needed for different locally based services and applications is being built as a part of the connectivity. Technical aspects, such as the use of global standards, interoperable vendor components, and open-source computing power needed for the mobile core network run in the port, on edge cloud, on radios, and on various end devices, provide a flexible architecture and integration strategies for existing blueprint solutions and IT architectures. The port is building an infrastructure to generate a digital twin of the port based on the managed and orchestrated service sets of the mobile network. The digital twin and its embedded algorithms and data will be used to create enhanced situational awareness of the port. The value of the digitalized ecosystem will be realized at higher layers through the integration of algorithms into the local private connectivity and computing platform.

On the content layer, a virtual data federation database managed by the port aggregates data from distributed sources, such as cameras, machines, and various end devices, comprising a common data model that forms a single source of data for the context and commerce layer applications. Since the data comes from a variety of stakeholders present in the port area, clearly defined data ownership, and controlled sharing and governance of data, it is essential to manage the different types and sources of data (e.g., open data for all [e.g., weather conditions] in the port for enhancing safety, proprietary company-internal data used in the port area coming from various sensors or humans to control and monitor robots or unmanned vehicles, data co-created by several stakeholders of the port for the digital twin, or data curated for the digital twin by the port) being utilized, for example, for predictive analytics and on-demand content and functionality for the deployment of contextualized services. Context-aware services are enabled and supported by the establishment of network connectivity and the extraction, collection, and storage of data. Information streams support a broad spectrum of real-time analysis, such as video data analysis and actuation algorithms.

The planned activities at the commerce layer will support extreme service agility for a high number of new services to be introduced and lower the entry barrier for new service providers. To enable multi-tenant use cases, that is, several stakeholders that share the same infrastructure, the to-be-built analytics platforms need to allow for easy specialization and onboarding of tenant-specific analysis algorithms. The fundamental purpose of the digital twin is to enable flexible access to data on demand and create a marketplace for data inside and outside the port.

Table 1. 4C/platform -analysis summary of the Port of Oulu platform

	Components	Interfaces	Data	Algorithms
Commerce	Digital twin Local computing services	Access to data	Marketplace for data (raw data, curated data) Data governance	Data analytics services, e.g., digital twin user interface
Context	Situational awareness High availability/ quality local services	Firewalls, cyber security Physical gates	Control and monitoring data for robots, unmanned vehicles	Video analytics, awareness user interface visualization of digital twin
Content	Sensors 360 HD video cameras Machines collecting and using data, Analytics tools, User equipment	Cloud and device interfaces	Machine collected data IoT sensor data Humans as sensors Open data, e.g. weather, water, ice From port, stevedoring, customs, shipping line, Exp./importers	Video analytics at gates 3D map of harbor area as digital twin
Connectivity Computing	Closed private mobile network, public mobile network Private computing platform Devices: mobiles, tablets, augmented reality glasses	Global standards Service-oriented architecture Network management and orchestration for service tailoring Open interfaces for applications	Local data warehousing "Digital Twin"	Operational awareness and optimization Privacy and security "trust" management Computing algorithms

Table 1 depicts an ideal situation created in the workshops by the port stakeholders. In practice, the hardware and infrastructures, platforms and data, equipment and devices, and applications and user interfaces needed for the whole digital platform might be developed, owned, managed, and utilized by different stakeholders, even new entrants not currently active in the port. This is expected to bring about questions and issues related to managing innovation and complementarity of services in the port, coordination of activities and collaboration between the stakeholders, as well as openness and transparency between the activities, stakeholders, and services. The question of the scalability and sustainability of the business model developed for the ecosystem is especially important. At the connection layer, stakeholders expect the business model will be rather straightforward, as the existing connectivity services of mobile network operators can be benchmarked. However, the value of content-related services and respective business models appears less clear for the ecosystem stakeholders. The context-related services appeared to provide rather clear direct value to the ecosystem stakeholders. In addition, the commerce-related services and respective business models appeared to be more for the port itself, although some of the stakeholders have activities in other ports, too. Later, this might open new opportunities to scale or replicate the digital part of the port ecosystem outside its current area.

OPENING OF CLOSED ECOSYSTEMS VIA DIGITAL PLATFORMS

To answer the research question—how can we deal with the controversies stemming from bringing openness to closed ecosystems via digital platforms?—the key elements identified in the literature are reflected on in this section: the empirical case of the port ecosystem. The authors argue that these controversies can be approached via business model thinking. In the case of a platform-based business model, the choices regarding opportunities, value, and advantages have direct and indirect consequences for the scalability, replicability, and sustainability of business models, as exemplified by the data (see Yrjölä et al., 2019b). Sustainability is central for the port ecosystem, as the boundaries for scalability and replicability are naturally limited in closed ecosystems. The development and utilization of a digital platform enables the scalability and replicability of various types of previously closed data, algorithms, interfaces, and components, directly impacting the innovative output and value delivery of the ecosystem (*cf.* Thomas & Autio, 2019; Cennamo, 2019).

Economies of Scale and Scope

Aligning the scale on the platforms relates both to service provisioning (Teece, 2018) and business models (Nielsen & Lund, 2018). Aligning the scope of the platforms extends service provisioning to innovation (Gawer, 2014). In the case of the port ecosystem, the softwarization and virtualization of the connectivity and computing layers of the platform will make it possible to separate the software from the hardware. This offers the further possibility of instantiating many novel functions on a common platform infrastructure, leveraging a commodity-of-the-shelf approach. The value of platforms is realized, for example, through the development of open interfaces for applications and devices, which in turn improve operational awareness and optimization for general services in the port and further contributes to increased privacy and security. The introduced network elasticity and scalability makes it possible to adapt network and resource usage to needed capacity on demand when extending existing service provisioning and developing completely new products and services. As a result, business agility is improved.

Competition and Cooperation

Competition in platforms may appear at three levels: between platforms, between a platform and its partners, and between complementors (Teece, 2018). In the port case, competition occurs within the platform while the port itself competes with other ports. The platform in the port context requires a careful balancing of cooperation and competition, particularly in relation to platform partners and between complementors. Exposing valuable infrastructure, data assets, and analytics services to stakeholders through a set of APIs and setting up effective partnerships will allow service providers to grow their businesses by sharing their services with partners. 4G/5G wireless networks and digital twin data federation architectures enable different levels of exposure to network resources and data between actors. Depending on the relationships between business actors and customers, there may exist different levels of transparency in network service provisioning and in the related forms of cooperation.

Organization and Governance

In the platform governance discussion, Gawer (2014), de Reuver et al. (2017), and Teece (2018) raise the questions of how to organize the openness of interfaces, what capabilities are accessible, and from where, by, or through the platform, and whether the governance is based on ownership, contractual relationships, or ecosystem governance. In the port case, the standardization of connectivity and computing technologies ensure multi-vendor interoperability and economies of scale and minimize complexity—thereby reducing the cost of interfaces. The key domains of the vertical industry platform, like the port, are wider than those of the previous platform generations, including support for virtualized network functions, slicing (of network services), converged wireless and wired access, transport, cloud, applications, and service orchestration. Diversity in use cases, along with standardized open-source platforms, will become an essential new cross-domain collaboration and interoperability tool for the industry and for a business's agility at providing tailored solutions. However, governance relates especially to data access and ownership in the port case, impacting the commerce layer the most: there needs to be clear rules and boundaries for what kind of data can be sold in the marketplace.

Openness and Transparency

Casadesus-Masanell and Llanes (2011) see the openness of a business model in the digital context starting from closed and extending toward open-edge, open-core, and open-source models. A software-based, service-oriented, cloud-native, common local connectivity and edge computing platform—as exemplified by the connection/computing layer—enables efficient infrastructure and resource sharing by different tenants, it can open the ecosystem to new players, and it can accelerate time to market by reducing service creation and activation times. However, in the case of a port ecosystem, the kinds of data, interfaces, algorithms, or components that can be opened or shared need to be clearly defined. Openness as a concept refers not only to constantly increasing levels of openness (Iivari, 2015), but also that some aspects of the platform need to remain closed if they are crucial for the ecosystem's sustainability. Security-related data (both physical and cyber security) or the privacy of individuals and the use of video analytics for commercial purposes is one such example. The port as the network and cloud service orchestrator, or as the platform owner, thus acts as the logical interface between network and business applications. An orchestrator can provide abstraction for the platform users of the network and applications and interfaces for easy service creation and optimization and it can expose actionable network insights to application and content providers, enterprises, and industry verticals.

Complementarity and Configuration

Teece (2018) relates complementarity to production, customers, asset prices, inputs, technologies, or innovation, and Gawer (2014) acknowledges that different types of platforms (internal, supply-chain, or industry) may exhibit different types and levels (lightly or loosely coupled) of complementarity. Lepore, Nambisan, Tucci, and Zahra (2019) discuss complementarity in connection with competencies and knowledge structures. As such, the physical port functions as a transport hub, thus representing a supply chain hub; hence, there is a natural complementarity among ecosystem players due to industrial linkages. However, it is not automatic that the complementarity extends to the digital platform. Complementarity within the digital platform relates especially to both internal and external sources of data, such as weather, ice, or water conditions, or to inland logistics data. Equally, local authorities, such as customs or border control, not only utilize internal data, but also work in a national, but closed, environment. The management and orchestration functionality at the connection/computing layer can incorporate an exposure function that opens the connectivity, computing, data, and analytics assets of a network to the stakeholders in the port.

Innovation and Managing Complexity

The engineering approach to platforms highlights innovation through modularity, which makes managing innovation easier and incremental in complex systems (Teece, 2018). Service-oriented open architecture and open collaboration that use open common interfaces and toolkits are essential at every level of the digital architectures, from hardware to services and applications. Through the softwarization and virtualization of network functions and the opening of interfaces, economy concepts can be shared not only at higher platform business layers, but more broadly with respect to the use of spectrum, network connectivities, and data. Value appropriation and positive spillover effects can be ensured precisely because the port area handles so much sensitive data and enabling and general-purpose technologies (Gawer, 2014; Teece, 2018). Ecosystem stakeholders identified this fact as one of the key motivators for seeking to develop a digital platform and transform their use of data and technologies. By using the right kinds of tools and systems, complexities can also be reduced for other innovations that can be commercialized or replicated from within the ecosystem.

Platformic Interaction

Traditionally, both the wireless and computing contexts have been dominated by supply-side business models (Priem et al., 2018) of the mobile operators. In the port ecosystem, different types of distinct demands will be placed on the 4C layers and related platforms, anticipating an increase in the use of multi-sided business models. The nature of future port applications will range from simple low-power sensors to high-resolution, contextualized, immersive video content and 3D location context data needed for mission-critical control operations, putting unprecedented demands on service tailoring and scalability. Interaction within the ecosystem is thus a crucial antecedent for all business. Through interaction, ecosystem members will better identify not only their current needs and challenges, but also future opportunities for value creation for the ecosystem and its stakeholders. Interaction fosters better skills for configuration and interoperability, and it helps stakeholders identify the boundaries of collaboration at the organizational, service/product, and business model level. Interaction also addresses the different needs and challenges related to openness and transparency within the ecosystem. There, our port case exemplifies a clear shift from supply-side and two-sided closed platforms and business models to more open, multi-sided, and oblique business models and platforms. Thus, interaction will aid in conceptualizing the role of the platform for the port ecosystem as a whole, how to manage the platform, and how to utilize data in the future (Yrjölä et al., 2019a, 2019b). Platformic interaction thus relates to the use of data and technologies at the various layers of the 4C model, whereas ecosystemic interaction relates to the "sum of all things," thus fostering competitive advantage for the Port of Oulu.

A Conceptual Framework for Opening Closed Ecosystems With Digital Platforms

Despite the underlying idea of openness in platforms, ecosystems, and business models alike, certain boundary conditions determine the degree of openness. Controversies arise when the physical limitations and realities of the ecosystem, as in the case of the port, and the nature and roles of its stakeholders clash at the different layers of the digital platform and its respective business model enablers. Business model thinking as an approach helps to define the internal and external contexts of the ecosystem—and its relationship to the digital platform. The authors argue that these controversies result in so-called mixed ecosystems and mixed platforms, as depicted in figure 2. To this way of thinking, *at the platform level* both platform conceptualization and platformic interaction provide the basis for managing innovation-related complexities, complementarity, configurations, openness, and transparency. Organization and governance, managing competition and cooperation, and dealing with scale and scope are *ecosystem-level* activities related to the platform.

Figure 2. From physical to digital: controversies in bringing openness to ecosystems and platforms

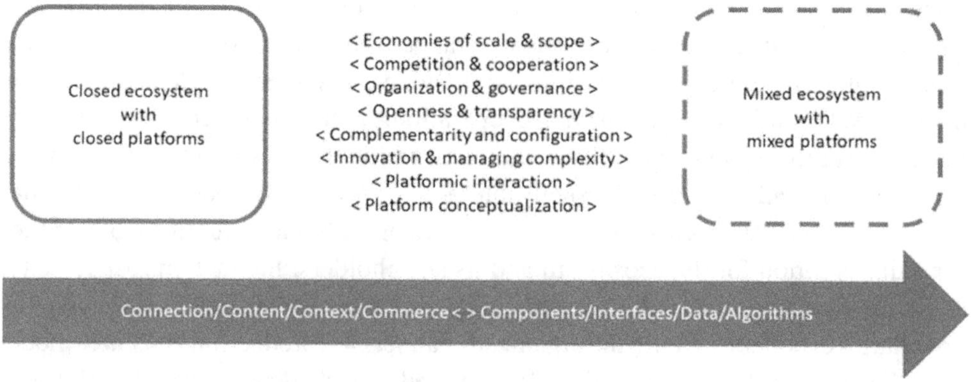

This study has demonstrated that despite the multi-sided nature of platforms and the open nature of digital business ecosystems, ports need to clearly define *how* external parties are incorporated (Iivari, 2015) and *what* are the rules for interaction (van Alstyne et al., 2016). This makes the role of the platform owner critical. A central player (Zahra & Nambisan, 2012) is needed to govern the process of transformation, and this player needs to consciously define the degree of openness within the platform. This is to ensure the sustainability of the existing ecosystem and set the prerequisites for the scalability and replicability of the digital platform and the whole ecosystem.

CONCLUDING REMARKS

This chapter illustrates the controversies arising when a physical, closed ecosystem seeks to utilize digital platforms to tap new kinds of opportunities, value, and advantages. The study indicates that only a mixed level of openness can be achieved when different organizations maintain and seek different degrees of openness. These controversies impact the design and development of a platform-based, ecosystemic business model in the long term, but also act as the prerequisites for and consequences of its successful transformation.

The practical implications of this study relate to platform ownership and management and the governance of ecosystems. Ecosystem or platform developers need to acknowledge how they are able to identify novel opportunities, what kinds of value propositions can be built based on these opportunities, and how to utilize the processes of value creation and capture to create competitive advantages. Equally, ecosystem and platform developers need to consider the implications of their decisions on sustainability, scalability, and replicability that further influence the different roles within the platform, namely those of owners, developers, managers, and users. Roles help ecosystem and platform developers identify the resources already present or accessible within the ecosystem, and the resources, skills, or knowhow they need to acquire outside their existing boundaries. The chapter highlights that the identified controversies can be utilized as a "check list" for ecosystem orchestrators and a "risk list" for ecosystem stakeholders.

The theoretical contribution of the chapter relates specifically to transforming ecosystems. Earlier, transformation in business ecosystems was primarily approached from a technological point of view. Platforms grow ecosystems around them, but ecosystems also build and integrate platforms, as exemplified by the empirical research case. Thus, this study contributes to scientific discussion by having studied a closed but self-sustained ecosystem with clear boundaries, where digitalization is not a driver but an enabler. This study also contributes to discussions on differentiating the concepts of ecosystems and platforms, bringing clarity and applied usage to both concepts. The study further helps to determine the interplay between these concepts at different levels of analysis. Most importantly, this chapter contributes to the purpose of this book and the emergence of ecosystem-centric business models that look at the joint value creation and capture in ecosystemic contexts. This particular study presents business models as an approach through which openness in ecosystems can be studied theoretically and empirically with an aligned methodological perspective.

Even though academia calls for longitudinal studies on ecosystems, such a longitudinal aspect cannot be fully addressed in a single study. Validation of the methodology occurred in parallel with data collection via the action research method, where a uniform understanding of the ecosystem's development was built. This is also a limitation of the study, as some of the empirical issues, such as security or physical access, may be highly contextual. Therefore, utilizing the framework provided by the literature, similar studies on other types of closed ecosystems should be done to compare the controversies discovered in the port case.

Extant research acknowledges different roles within ecosystem/platform management (van Alstyne et al., 2016; Zahra & Nambisan, 2012; Dedehayir et al., 2018; Krčo et al., 2019). The chapter also highlights the central role of a focal player, yet only briefly touched on its role in governing the transformation process. It would be important to explore further how focal players are able to facilitate, orchestrate, and support the opening of closed ecosystems and what kind of role they play in the context of digital platforms. Also, this study applied the concept of business models as an approach and identified the antecedents of business model design for ecosystems. Further studies are needed to explore how business model design, creation, and experimentation takes place in ecosystemic/platformic context. How to define the mutual opportunities identified via digitalization and how to turn such opportunities into solid value propositions and competitive advantages for the ecosystem will be an interesting future avenue of research.

Acknowledgment

The authors would like to acknowledge the contributions of the 5GViima project consortium.

REFERENCES

Adner, R. (2006). Match your innovation strategy to your innovation ecosystem. *Harvard Business Review*, *84*(4), 98–107.

Adner, R., & Kapoor, R. (2010). Value creation in innovation ecosystems: How the structure of technological interdependence affects firm performance in new technology generations. *Strategic Management Journal*, *31*(3), 306–333.

Ahokangas, P., Boter, H., & Iivari, M. (2018). Ecosystems Perspective on Entrepreneurship. In R. Turcan & N. M. Fraser (Eds.), *The Palgrave Handbook of Multidisciplinary Perspectives on Entrepreneurship* (pp. 387–407). Palgrave Macmillan.

Ahokangas, P., Matinmikko-Blue, M., Yrjölä, S., Seppänen, V., Hämmäinen, H., Jurva, R., & Latva-aho, M. (2019). Generic Business Models for Local 5G Micro Operators. *IEEE Transactions on Cognitive Communications and Networking*, *5*(3), 730–740.

Amit, R., & Zott, C. (2001). Value creation in E-business. *Strategic Management Journal*, *22*(6-7), 493–520.

Andrade, A. D. (2009). Interpretive Research Aiming at Theory Building: Adopting and Adapting the Case Study Design. *Qualitative Report*, *14*(1), 42–60.

Aspara, J., Hietanen, J., & Tikkanen, H. (2010). Business model innovation vs replication: Financial performance implications of strategic emphases. *Journal of Strategic Marketing*, *18*(1), 39–56.

Autio, E., Nambisan, S., Thomas, L. D., & Wright, M. (2018). Digital affordances, spatial affordances, and the genesis of entrepreneurial ecosystems. *Strategic Entrepreneurship Journal*, *12*(1), 72–95.

Baldwin, C. (2008). Where Do Transactions Come From? Modularity, Transactions, and the Boundaries of Firms. *Industrial and Corporate Change*, *17*(1), 155–195.

Baldwin, C., & Clark, K. (2000). *Design Rules: The Power of Modularity*. MIT Press.

Baldwin, C., & Woodard, J. (2009). The Architecture of Platforms: A Unified View. InPlatforms, Riding in the Open Source Development Model? *Management Science*, *52*(7), 1116–1127.

Bengtsson, M., & Kock, S. (2000). "Coopetition" in business networks—To cooperate and compete simultaneously. *Industrial Marketing Management*, (29), 411–426.

Bharadwaj, A., El Sawy, O., Pavlou, P., & Venkataraman, N. (2013). Digital business strategy: Toward a next generation of insights. *Management Information Systems Quarterly*, *37*(2), 471–482.

Bhattacharya, H. (2012). Interpretive Research. In L. M. Given (Ed.), *The SAGE Encyclopedia of Qualitative Research Methods* (pp. 465–467). SAGE Publications.

Bocken, N. M., Rana, P., & Short, S. W. (2015). Value mapping for sustainable business thinking. *Journal of Industrial and Production Engineering*, *32*(1), 67–81.

Casadesus-Masanell, R., & Llanes, G. (2011). Mixed source. *Management Science, 57*(7), 1212–1230.

Cennamo, C. (2019). Competing in digital markets: A platform-based perspective. *The Academy of Management Perspectives.*

Chan, H. C. (2015). Internet of things business models. *Journal of Service Science and Management, 8*(4), 552.

Chesbrough, H. (2012). Open innovation: Where we've been and where we're going. *Research Technology Management, 55*(4), 20–27.

Coghlan, D., & Brannick, T. (2010). *Doing Action Research in your own organization* (3rd ed.). Sage.

Cusumano, M., & Gawer, A. (2002). The elements of platform leadership. *MIT Sloan Management Review, 43*(3), 51–58.

Davis, J. P. (2016). The Group Dynamics of Interorganizational Relationships: Collaborating with Multiple Partners in Innovation Ecosystems. *Administrative Science Quarterly, 61*(4), 621–661.

De Langen, P. W. (2006). Stakeholders, conflicting interests and governance in port clusters. *Research in Transportation Economics, 17*, 457–477.

de Reuver, M., Sørensen, C., & Basole, R. C. (2017). The digital platform: A research agenda. *Journal of Information Technology, 33*(2), 124–135.

Dedehayir, O., Mäkinen, S. J., & Ortt, J. R. (2018). Roles during innovation ecosystem genesis: A literature review. *Technological Forecasting and Social Change, 136*, 18–29.

Demil, B., Lecocq, X., & Warnier, V. (2018). Business model thinking, business ecosystems and platforms: the new perspective on the environment of the organization. *M@n@gement, 21*(4).

Doganova, L., & Eyquem-Renault, M. (2009). What do business models do? Innovation devices in technology entrepreneurship. *Research Policy, 38*(10), 1559–1570.

Eden, C., & Huxham, C. (2006). Researching organizations using action research. In S. R. Clegg, C. Hardy, T. B. Lawrence, & W. R. Nord (Eds.), *The Sage handbook of organization studies* (pp. 389–408). Sage Publications.

Floyd, J. (2012). Action research and integral futures studies: A path to embodied foresight. *Futures, 44*(10), 870–882.

Frankenberger, K., Weiblen, T., & Gassmann, O. (2014). The antecedents of open business models: An exploratory study of incumbent firms. *R & D Management*, *44*(2), 173–188.

Frosch, R. A., & Gallopoulos, N. E. (1989). Strategies for Manufacturing. *Scientific American*, *261*(3), 144–152.

Galateanu, E., & Avasilcai, S. (2013). Business ecosystems architecture. *Annals of the Oradea University*, *1*(May), 79–84.

Gawer, A. (2014). Bridging differing perspectives on technological platforms: Toward an integrative framework. *Research Policy*, *43*(7), 1239–1249.

Gawer, A. (2014). Bridging differing perspectives on technological platforms: Toward an integrative framework. *Research Policy*, *43*(7), 1239–1249.

Gawer, A., & Cusumano, M. A. (2014). Industry platforms and ecosystem innovation. *Journal of Product Innovation Management*, *31*(3), 417–433.

Gomes, J. F., Iivari, M., Pikkarainen, M., & Ahokangas, P. (2018). Business Models as Enablers of Ecosystemic Interaction: A Dynamic Capability Perspective. *International Journal of Social Ecology and Sustainable Development*, *9*(3), 1–13.

Iansiti, M., & Levien, R. (2004). *The Keystone Advantage: What the New Dynamics of Business Ecosystems Mean for Strategy, Innovation and Sustainability*. Harvard Business Press.

Iansiti, M., & Richards, G. L. (2006). The Information Technology Ecosystem: Structure, Health, and Performance. *The Antitrust Bulletin*, *51*(1), 77–110.

Iivari, M. (2015). Dynamics of Openness in SMEs: A business model and innovation strategy perspective. *Journal of Business Models*, *3*(2), 30–50.

Iivari, M., Ahokangas, P., Komi, M., Tihinen, M., & Valtanen, K. (2016). Toward ecosystemic business models in the context of industrial internet. *Journal of Business Models*, *4*(2), 42–59.

Inayatullah, S. (2006). Anticipatory action learning: Theory and practice. *Futures*, *38*, 656–666.

Isenberg, D. J. (2010). How to Start an Entrepreneurial Revolution. *Harvard Business Review*, *88*(6), 41–50.

Jacobides, M. G., Cennamo, C., & Gawer, A. (2018). Towards a theory of ecosystems. *Strategic Management Journal*, *39*(8), 2255–2276.

Jansson, N., Ahokangas, P., Iivari, M., Perälä-Heape, M., & Salo, S. (2014). The competitive advantage of an ecosystemic business model: The Case of OuluHealth. *Interdisciplinary Studies Journal, 3*(4), 282–294.

Jeble, S., Kumari, S., & Patil, Y. (2018). Role of Big Data in Decision Making. *Operations and Supply Chain Management, 11*(1), 36–44.

Katz, M., & Shapiro, C. (1994). Systems Competition and Network Effects. *The Journal of Economic Perspectives, 8*(2), 93–115.

Krčo, S., von Kranenburg, R., Lončar, M., Ziouvelou, X., & McGroarty, F. (2019). Digitalization of Value Chains and Ecosystems. In A. Aagaard (Ed.), *Digital Business Models* (pp. 81–116). Palgrave MacMillan.

Lanzolla, G., Pesce, D., & Tucci, C. L. (forthcoming). The digital transformation of search and recombination in the innovation function: Tensions and an integrative framework. *Journal of Product Innovation Management.*

Lepore, D., Nambisan, S., Tucci, C. L., & Zahra, S. A. (2019, July). Digital Transformation & Firms' Innovative Strategies: Capabilities, Ecosystems, and Business Models. In Academy of Management Proceedings (Vol. 2019, No. 1, p. 14623). Briarcliff Manor, NY: Academy of Management.

Lincoln, Y. S., & Guba, E. G. (1985). *Naturalistic inquiry* (vol. 75). Academic Press.

Mackewn, J. (2008). *Facilitation as action research in the moment. The Sage Handbook of Action Research. Participative Inquiry and Practice*. Sage Publications.

Martins, L., Rindova, V., & Greenbaum, B. (2015). Unlocking the hidden value of concepts: A cognitive approach to business model innovation. *Strategic Entrepreneurship Journal, 9*(1), 99–117.

McAfee, A., Brynjolfsson, E., Davenport, T. H., Patil, D. J., & Barton, D. (2012). Big data: The management revolution. *Harvard Business Review, 90*(10), 60–68.

McGrath, R. (2010). Business models: A discovery driven approach. *Long Range Planning, 43*(2–3), 247–261.

Miles, M. B., & Huberman, A. M. (1994). *Qualitative data analysis*. Sage publications.

Moore, J. (1993). Predators and Prey: The New Ecology of Competition. *Harvard Business Review, 71*(3), 75–86.

Morris, M., Schindehutte, M., & Allen, J. (2005). The entrepreneur's business model: Toward a unified perspective. *Journal of Business Research, 58*(6), 726–735.

Nachira, F., Dini, P. & Nicolai, A. (2007). *A network for digital business ecosystems in Europe: Roots, processes and perspectives*. European Commission, Information Society and Media.

Nielsen, C., & Lund, M. (2018). Building scalable business models. *MIT Sloan Management Review*, *59*(2), 65–69.

Onetti, A., Zucchella, A., Jones, M., & McDougal-Covin, P. (2012). Internationalization, innovation and entrepreneurship: Business models for new technology-based firms. *The Journal of Management and Governance*, *16*(3), 337–368.

Osterwalder, A., & Pigneur, Y. (2010). *Business Model Generation: A Handbook for Visionaries, Game Changers, and Challengers*. John Wiley & Sons.

Paulus-Rohmer, D., Schatton, H., & Bauernhansl, T. (2016). Ecosystems, strategy and business models in the age of digitization - How the manufacturing industry is going to change its logic. *Procedia CIRP*, *57*, 8–13.

Phillips, M. A., & Ritala, P. (2019). A complex adaptive systems agenda for ecosystem research methodology. *Technological Forecasting and Social Change*, *148*, 119739.

Pikkarainen, M., Ervasti, M., Hurmelinna-Laukkanen, P., & Nätti, S. (2017). Orchestration Roles to Facilitate Networked Innovation in a Healthcare Ecosystem. *Technology Innovation Management Review*, *7*(9), 30–43.

Pilinkienė, V., & Maciulis, P. (2014). Comparison of different ecosystem analogies: The main economic determinants and levels of impact. *Procedia: Social and Behavioral Sciences*, *156*, 365–370.

Priem, R. L., Wenzel, M., & Koch, J. (2018). Demand-side strategy and business models: Putting value creation for consumers center stage. *Long Range Planning*, *51*(1), 22–31.

Reason, P., & Bradbury, H. (2008). *The SAGE Handbook of Action Research* (2nd ed.). SAGE.

Sanchez, R., & Mahoney, J. (1996). Modularity, Flexibility, and Knowledge Management in Product Contingencies. *Management Information Systems Quarterly*, *23*(2), 261–290.

Scaringella, L., & Radziwon, A. (2018). Innovation, entrepreneurial, knowledge, and business ecosystems: Old wine in new bottles? *Technological Forecasting and Social Change*, *136*, 59–87.

Schaltegger, S., Hansen, E., & Lüdeke-Freund, F. (2016). Business models for sustainability: Origins, present research, and future avenues. *Organization & Environment*, *29*(1), 3–10.

Schilling, M. (2000). Toward a General Modular Systems Theory and Its Application to Interfirm Product Organization and Design. *Strategic Management Journal*, *17*(1), 63–76.

Stampfl, G., Prügl, R., & Osterloh, V. (2013). An explorative model of business model scalability. *International Journal of Product Development*, *18*(3-4), 226–248.

Stevenson, T. (2002). Anticipatory action learning: Conversations about the future. *Futures*, *34*(5), 417–425.

Stevenson, T. (2006). From vision into action. *Futures*, *38*(6), 667–672.

Talmar, M., Walrave, B., Podoynitsyna, X., Holmström, J., & Romme, G. L. (2018). (in press). Mapping, analyzing and designing innovation ecosystems: The Ecosystem pie model. *Long Range Planning*.

Teece, D. (2010). Business models, business strategy and innovation. *Long Range Planning*, *43*(2-3), 172–194.

Teece, D. J. (2018). Profiting from innovation in the digital economy: Enabling technologies, standards, and licensing models in the wireless world. *Research Policy*, *47*, 1367–1387.

Thomas, L.D.W. & Autio, E. (2019) *Innovation ecosystems*. Academic Press.

Tsujimoto, M., Kajikawa, Y., Tomita, J., & Matsumoto, Y. (2018). A review of the ecosystem concept—Towards coherent ecosystem design. *Technological Forecasting and Social Change*, *136*, 49–58.

Van Alstyne, M. W., Parker, G. G., & Choudary, S. P. (2016). Pipelines, platforms, and the new rules of strategy. *Harvard Business Review*, *94*(4), 54–62.

Van der Borgh, M., Cloodt, M., & Romme, A. G. L. (2012). Value-creation by knowledge-based ecosystems: Evidence from a field study. *R & D Management*, *42*(2), 150–169.

Verstraete, T., & Jouison-Laffitte, E. (2011). A conventionalist theory of the business model in the context of business creation for understanding organizational impetus. *Management International*, *15*(2), 109–124.

Voros, J. (2008). Integral futures: An approach to futures inquiry. *Futures*, *40*(2), 190–201.

Walrave, B., Talmar, M., Podoynitsyna, K. S., Romme, A. G. L., & Verbong, G. P. (2018). A multi-level perspective on innovation ecosystems for path-breaking innovation. *Technological Forecasting and Social Change, 136*, 103–113.

Weill, P., & Woerner, S. L. (2015). Thriving in an increasingly digital ecosystem. *MIT Sloan Management Review, 56*(4), 27.

Wirtz, B. W., Schilke, O., & Ullrich, S. (2010). Strategic development of business models: Implications of the Web 2.0 for creating value on the internet. *Long Range Planning, 43*(2), 272–290.

Yrjölä, S., Ahokangas, P., & Matinmikko, M. (2015). Evaluation of recent spectrum sharing concepts from business model scalability point of view. *Dynamic Spectrum Access Networks (DySPAN), 2015 IEEE International Symposium*, 241-250. doi:10.1109/DySPAN.2015.7343907

Yrjölä, S., Ahokangas, P., & Matinmikko-Blue, M. (2019a). *Novel Platform-based Ecosystemic Business Models in the Future Mobile Operator Business.* Paper presented at the 3rd Business Model Conference, New York, NY.

Yrjölä, S., Ahokangas, P., & Matinmikko-Blue, M. (2019b). *Novel platform ecosystem business models for future wireless communications services and networks.* Paper presented at NFF 2019 Conference, Vaasa, Finland.

Zahra, S. A., & Nambisan, S. (2012). Entrepreneurship and strategic thinking in business ecosystems. *Business Horizons, 55*(3), 219–229.

Zott, C., & Amit, R. (2010). Designing your future business model: An activity system perspective. *Long Range Planning, 43*(2–3), 216–226.

Zott, C., Amit, R., & Massa, L. (2011). The business model: Recent developments and future research. *Journal of Management, 37*(4), 1019–1042.

ADDITIONAL READING

Ahokangas, P., & Atkova, I. (forthcoming). Business Model - A New Theory of the Firm? In D. Korten, M. Pirson, D. Wasieleski, E. Steckler, & R. Aguado (Eds.), *Alternatives to the Theory of the Firm / Alternative Theories of the Firm, Humanistic Management Series.* Routledge Publishers.

Amit, R., & Han, X. (2017). Value Creation through Novel Resource Configurations in a Digitally Enabled World. *Strategic Entrepreneurship Journal, 11*(3), 228–242. doi:10.1002ej.1256

Iivari, M. (2016). *Exploring Business Models in Ecosystemic Contexts*. Doctoral Dissertation. Acta Universitatis Ouluensis

Lund, M., & Nielsen, C. (2018). The Concept of Business Model Scalability. *Journal of Business Models*, *6*(1), 1–18.

Luo, J. (2018). Architecture and evolvability of innovation ecosystems. *Technological Forecasting and Social Change*, *136*, 132–144. doi:10.1016/j.techfore.2017.06.033

Massa, L., Tucci, C., & Afuah, A. (2017). A critical assessment of business model research. *The Academy of Management Annals*, *11*(1), 73–104. doi:10.5465/annals.2014.0072

Xu, Y. (2019). *Business model opened? The value configuration of future smart energy*. Doctoral Dissertation. Acta Universitatis Ouluensis.

Xu, Y., Ahokangas, P., Turunen, M., Mäntymäki, M., & Heikkilä, J. (2019). Platform-based business models: Insights from an emerging AI-enabled smart building ecosystem. *Electronics (Basel)*, *8*(10), 1150. doi:10.3390/electronics8101150

KEY TERMS AND DEFINITIONS

Business Ecosystem: A collection of organizations involved in the development and delivery of a specific product or service through simultaneous competition and cooperation.

Business Model: Tool that helps organizations and ecosystems to define how they create and capture value from identified business opportunities.

Business Opportunity: Exploration and exploitation of ideas and inventions and their development into any commercialized product, service, equipment, process, or system.

Competitive Advantage: The ability to generate greater value for an organization, shareholders, and stakeholders than competitors.

Ecosystemic Business Model: A business model that combines different goals and drivers under a mutually connected, joint opportunity and a common motive that drives value co-creation and co-capture.

Platform: An integrated set of components, interfaces, algorithms, and data that enables service provisioning and utilization.

Platform-Based Business Model: A business model that combines value creation and capture by channeling communication and transactions between buyers and sellers.

Chapter 5
Emerging Ecosystems Empowered by AI and IoT Technologies

Charilaos Akasiadis
National Centre for Scientific Research "Demokritos", Greece

ABSTRACT

As latest advancements signify the fourth industrial revolution, artificial intelligence (AI) and internet of things (IoT) became the focal points for innovators. IoT-enabled technology can be used to gather and explore huge amounts of data from both virtual and physical environments, and AI provides the means for effectively processing and manipulating resulting information to optimize or automate processes. In this chapter, the related state of the art is presented, along with the characteristics that enable the creation of hybrid innovation ecosystems. An overview of IoT and AI platforms is included, which can be utilized even by non-experts to compose advanced cost-effective services. Also, related notions such as interoperability and engagement are also discussed. Although such components can be applied in a multitude of domains, to provide a concrete example of innovation enablement, the smart grid ecosystem is employed. Here, participants, either from the supply or the demand side, take advantage of IoT and AI technology to address new business requirements that arise.

DOI: 10.4018/978-1-7998-4843-1.ch005

INTRODUCTION

During the recent years, quite a few technological achievements that were once deemed as fiction now exist, either as laboratory prototypes, or as products with high technology readiness levels. Examples include autonomous vehicles and mobile robots of advanced capability, home and personal assistants that simplify a number of every-day processes, machines that are by far faster than humans in solving specific problems, and so on. Although such ideas have already been introduced during the past few decades (Kurzweil, 1992), their manifestation into real-world products and solutions was made possible only recently, mainly due to advancements in two broad domains of electronics and computer science, the Internet of Things (IoT), and Artificial Intelligence (AI).

Internet of Things is a result of breakthroughs in a multitude of fields, e.g. electronics and telecommunications, embedded systems, software engineering, web and cloud services, as well as finance and marketing (Ibarra-Esquer et al., 2012). Nevertheless, the main market requirement that provides a boost for IoT adoption is the fact that it enables enterprises to gather and make effective use of huge amounts of data originating from the real, physical world. This collected data is then turned into usable information and actionable knowledge regarding improvements in products and services, market analysis and various predictions, and can be employed for the optimization of a number of business and production processes within the enterprise or organization (Erevelles et al., 2016).

However, very large amounts of collected measurements and calculated indices cannot be easily processed and analyzed by the human brain. Thus, in parallel to the outspread of IoT technology adoption, the requirement for efficient manipulation and processing of the available data has also appeared. For this purpose, scientists, engineers, and decision makers turn their attention mainly to AI. AI is far from a new term and notion, as it has been conceptualized from the middle of the last century as computational methods that simulate the human brain's operations with respect to learning and decision making (Russel & Norvig, 2019). Occasionally being in and out of researchers' spotlights, AI is currently an "umbrella" term covering multiple sub-fields, such as natural language processing, machine learning, symbolic computation, intelligent agents, and multi-agent systems, among others.

Generally, such technologies can be considered as innovation enablers, e.g. concepts of the fourth industrial revolution can be made possible with the advent of 5G communications (Gundall et al., 2018), and adaptive/personalizable mechanisms can be improved by using machine learning techniques (Vermesan, 2017). Furthermore, these approaches are also characterized as disrupting, introducing this way the need for novelties in business model design and assessment as well (Amshoff et al., 2015), (Renda, 2019). However, this disruption is regarded by business and industries differently in each case, according to the application domain and the strategy that each party decides to adopt, and vary from partial, to full integration of such novel technologies (Laudien & Daxböck, 2016).

Now, IoT and AI, like other technologies, follow the hype cycle, and after a "Media exposure" period, when increased public attention is given, comes the "Peak of inflated Expectations" (Hahanov, 2018). Currently, most SMEs or even larger organizations do not have a complete and realistic perspective of what such technologies and related products and services are actually capable of, and how they can be integrated into their processes to their benefit one hand, and that of society in general on the other.

Moreover, since AI and IoT are mainly dealt with in the scope of research and academic activities, there are certain constraints that make their transformation into industrial and commercial products difficult. Experts ask for actual incentives towards their commercialization and the formation of funding bodies that will set the grounds for startup creation and innovation more fertile. Now, in order to deliver innovation, different technologies must be exploited and be subjects of exhaustive testing. This can be achieved by large hybrid ecosystems consisting of numerous types of actors, either contributing as providers, end-users, or both at the same time. Such ecosystems mainly refer to activities around certain application areas or business objectives that aim to capture value (Ritala et al., 2013). The impact on innovation by such ecosystems can be substantial, since adoption rate is increased by the large number of participants, and emerging technologies such as AI and IoT induce major shifts in the techno-economic paradigm. To allow more broad applicability though, the incentives of different types of participants must be aligned, to render their active and long-term engagement. This can be made possible by employing solutions from the field of Mechanism Design (MD), where notions such as truthfulness in participation, fair reward distribution, and incentive compatibility are mathematically guaranteed.

The aim of this chapter is to briefly review advancements in 'viral' fields of information and telecommunication technology, i.e. Artificial Intelligence and Internet of Things, and to highlight how their incorporation in hybrid innovation ecosystems can allow the realization of large-scale cyber-physical systems and human-agent collectives. Enabling concepts such as X-on-Demand and X-as-a-Service paradigms are examined, and focus is given on existing examples of related platforms that can be combined to deliver solutions to complex problems. To better illustrate the means of application of such technologies, two use-cases related to energy management in Smart Grid scenarios are analyzed, in particular an application for large scale Demand-Side Management (DSM), and for Vehicle-to-Grid/Grid-to-Vehicle (V2G/G2V) charging and energy exchange. Both these cases include (a) actors of various types and categories---often with contradicting interests, (b) the incorporation of interoperable IoT and AI tools, methods, and platforms that significantly reduce the difficulties of realization, and (c) requirements for carefully designed incentivization mechanisms to maximize stakeholder participation, social welfare, and fairness.

The chapter is structured as follows: First, a brief overview of the state of the art in IoT, AI, Hybrid Ecosystems, and applied MD is provided, highlighting the current opportunities for innovation related to each sub-field. Next, existing ecosystem-enabling platforms are presented, i.e. the AI4EU the European AI-on Demand platform, the architectural and interoperability guidelines of the BigIoT API and marketplace, and SYNAISTHISI, an application enabling IoT platform based on open-source frameworks. Their capabilities are analyzed from an innovation enablement aspect, and to better illustrate their applicability, focus is put on the complex case of the Smart Electricity Grid. Here, multiple stakeholders of various types need to interact and reschedule processes in a collective manner to reduce monetary costs and environmental impacts. Although a complex domain, by taking advantage of the discussed emerging technologies, effective marketable solutions can be realised to the benefit of every participant type.

BACKGROUND

In this part we provide some basic background regarding IoT and AI, two horizontal technologies that can be applied among different sectors. Also, we refer to the concept of Mechanism Design, which can be used to align the incentives of various types of stakeholders, and and analyze how these can be combined altogether to form crowdsourced Hybrid Innovation Ecosystems. We begin with AI, since it is an "older" notion with significantly longer history.

Artificial Intelligence

Many attempts have been made towards defining what the term AI actually includes. The book that is used by many universities around the world to introduce undergraduates to AI (Russel & Norvig, 2009), presents four different definition categories, which characterize a system's behaviour according to, i.e. if it is thinking like humans, if it acts like them, if it thinks in a strictly rational way, and if it acts like so. According to the more recent definition of EC (2018), "AI refers to systems that display intelligent behaviour by analyzing their environment and taking actions --- with some degree of autonomy --- to achieve specific goals. AI-based systems can be purely software-based, acting in the virtual world (e.g. voice assistants, image analysis software, search engines, speech and face recognition systems) or AI can be embedded in hardware devices (e.g. advanced robots, autonomous cars, drones, or Internet of Things applications)."

The subfields that roughly constitute AI are: Computational Logic, Decision Support Systems, Search and Planning, Knowledge Representation and Reasoning, Multiagent Systems, Machine Learning, Computer Vision, and Natural Language Processing. Methods originating from these subfields, often in combination, are used in a plethora of application areas, such as health, education, telecommunications, security, manufacturing, and so on (Ramos, 20007). Now, although it may appear that AI methods can readily be adopted in a generic way to any aspect of business or process, there are still limitations when transiting in real world applications. Take as an example a trained neural network black box that can provide 99 correct answers out of 100 times, though it fails to sufficiently explain why a particular answer is given, or another case, where the 1% error rate might not be acceptable, e.g. when human lives depend on an erroneous decision. Thus, recently, there is an urge in the research community to explore respective features and properties towards AI methods applicability in the real world, that should be considered in any approach incorporating AI, despite the application vertical, such as, explainability, verifiability, trustworthiness, and human centricity (Renda, 2019).

Kaplan & Haenlein (2019) classify AI approaches from a business-wise aspect, based on the capabilities that successful humans also possess, those that make them perform above average in corporate environments, i.e. *Analytical AI*, *Human-inspired AI*, and *Humanized AI*. Authors discuss existing systems of the first two categories and their application in academic, corporate, and governmental environments. Focus is also given on the implications of wide adoption of AI-related tools. The implications are further categorized into the three Cs, *confidence*, *change*, and *control*. Authors argue that in the following years, innovative approaches will be required for managers to decide which positions suits an employee better, in hybrid cyber-physical business mechanisms. Also, employees themselves will have to be able to face new challenges, and keep improving on their skills in order to complement the advances in AI. Apart from professionals, consumers as well will have to put trust and confidence on AI, competing companies and corporations will have to change their processes and adoption strategies, and, finally, states should be able to control how much of citizen and customer privacy will be constricted, in order to leave space for further economic growth. Note that this trade-off is quite important and will be a key decision for the control of future developments.

Kruse et al. (2019) focus on the financial sector, and investigate how modern AI can be applied to this complex and highly data driven business field. Reports show that AI techniques have been successfully applied to reduce costs, increase customer orientation and satisfaction, and have driven major innovations in payments and wealth management. Chatbots in particular, although being capable to answer only simple questions, currently engage in conversations with customers and achieve faster response times with reduced cost for real-world banks and insurance companies.

Hager et al. (2019) discuss the notion AI for social good, and the further implications that accrue. Ongoing work in the fields of urban computing, sustainability, health, public welfare is also discussed. Transportation in particular, is a sector that has been significantly impacted by technological advancements, and many pilot demonstrations have been set up that optimize traffic flow, and provide on-demand transportation systems with fleets of small vehicles. Also, large-scale data collection and the training of models can lead to policy optimization approaches. Interestingly, the role of data science platforms is highlighted, i.e. cloud based infrastructure that can be used to collect and share data, define common data models, and conduct experiments in shared experimental test-beds. It is argued that such approaches will help lowering the barrier of entry for researchers and enterprises.

Potentials for Innovation

Cockburn et al. (2018) highlight the impact that AI has on innovation and further advancements in research on different application areas. Taking into account the breakthroughs in key sectors, e.g. Robotics and Deep Learning, there are limitless cases where general purpose AI methods can be integrated into and improve production processes, for example highly accurate predictors trained over very large pools of unstructured data, industrial automations etc. Importantly, AI can be considered as an "invention of a method for inventing", and as such it is not limited to just reducing costs of innovation activities, but it introduces new approaches to innovation itself.

Of course, AI has found its place in multiple verticals in the form of special purpose approaches as well, and will definitely continue to do so in the future. Examples of verticals that have been impacted so far are the following (Vocke et al., 2019):

- In smart energy grids, for monitoring, management, and maintenance (Santofimia-Romero et al., 2011)(Akasiadis & Chalkiadakis, 2017).
- In autonomous vehicle design, for planning, autonomous coordination, and intelligent driver assistance (Driankov & Saffiotti, 2013) (Schwarting et al., 2018).
- In healthcare, for diagnosis, drug design, and genome interpretation (Nichols et al., 2019) (Hessler & Baringhaus, 2018) (Yu et al., 2018).
- In financial services, for fraud detection, and decision support for planning (Bahrammirzaee, 2010) (Ryman-Tubb et al., 2018).
- In manufacturing, for operations monitoring, predictive maintenance, and supply chain optimization (Lee et al., 2018) (Li et al., 2017)

- In advanced cyber-physical systems, and transportation/logistics (Klumpp, 2018)
- In crowd intelligence (Pan, 2016)

Moreover, Quan et al. (2018) characterize the various business applications that AI enables, as an ecosystem by itself. Various categories include open source software platforms, core technology algorithms, AI-specific open platforms, and applications incorporating AI. Such components are used by the industry to identify fruitful domains and particular novel application scenarios that can be built upon existing infrastructure, e.g. AI applications provided via the use of smart phones.

Internet of Things

According to a European commission staff working document (CSWD, 2016), IoT is defined as "a dynamic global network infrastructure with self-configuring capabilities based on standard and interoperable communication protocols where physical and virtual things have identities, physical attributes, and virtual personalities and use intelligent interfaces, and are seamlessly integrated into the information network". Similarly to AI, IoT research directions focus too on human centricity and trustworthiness. Moreover, it has also overlapping areas of application, i.e. smart energy, smart manufacturing, automated driving, etc. In other words, IoT can be considered as the layer that links physically isolated and virtual processes (e.g. AI modules) with the real world by employing heterogeneous sensory, processing, and actuation equipment, and effectively interconnecting it.

By definition, IoT is strongly related to actual objects that are placed in the physical environment (Mazhelis et al., 2012). In contrast to the virtual domain, where a software process can very easily be duplicated or destroyed, the same does not hold for the physical devices and objects related to the IoT ecosystem. Devices and hardware are created and destroyed (or recycled) following complex processes that require significant effort and infrastructure to be completed. Thus, when designing IoT systems one should keep in mind that the components utilized should be reused for additional purposes, possibly different than those that we originally planned to use them for (Jarwar et al., 2018).

Apart from being reusable, IoT-enabled systems should also be interoperable. This means that (a) the interconnection of heterogeneous platforms, systems, and services, should be seamless, and (b) it is possible to orchestrate the functionality of these components, in every aspect of their operation, e.g. turning on / off, reconfiguration, exchange of sensor information, etc. (Fortino et al., 2018). The vision is to also provide an infrastructure for the automatic discoverability, configuration, and execution of complex IoT services and platforms. However, still, recent works highlight the interoperability requirement, and convergence to specific technologies, e.g. a single standard, is deemed unlikely (Soursos et al., 2016).

To facilitate IoT and to overcome the vertical barriers of the use-case specific solutions that mainly emerge, attention is given to the so-called IoT platforms. This kind of solutions are used to discover, manage, and interconnect vast numbers of IoT-enabled devices and data sources via single (web)portals, and aggregate the available information as well as the monitoring and control capabilities for every IoT resource available. The key features of IoT platforms are scalability, high availability, interoperability, and support for a multitude of open protocols for communication, monitoring, and device control. IoT platforms mainly aim to create IoT services marketplaces and give the opportunity to developers and end-users to participate with devices, data, and algorithms, where such resources can be discovered and used by others as well.

The FP7-ICT project "Internet of Things Architecture" (IoT-A), managed to set a reference architecture for IoT platforms in 2013, with the main goal to promote the interoperability of IoT systems and outline the principles and guidelines for the creation of appropriate protocols, interfaces, and algorithms (Bauer et al., 2013). In this approach, abstract functional components are divided into seven functional groups, management, security, communication, IoT service, virtual entity, service organization and IoT process management.

Apart from IoT-A, which defines the modules from a computer-engineering point of view, additional reference architectures have been defined in the later years, which highlight industrial and business process aspects as well. Particularly, in 2015, the Industrial Internet Consortium introduced the Industrial Internet Reference Architecture (IIRA), which in 2017 became part of the Industrial Internet of Things (IIC-IIoT) collection of specifications (Lin et al., 2017). IIRA aims to provide an open and standards-based architecture for industrial IoT systems, which has broad industry applicability regarding interoperability, mapping of applicable technologies, and general guidance in systems development. Descriptions of components come in a generic and highly abstract way in order for it to be more comprehensive by various industry-related parties. A characteristic of IIRA is that it constitutes a distillation of common characteristics, patterns, and features that exist in the industrial sector in general. Similarly to the "divide and conquer" approach, IIRA decomposes the main solution into various models, as seen from different viewpoints, i.e., according to its implementation, functional, usage, and business aspects. Taking these categories into account, respective concerns are analyzed, and guidance is provided towards their resolution.

In a similar approach to the IIRA, the Industry 4.0 technical committee introduced the Reference Architecture Model for Industry 4.0 (RAMI 4.0), which highlights the development layers of a product, system, or service, under the scope of smart industries and factories (Hankel et al., 2015). The difference in RAMI 4.0 however, is that it defines a three-dimensional schema, where each axis represents different dimensions of the design requirements of smart industry solutions: smart factory hierarchy, product life-cycle, and the IT architecture of the solution.

In 2015, the Alliance for Internet of Things Innovation (AIOTI - https://aioti.eu) was launched, with the aim to to strengthen the dialogue and interaction among stakeholders in the European Internet of Things (IoT) domain, and to speed up the uptake of IoT by contributing to the creation of a dynamic European IoT ecosystem including industry, academia, and regulators. Members are structured into horizontal and vertical working groups intersecting this way every area of interest. AIOTI issues studies and recommendations, and organizes events and large scale pilots in order to build trustworthy IoT solutions for worldwide usage.

Ray (2018) presents a survey on the most recent advancements in the IoT reference architectures in various domains of application, such as, app development, devices, systems, heterogeneity, and data management, analytics, deployment management, monitoring management, visualization, and research. The important aspect of IoT is that it can enable interoperable ecosystems that include hardware devices, software components, as well as humans.

Potentials for Innovation

Even from the beginning of this decade, Bucherer & Uckelmann (2011) have highlighted the value of IoT technologies as an innovation enabler in a number of example cases such as information service providers, right-time business analysis and decision making, etc. The most important enabler feature though is the fact that a product is still interconnected and can provide information to manufacturers and enterprises, even after it is sold and ownership is transferred to the end-user. This property allows higher visibility and advanced control mechanisms. Moreover, the generated data and information can be shared with third parties without loss in value, which actually increases when combined with other information, and, additionally, it is not a depletable resource. Thus, the potentials of added value creation are indeed very high and, importantly, can be combined with the possibilities that AI enables, as discussed in the previous subsection, and provide the means for incorporation of crowd-driven factors, such as sharing individually owned data and devices. Additionally, IoT can be employed to support Product-as-a-Service (PaaS) approaches. Sensors can track a product's position, precisely monitor usage time, the environmental conditions, as well as the health of specific parts or submodules, leading also to predictive maintenance solutions.

Also, application enabler platforms give the possibility to generate crowdsourced service ecosystems in a marketplace-like form. In such cases, various types of stakeholders, either individual developers, or entire R&D departments, can share data, devices, and algorithms with the appropriate pricing, which can be combined with other available and compatible modules to deliver solutions to even more complex problems involving actors in large numbers, such as designing smart environments, web enhanced automation systems, emergency response, and so on (Bessis & Dobre, 2014).

A good example area that can be significantly impacted is that of the industry. Industrial IoT (IIoT) in particular, refers to interconnected and interoperable factories, production lines, and reconfigurable appliances, which gather and exchange information and commands to deliver advanced application scenarios. Improvements include intelligent automation, high resolution and predictable production planning and execution, sustainability, and multi-level feedback to designers, engineers, and operators. IIoT can also enable the implementation of new business models that make effective use of the transparent pipeline from the customer requirements and feedback, to product manufacturing, and delivery (Jeschke et al., 2016).

In another study, Andersson & Mattsson (2015) focus on cases of service innovation, and present a conceptual framework using reference cases enabled by IoT technologies. Authors argue that to deliver innovation, the community must focus on the innovative services themselves, instead of the underlying technologies that enable them, and that new cooperation schemes between the stakeholders and the different contexts must be established.

The Concept of Applied Mechanism Design

The resulting ecosystem of intelligent and physically-capable services should most probably operate under specific regulations and rules. However, even since the emergence of the internet, it has become impossible to expect that every part or module of a complex application will precisely act as instructed, e.g. due to malfunctions or malicious behavior (Nisan & Ronen, 2001). In the current circumstances, this issue is exaggerated when taking into account the nature of AI models, which are trained using different data sources---thus might provide different output for the same input, and, even worse, for some black-box approaches, there is lack of explainability of results, i.e. humans are not able to understand why a particular decision or result has been obtained (Holzinger, 2018).

A possible answer to the above concerns regarding the uncontrollability of intelligent rational agents behavior, is the concept of Mechanism Design (MD). MD is a subdomain of game theory that explores how to design rules and regulations so that individual actors that act rationally adopt desired behaviours from the designer's perspective (Nisan, 2007). For example, in a crowdsensing scenario where multiple individuals are called in to provide measurements via mobile sensors, the objective is to offer the appropriate incentives to the individuals to keep participating constantly (Nava Auza et al., 2019). In other settings, the mechanism should select only the most appropriate candidates, and exclude those that systemically misbehave, e.g. prefer accurate measurements to inaccurate ones, or penalize "bad" players and in parallel reward the "good", so that gradually, "bad" players tend to lose more, than what they would gain.

Apart from application specific settings, MD can be employed in more generic forms, e.g. by governments and regulators. In their work, Mukherjee et al. (2017) illustrate the effect of corporate taxes on future innovations of corporates in the US, showing that increasing taxation results to reduced output of corporate patents; and decreasing taxes on the other hand, does not have proportionally the same positive impact. Thus, the provision of state incentives must be very carefully designed and provide guarantees that would allow innovators to overcome uncertainty and risks, reduce the variability of rewards, and to constantly conduct quality R&D operations. Except for tax regulation, other incentives that could foster innovation include additional subsidies for AI- and IoT-enabled equipment acquisition, or for subscriptions in respective platforms. Sophisticated "win-win" mechanisms that aim to maximize the social welfare on the long-run can be the answer to how governments and NGOs are invovled in innovation ecosystems (Oh et al., 2016), and how the concept of value co-creation can be promoted (Smorodinskaya et al., 2017). MD can be seen as an engineered higher level aspect of the ecosystem from a market perspective, so that the involved parties can self-organize in fruitful ways.

Hybrid Innovation Ecosystems

In existing business literature, the term ecosystem mainly refers to groups of interlinked organizations operating on a specific subject, that also include the consumer side in the process of designing and delivering novel products, processes, or services (Autio & Thomas, 2014) (Smorodinskaya et al., 2017) (Venkatraman et al., 2014) (Zahra & Nambisan, 2011). Typically, the impact that such activities result to is pooling of complementary skills, the refinement of production processes, and the solutions' extended application to a horizontal scope, which includes multiple industries and domains. Now, considering the extended capabilities that AI and IoT resources 'unlock', innovation ecosystems that incorporate these are composed of businesses, regulators, end-users, as well as intelligent cyber components and physical devices that interact and can learn to behave collectively. To ensure that the desired equilibrium in the innovation ecosystems---which is one of their basic components (Jackson, 2011)---is reached, MD techniques can be included. This way, hybrid innovation ecosystems emerge that include heterogeneous sets of participants, i.e. humans, devices, and processes (both business and software), all aiming to cooperate, optimize processes, deliver innovative products and services, and doing so in an relatively quick, worthwhile, and scalable manner.

Furthermore, parts of the resources of an ecosystem can be crowdsourced. Respectively to what the 'crowd' is asked to provide for, different subcategories of crowdsourcing exist, such as crowdsensing for gathering measurements and crowdfunding for collecting funds (Komninos, 2013). Crowdsourced approaches are expected to be able to match dynamically varying user needs, and to achieve shorter production cycles (Kohler, 2015). Here, the IoT and AI layers can be used to gather information from the crowd, and communicate back results after analysis and decision-making. The value of each contribution and the price that each requester would pay for each result can be balanced and considered objectively fairly, after performing game theoretic analysis from the scope of MD. Taking this into account, the 'hybrid' term in an innovation ecosystem can also refer to the combination of human and artificial actors working together towards a specific goal in the so-called cyber-physical systems.

A good example of such types of systems operating in large scale is the case of the Smart Electricity Grid. As is further explained in a later section, the operation of region-wide electricity systems require the coordination of many different stakeholder types, including the large numbers of individual customers. To sustain a more environmental-friendly behavior, complex pricing mechanisms are established by regulators and companies to induce changes in end-users energy consumption profiles so that it matches the production levels of renewable sources. To make this process possible, a series of AI- and IoT-oriented components need to be utilized, such as smart meters and other sensors, and autonomous agents that take into account user preferences and ambient conditions.

In the following, we explain how open digital innovation platforms can contribute to the formation of crowdsourced hybrid ecosystems by taking advantage of the dynamic ICT-enabled "on-demand" and "as-a-service" features that are currently thriving in the global market (Duan et al., 2015) (Lindner et al., 2010).

X-on-Demand and X-as-a-Service: Platforms and Ecosystems

Originating from the Cloud domain, the terms "as-a-Service" and "on-Demand" indicate respectively, the ability to deliver offerings over the network in the form of off-the-shelf services, and the ability to dynamically assign resources based on the real-time needs of the end-user (Duan et al., 2015) (Počuča et al., 2012). In our case, the technologies that we are describing have all the required characteristics to be offered as services, and if the relevant stakeholders choose, can make them available on-demand, based on the time-varying user needs. Attention is first drawn by platform offering capabilities, since platforms have become the main building block of contemporary solutions, and, as also stressed by Kenney & Zysman (2015), constitute a new type of emerging economy.

The importance of platforms as an instrument for industrial research and management has also been highlighted by Gawer & Cusumano (2014). Industrial platforms are categorized as (a) internal, which refers to company assets, such as new products that are continuously developed and reused to deliver a family of incrementally innovative products or services, and (b) external, i.e. products, services, or technologies that serve as foundations upon which several firms develop complementary innovations, and which come in different levels of openness, e.g. varying access levels to information or platform components, usage policy, etc. Either way, increasing interests ask for X-on-Demand and X-as-a-Service approaches, where X represents any type of technology, e.g. AI, IoT, Platforms, etc.

In the following, an overview of existing platforms is provided, and specific desirable characteristics that enable innovation are highlighted, such as high availability, polymorphism with respect to application areas, remote access and management, as well as interoperability. In particular, such platforms are able to utilize crowdsourced ecosystems that co-create value outside the boundaries of company-specific production processes (Hein et. al, 2019).

Digital platform ecosystems consist of three main components, (a) the platform ownership processes, (b) the value-creating mechanisms, and (c) complementor autonomy. This means that, first, a platform is supposed to have responsible bodies for its management, such as hosting, maintenance, and administration, and the policies via which added value is created or co-created should be clear; and, second, the ecosystem should be open so that end-users and contributors have the freedom to innovate according to respective needs, which most probably cannot be foreseen a priori when the platform is designed in the first place.

Next, specific examples of modern digital platforms that enable innovation ecosystems are described, which focus mainly on the exploitation of AI and IoT technologies. Specifically, we refer to AI4EU, a European on-demand platform for AI resources, BigIoT, a marketplace approach that aims to establish common protocols for interoperability, and a case of an IoT application enabler platform, named SYNAISTHISI, that can be used to interconnect data and processing components to form complex services whose availability to third parties can be directly controlled by the end-users that design them. Such approaches can satisfy both main needs of innovation ecosystems creation as described by Ritala et al. (2013) that is, the ability to gather all relevant actors for building the ecosystem and promoting the application of key technologies in other sectors, and the ability to integrate open collaborative structures into the industry to enable their creation and maintenance. Also, their combination can address all the dimensions of the factors that drive digital business innovation, i.e. intelligent data, interoperable technologies, and input from co-creators. Note that a number of platform implementations that are similar to those we include in this analysis are currently being researched and are in the stage of development, e.g. Bonseyes, European Language Grid, etc. However, the cases that are presented here adopt a more generic model and are not specialized towards specific business application areas, enabling this way more innovation potential.

AI4EU

In an advent to create an integrated European Artificial Intelligence on-demand platform, the AI4EU project (https://www.ai4eu.eu/) was initiated in the beginning of 2019, with funding from the H2020 European Commission programme. By bringing together more than 80 partners from all around Europe, AI4EU aims to create an "one-stop-shop" that enables knowledge transfer, both among the research community, and to non-expert innovators from any business area as well. The main goals of AI4EU are:

- To create and support a large ecosystem of European AI for promoting collaboration between various actor categories, such as scientists, entrepreneurs, SMEs, industrial, funding organizations, and so on.
- To design and implement a platform that supports such an ecosystem, and via which effective and applicable AI resources of high technology readiness level are shared and made available. Examples of AI resources include trained models, expertise in AI, executable components, datasets, high performance computation resources, and seed funding for innovative projects.
- To implement industrial pilots that make effective use of the platform, and demonstrate the potentials of innovation enablement.
- To bridge technological gaps in five key AI-related scientific areas that have come up from real-world applications requirements: Explainable AI, Verifiable AI, Collaborative AI, Integrative AI, and Physical AI.
- To fund SMEs and start-ups that effectively employ the available AI resources to their business processes.
- To create a European Ethical Observatory that will monitor European AI developments and make sure that they adhere to high ethical, legal, and socio-economic standards.
- To work towards a comprehensive Strategic Research Innovation Agenda for Europe.
- To establish AI4EU Foundation, which will ensure the sustainable platform structure and operability in the long run.

Additionally, AI4EU employs the instrument of open calls and will distribute 3 million Euro, equity-free, among individuals, start-ups, and SMEs. There will be two different types of calls, (a) AI Prototypes, where 25 individuals will be granted up to 30.000 and 4-month support programs to develop AI-based prototypes, and (b) Technology Transfer Programs, where 20 scale-ups will be selected, to be funded up to 180.000 Euro and online premium acceleration programs, i.e. mentoring from top entrepreneurs, training, and access to technology and investment.

With the successful delivery of the AI4EU project, end users of multiple categories will be able to compose pipelines of various executable AI resources, for research and innovation purposes. By browsing a catalogue of AI resources that include both datasets and executable tools, and by discovering related information such as past cases of application, publications, tutorials, and experts' opinions, non-specialized individuals can very quickly educate themselves and gain intuition on how available tools and resources may contribute in the improvement of their own business processes and lead to products of increased quality. Additionally, by combining funding instruments such as open calls and venture capitals, AI4EU can significantly boost innovators to design and deliver new products that are of higher quality and value. Thus, end-users will have the possibility to test and compare their solutions to other benchmarks, and define workflows of composite AI solutions, which can be easily deployed in high performance computers or other experimentation infrastructure.

AI4EU offers interoperability on functional and semantic levels between various other platforms, e.g. Acumos, Bonseyes, European Language Grid, and Mundi. Functional interoperability, i.e. the ability of modules of different implementations and origin to work together and interconnect seamlessly, is achieved by utilizing open standards and interfaces. Syntactic interoperability, on the other hand, refers to the incorporation of open semantic models and ontologies, which allows the meaningful and accurate interpretation of data and results from processes by any platform or framework. In AI4EU, this is achieved by the definition of a common AI Resource Semantic Model that extends well known ontologies and also introduces new concepts related to AI resources. A respective knowledge graph has been developed using the open and well established RDF and RDFS W3C specifications.

Apart from the networking and communication capabilities, AI4EU offers an AI-as-a-Service infrastructure, where any user can create an account, be granted access to the AI resources catalogue, and educate themselves around the functionality of each, the usage, and application scenario recommendations. Then, they can choose the most suitable ones for their case and download a 'production' copy to be readily deployed and integrated into their business processes. Also, AI4EU offers AI-on-Demand services, since selected AI resources can be deployed in the form of composite workflows in in the form of composite workflows in available high performance computing infrastructure.

BigIoT

A few years earlier than AI4EU, in the scope of another European research project, the BigIoT (http://big-iot.eu/), an approach based on three key enablers to deliver a unified IoT ecosystem has been proposed. These enablers are (a) a common application programming interface (API) that supports identity management, the discovery of available IoT offerings, and the communication and information exchange between them and other resources, external to the BigIoT platform, (b) well defined semantic descriptions and information models so that offerings are clearly described and can be easily reused, and (c) a marketplace to help with the monetization and promotion of such offerings' usage (Bröring et. al, 2017).

Focus is put on BigIoT here since the interoperability feature is of utmost importance for allowing collective functionality between platforms, AI and IoT resources, as well as end-users. In particular, BigIoT defined five different patterns for achieving interoperability between heterogeneous services and platforms, that allow different schemes of communication between the modules, as well as various deployment configurations. By distinguishing among basic and advanced interoperability modes of IoT ecosystems, third-party developers and integrators may choose the one that fits most to their needs, among 'cross platform access', 'cross application domain access', 'platform independence', 'platform scale independence', and 'higher level service facades'. The results of adopting any of these patterns are the easy integration of services and data from heterogeneous devices and providers, dynamic discovery and orchestration of modules offered by different vendors, and increased compliance of solutions.

Apart from the interoperability patterns, an important factor is also the semantic framework by which data and services are described. Apart from matching context and prevention of incompatible interconnections, semantic descriptions can be also utilized for automatic reasoning and manipulation of unforeseen combinations of data and services (Tzortzis et. al, 2017). For example, consider the case of a future domestic energy usage predictor. Such an application would utilize sensors that collect real-time measurements and create historical profiles, a learning module that manipulates these measurements and generates predictions, and perhaps a graphical interface component that is used to interact with the end-users. Now, the performance of the predictor is very important and significantly impacts the overall accuracy of the forecasts. Meanwhile, there can be different types of predictors with respect to their internal functionality, and it is hard to manually evaluate and compare them all, one by one. In case the various available modules are adequately described semantically, the platform could automatically determine compatible candidates and perform an 'ex officio' evaluation to recommend for incorporation the most well performing ones for each case.

The third aspect of BigIoT that integrates the two others is the marketplace architecture. In such a setting, third party platforms and developers can be content providers and share resources with others and receive monetary gains in return. To achieve wide market adoption, participation opportunities should be as open as possible, e.g. for providers or consumers from different application domain verticals and for resources hosted on different IoT platforms, both in terms of the underlying technology and platform geographical placement.

Overall, the potentials for innovation in these cases are multiple, and include various stakeholder types. In the discussed scenarios there are data owners, providers of sensors and devices, providers of platforms, marketplaces, of services and applications, as well as of standardizations. The availability of commonly used and open marketplaces enable inter- and intra-segment interactions for value creation and revenue generation across multiple vertical application areas (Schladofsky et al., 2017). For example, a predictor that has been proven valuable in the energy domain in one pilot case, can easily be integrated to other geographical regions' energy systems, or be utilized in solutions for other business areas, e.g. for the financial sector.

SYNAISTHISI IoT platform

SYNAISTHISI (http://iot.synaisthisi.iit.demokritos.gr/) is an application enabler IoT platform developed by the Institute of Informatics and Telecommunications of NCSR "Demokritos". The platform is equipped with open and commonly used APIs for communication between objects, such as sensors exposed via gateways, processing systems running on the cloud, user interfaces executing on end-users' devices, or decision making mechanisms, etc. These objects are virtualized as vendor/technology-agnostic services, and can be published on cloud, local, or edge infrastructures for further use. Developers can create services on-the-fly by integrating humans, sensors, devices, data and processing systems (Akasiadis et. al, 2019).

The communication among services is realized by a middleware mechanism composed by distributed message brokers that can support multiple protocols which are widely used in the IoT domain. The platform also provides storage capabilities using database agnostic interfaces for storing, managing and recovering the distributed data generated. Having this, it is possible to create analytics and reports that monitor various key performance indicators for every use-case. Also, platform operations and data exchange are processes governed by appropriate authentication and authorization policies.

SYNAISTHISI platform has so far been used as the basis for five different pilot use-cases categories. In particular, it was employed to deliver smart meeting room applications, which combine a multitude of sensors placed in a room (depth PTZ cameras, microphone arrays, power consumption meters, temperature and humidity sensors, motion detectors, etc.), a number of processing cloud services (person counting, data storage and fusion, decision making, energy usage optimizers, text-to-speech modules, resource management and monitoring dashboards, complex event recognition modules, etc.), as well as multiple actuators (lights and plugs switches, infrared remote controls, and speakers). Also, prototype applications have been developed for the automatic lighting and HVAC control in common building areas, for visitor management scenarios, for safety and surveillance, and energy management applications (Pierris et. al, 2015). By combining available IoT resources, integrated solutions can be quickly composed and instantly redeployed for any similar use case that includes respective physical equipment, or just parts of it.

Currently, SYNAISTHISI is available in containerized versions for end-users, so that they can deploy the platform on a local level. This way, apart from being able to directly control, customize, and enrich platform components, developers can test and evaluate newly developed IoT services and solution candidates before releasing them to the marketplace and making them available for use by third parties under preferred sharing policies. Additionally, the marketplace-oriented architecture that the platform adopts allows advanced capabilities for the participants to discover, use, and rate IoT services and resources that have been provided by others, so that their reusability is promoted in the presence of well defined financial and social incentives.

Another feature of the platform that further simplifies usage and IoT resource discoverability is the utilization of semantic annotations for services and datastreams. SYNAISTHISI incorporates RDF triplestores that hold descriptions of IoT resources, based on ontologies of specific standardizations. Additional specialized modules and enriched relevant ontologies can also be equipped according to the priorities of the platform administrator. As discussed earlier, semantic annotations may be used in the future for the delivery of automatic service composition techniques, where existing services are automatically combined, deployed, and evaluated to be offered for further use.

Moreover, SYNAISTHISI can be used to define complex application blueprints, that is abstract descriptions of complex IoT services constituting of simpler microservices, which are interconnected and demonstrate desired behaviors. The blueprints include details of the input and output datastreams for each of the composing microservices, and of the nature that each of them has, e.g. lighting optimization, face recognition, etc., and incorporate semantics. Also, they can be equipped by other end-users of the platform, apart from their creators themselves, and this way make the deployment of complex applications much easier and faster.

Innovation is enabled by SYNAISTHISI as it constitutes an IoT Platform as a Service (IoT-PaaS) solution based on open-source frameworks that allows businesses and developers with limited technical expertise or lacking the necessary resources, to convert custom or third party internet-ready devices to web-services in their internal infrastructure. These services can then be directly incorporated in B2B or B2C schemes any time and from anywhere without limitations. User authentication and authorization processes guarantee privacy and direct control of third-party access by resource owners, as an answer to disputes on practices followed by large corporations regarding private data usage and sharing (Parra-Arnau et al., 2018). Additionally, the resources available on the platform can be offered via flexible deployments to clients and collaborators of the integrating businesses or organizations for various use-cases. Excluding the lower level of things and devices that in most cases must have been physically installed to begin functioning, the other layers, i.e. management platform, processing type services, and computational resources, can be available on a 'IoT-on-Demand' basis.

Potential Barriers and Issues

Naturally, apart from all the opportunities that this chapter so far presented, there also exist specific barriers that decelerate wide AI and IoT adoption, mainly generated by the lack of willingness of people to put their trust on such systems.

Ragarding AI, to characterize an approach as trustworthy, systems must be clear with respect to their functionality and goals. Yampolskiy (2016) provides a taxonomy of AI related risks, and distinguishes eight different pathways towards a potentially dangerous AI system, either by external or internal causes, prior to deployment, or after. The author argues that unless legal limitations against malevolent AI systems development are applied, the risk of dangerous AI deployments is high.

Apart from security issues, the property of explainability is also very important to gain trust in AI-based computer systems. Decisions, especially when impacting human lives, should not be taken thoughtlessly even if the suggestion was based on the most accurate predictor. Currently, there are legal implications behind decisions, which should be taken by humans. Before taking a decision, the decision maker should clearly monitor and examine all factors that can and should influence the outcome. With respect to trustworthiness in general, it is on the hands of societies and states to decide on the trade-off between fast and wide market adoption, or ethicality and human-centricity.

In the IoT domain, the trustworthiness risks are mostly related to privacy and security, since if unauthorized access to sensitive data and equipment is granted, then many types of life- and prosperity-threatening issues might come up (Macaulay, 2016). Examples include cases that could have large negative impacts to public health and society, such as malicious access to critical infrastructure, or more narrow and personalized cases, such as unauthorized control of house door locks. It is very important to always keep in mind security, since it is often sidelined by the urge for fast and cheap market entrance.

Additionally to security and ethical barriers, there also exist technical ones for both AI- and IoT-related applications. In particular, there are increased accessibility costs for SMEs to new technologies, and this problem gets exaggerated when focusing on non technology related entities. Let alone the electronics equipment required to take a first leap, human force should also receive special training and get prepared, introducing this way huge difficulties in the adoption. With the emergence of X-on-Demand and X-as-a-Service solutions however, this situation will be improved, since less specialized personnel will also be able to get their hands on and experiment on a higher level, and also receive guidance via the platforms, towards delivering new technology enabled services. Furthermore, the remote access to such ecosystems will boost innovation in areas outside the large technological centres, as this is where innovation currently thrives the most, a fact that has been creating additional barriers to smaller SMEs that are not located in such large and technology friendly cities (Mulas et al., 2016).

Having the issues and barriers in mind, the next section illustrates how the examined platforms could be used to deliver solutions in complex real-world settings, where participants are different types of stakeholders with possibly contradicting interests. In particular, the domain of the Smart Electricity Grid is examined, and two related innovation use-cases are illustrated.

INNOVATION ENABLEMENT IN THE SMART GRID DOMAIN

A good example of how AI and IoT technology can be combined into hybrid innovation ecosystems to solve emerging real-world issues and in parallel generate innovation opportunities, is the domain of the Smart Electricity Grid (Fang et al., 2012). This term refers to the technological evolution in energy systems that end-up creating more secure, reliable and efficient networks infrastructure, with energy produced mostly by distributed and renewable sources, production costs minimized, and energy savings maximized. Smart Grid (SG) approaches assume bidirectional flow of energy and information between the various actors. Such a transition has significantly disrupted the energy market, as well as the related management processes, since in legacy energy systems the generation of energy was performed in large centralized facilities. Now, with the turn to renewable energy and energy harvesting sources, any consumer of energy can be also a producer, e.g. by installing arrays of photovoltaic panels in their premises, or by storing energy when availability is in excess to offer it later during periods of shortage, e.g. via employing domestic energy storage equipment or car parks of electric vehicles (Ramchurn et. al, 2017).

Specifically, two particular use-cases are introduced. First, a large-scale demand-side management setting is examined, where end-users are called in to take action for altering their individual energy demand profiles, in order to make aggregate demand match the available renewable production levels; and a second case, that of vehicle-to-grid and grid-to-vehicle energy exchange, which is used to optimize the process of charging large fleets of electric vehicles. Parties interested to be involved in such cases can benefit by utilizing XaaS and X-on-Demand solutions and deliver innovation in the SG ecosystem in a fast and cost-effective manner.

The SG ecosystem, involves a multitude of stakeholders:

- **Producers:** Utility companies and large energy production sites using fossil fuel, such as oil, nuclear and coal, or renewable sources, e.g. wind, or solar.
- **Consumers:** Residences, commercial, retail, or industrial corporates, any facility that uses energy.
- **Prosumers:** Buildings and facilities that have energy needs that can be fulfilled by the main grid, but also possess equipment for the production of energy, which is either consumed locally, or sold back to the main grid.
- **Aggregators:** Companies, organizations, or cooperatives that act as mediators between large numbers of smaller entities and represent them as a whole to regulators and other, larger entities.
- **Transmission System Operators:** Entities undertaking to transport energy on a national or regional level.
- **Distribution System Operators:** Owners or operating managers of distribution networks.
- **Regulators:** Entities that monitor the markets and the network to ensure that governmental laws are not violated and that policies are properly applied.

In the SG concept, communication infrastructure is utilized in all levels, from generators, to transmission systems, and, finally, to the end-users, with the IoT technology making this possible. The data and information gathered from large numbers of sensors and smart meters is exchanged at real-time and, apart from providing insights to managers and regulators via prediction models, it can also be used by individuals for other kinds of innovative crowdsourced operations. For example, with the increased penetration of renewable sources that often have intermittent output, generation is not controllable, thus one should focus on how to change demand to meet production. This is termed as Demand-Side Management (DSM), where instead of the producer side controlling the production levels, the end-users are asked to alter their demand profiles. DSM generally aims to induce changes to the consumers' individual demand curves via providing lower prices or other kinds of rebates and incentives, so that total demand levels match those of the available production (Gottwalt et. al, 2011).

However, even if a single consumer decides to alter their consumption profile and finally does so, this is only one drop in the ocean of the total demand of a region. Acting alone is not enough, and coordinated behaviour in the large-scale is required. As a first step, this can be achieved by the formation of cooperatives, or by subscribing to aggregator entities, which can issue demand-response requests or design appropriate incentivization mechanisms. Though, it is not easy for end-users to constantly take into account the respective constraints, and take last minute action, or reschedule pre planned tasks, even with advanced monitoring and remote control capabilities at hand enabled by IoT. This is a task for personalized AI applications that undertake to elicit end-user preferences and guarantee to pursue their best interests by acting in an autonomous manner. Akasiadis & Chalkiadakis (2017) put forward a multiagent systems and mechanism design approach to drive coordination of individual consumers organized in cooperatives in highly constrained large-scale DSM cases to maximize renewable energy usage, increase grid stability, and reduce energy consumption costs. Here, although pricing mechanisms and regulations might be universal means of incentivization at a regional level, different types of optimizer agents can be developed and deployed as seen fit for each case. This creates opportunities for innovative services that may take into account many different objectives, e.g. easy-to-use solutions, agents that pursue high comfort for the end-user, others that provide intuitive recommendations and seek to engage users in "greener" behaviours, etc.

Figure 1. Utilization of AI-on Demand and IoT Platform-as-a-Service for an Energy Usage Assistant Application

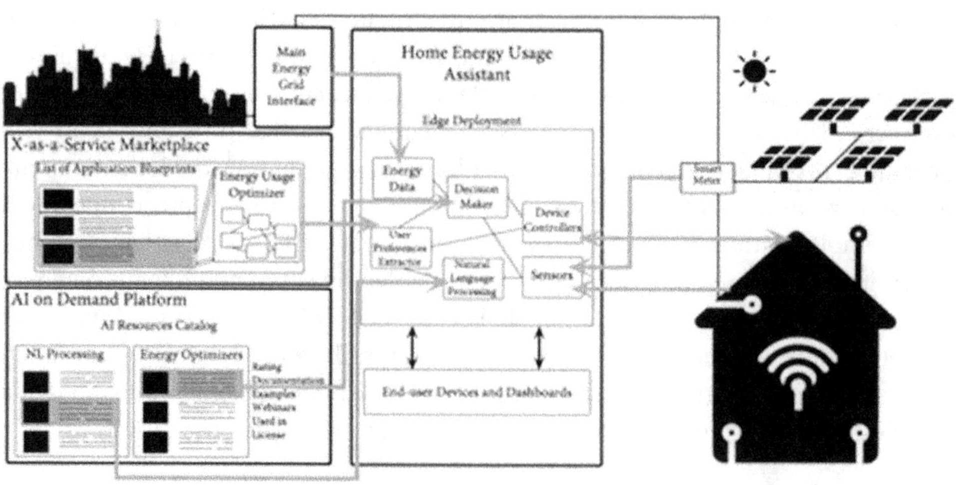

Moreover, aggregators may choose to select subsets of subscribers that have shown to be more reliable with less uncertainty with respect to their performance. In an attempt to engage individuals into participating truthfully, the aggregator or cooperative manager can also apply penalization mechanisms, which generate small but tangible profits for the aggregator, while still the majority of participants enjoy reduced rates for consumption (Akasiadis & Chalkiadakis, 2017b).

Cooperatives can also be formed by energy prosumers, necessitating fair reward sharing, transparency, and trustworthiness guarantees. The scientific literature is rich with methods that offer such guarantees and even more, however, the capability to integrate them in products and services is limited to the few large companies that are able to financially support R&D and pilot use-cases applications. This is expected to change with the wider availability of XaaS and X-on-Demand solutions that are used to boost knowledge transfer to SMEs and startups as well.

Figure 1 presents an example of a Home Energy Usage Assistant composition that can be used to enable ease-of-use in DSM and energy usage optimization scenarios. In this case, the corresponding complex application blueprint is discovered and deployed on a local-level IoT PaaS instance. This particular blueprint is composed of a Decision Maker, that monitors user preferences and optimization results, a Natural Language Processing component, that is used to engage in dialogs with the residents, a User Preferences Extractor, that can help to elicit user preferences in a non intrusive way, and various sensors, such as energy data, e.g. variable prices, levels of renewable production, etc., temperature meters, presence detectors, etc. and, finally, the device controller virtualizations that are used to enable, disable, or reconfigure electrical appliances, e.g. heating and lighting equipment. Note that for the Decision Making and the Natural Language Processing modules, existing AI resources from the AI on Demand platform catalogue can be selected for incorporation. In this case, the SG stakeholders combined with the smart equipment constitute a hybrid ecosystem, which co-operates to crowdsource energy usage promises of customers whose realization will result to reduced costs and 'greener' production.

Furthermore, another area that has not yet reached its peak and requires novel services energy network-wise, is the emerging market of electric vehicles. This kind of products will further alter electricity consumption baselines, and will require the development of a new family of services, termed as Grid-to-Vehicle/Vehicle-to-Grid (G2V/V2G) mechanisms. In such settings, simultaneous initiation of charging for large numbers of vehicles might induce serious problems in the network (Jain & Jain, 2014). Thus, the charging schedules must be shaped in an appropriate "smart charging" manner (G2V). Moreover, fleets of already charged electric vehicles that are not expected to be used for determined time intervals, e.g. not yet rented cars from a rental company, may collectively offer the energy stored in their batteries back to the grid in order to contribute to the network's stability (V2G). If the interaction protocols between the grid, the charging stations, and the vehicles are open, then customized applications following diverse business models can be composed, by manipulating available IoT and AI resources from the respective ecosystems appropriately (Spanoudakis et. al, 2019).

As an illustration example, Figure 2 presents a case of a car rental and parking SME, that aims to innovate in the field of green transportation, i.e. owns a fleet of electric vehicles and charges them using own renewable energy sources. The development of applications that solve the G2V/V2G problembecomes easier if a G2V/V2G optimizer application blueprint is utilized by the IoT Platform-as-a-Service marketplace. This complex application blueprint interconnects smart meters, smart chargers, and other data, e.g. end-user preferences, weather conditions etc., and predicts the output of the renewable energy sources, optimizes the charging schedules based on the predictions, and, if it is required, initiates negotiations with the customers. To realise this innovative service, an IoT PaaS instance is deployed on a local level within the SME's premises, and the equipment (i.e. smart chargers, smart meters, etc.) is virtualized and interconnected. To fill the various processing type components of the complex application, i.e. the predictor and the charging schedule optimizer, the catalogue of the AI on Demand platform is used, where the most preferable between the various available solutions are chosen for deployment.

Figure 2. Utilization of AI-on Demand and IoT Platform-as-a-Service in a G2V/V2G service case

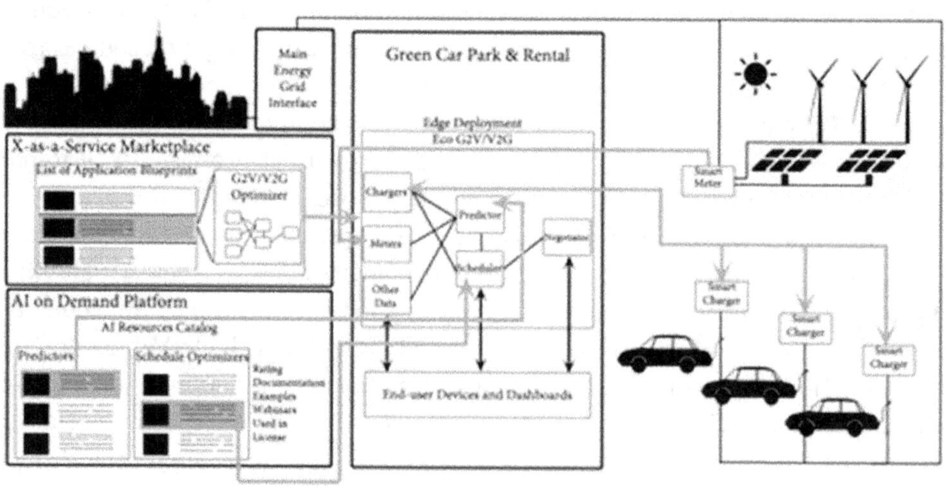

As can be observed by the previous use-cases, the generally applicable nature of IoT Platform-as-a-Service and AI-on-Demand allows the fast deployment of innovations with advanced capabilities. Less informed users can browse available solutions and educate themselves regarding existing approaches and choose and deploy the most appropriate ones for their case. Respective platforms, such as AI4EU and SYNAISTHISI, by following the necessary interoperability standards---e.g. those set by BigIoT, and incentivization mechanisms resulting from MD---make the deployment of composite applications a relatively easy task. In the first case, the interested party is composed of individuals in their residencies with the aim to minimize energy costs, as a crowdsourced solution that is used by themselves. The second one, includes business entities that aim to deliver innovative G2V/V2G services in an emerging field, and in a new set of customers, since such solutions are not deployed in the large-scale yet. Still, technology professionals are required for the deployment of the solutions and to tackle potential technical issues, but significantly less effort is needed regarding development and validation, than creating such applications from scratch. Although utilizing different components, both use-cases are enabled by XaaS and X-on-Demand hybrid approaches. Of course, these could also be utilized in a multitude of application areas, other than SG, e.g. in additive manufacturing, traffic management, supply-chain optimization, and so on.

The business components present in these two scenarios can be categorized according to the dimensions presented in Morris et al. (2005). First of all, value is created by leveraging on the price variances as a result of the balancing between supply and demand. Most countries have established variable pricing either on wholesale, or retail levels. By coordinating their consumption, end-users can collectively seek 'bargains' and thus reduce energy costs. Coordination can be performed by equipping AI-on-Demand services that analyze forecasts, prices, and consumption patterns. Automatic control of equipment is enabled by IoT platforms. Next, created value is enjoyed by energy end-users and the respective mediators (e.g. energy cooperatives, smart parking lots, etc.) that take part in such efforts. The source of competence of such business entities is mainly the innovative services that are based on cutting-edge technologies, such as AI and IoT. The same can be used for the competence positioning.

CONCLUSION

This chapter provided a brief overview of the latest advancements of innovation ecosystems combined with the fields of Artificial Intelligence and Internet of Things. The related background from a business aspect has been discussed and the potentials for innovation have been highlighted, together with the concept of Mechanism

Design, a subfield of economics and game theory that provides tools for trustworthy and large scale participation in various types of ecosystems. Next, focus was put on AI4EU, an AI-on Demand platform that aims to lower the barriers for widespread AI adoption even by individuals and SMEs that mainly do not possess strong scientific background and the technical expertise required to transform current processes to "smarter" versions. Also, the SYNAISTHISI IoT Platform-as-a-Service approach was presented that enables IoT applications and is based on open source frameworks. Finally, to showcase the applicability of X-on-Demand and X-as-a-Service platforms in delivering innovative services and applications, two use cases from the domain of Smart Grid were analyzed. It is expected that innovation ecosystems of various application areas will be invigorated by such platforms, enabling professionals and entrepreneurs to deliver smart products and services of advanced capabilities without having to go through long training and education programmes that require significant amount of time, effort, and money.

Still, appropriate policies and incentives must be put in place to engage individuals into large-scale participation, and to promote fair and trustworthy use of the newly emerging technologies. This is also a direction for future work, that is how to create fertile grounds from a regulation and economic perspective, to allow the fostering of such hybrid approaches. Also, more efforts should be put in place towards the establishment of new types of standards, which, although being restrictive by the definition of the term, should promote the diversibility of solutions, be as inclusive as possible, and aim to lower barriers for systems interoperability. In addition, further research is required in the field of semi- and fully automatic deployment and orchestration of complex services, as well as in the analysis and prediction regarding return on investments.

ACKNOWLEDGMENT

The author acknowledges partial funding from the European Union's Horizon 2020 research and innovation programme under grant agreement no. 825619 (AI4EU), and partial funding by the project SYNTELESIS "Innovative Technologies and Applications based on the Internet of Things (IoT) and the Cloud Computing" (MIS 5002521), which is implemented under the "Action for the Strategic Development on the Research and Technological Sector", funded by the Operational Programme "Competitiveness, Entrepreneurship and Innovation" (NSRF 2014-2020), and co-financed by Greece and the European Union (European Regional Development Fund).

REFERENCES

Akasiadis, C., & Chalkiadakis, G. (2017). Mechanism Design for Demand-Side Management. *IEEE Intelligent Systems*, *32*(1), 24–31. doi:10.1109/MIS.2017.6

Akasiadis, C., & Chalkiadakis, G. (2017b). Cooperative electricity consumption shifting. *Sustainable Energy. Grids and Networks*, *9*, 38–58.

Akasiadis, C., Pitsilis, V., & Spyropoulos, C. D. (2019). A Multi-Protocol IoT Platform Based on Open-Source Frameworks. *Sensors (Basel)*, *19*(19), E4217. doi:10.339019194217 PMID:31569338

Amshoff, B., Dülme, C., Echterfeld, J., & Gausemeier, J. (2015). Business Model Patterns for Disruptive Technologies. *International Journal of Innovation Management*, *19*(03), 1540002. doi:10.1142/S1363919615400022

Andersson, P., & Mattsson, L. G. (2015). Service Innovations Enabled by the "Internet of Things". *IMP Journal*, *9*(1), 85–106. doi:10.1108/IMP-01-2015-0002

Autio, E., & Thomas, L. (2014). Innovation ecosystems. The Oxford handbook of innovation management, 204-288.

Bahrammirzaee, A. (2010). A comparative survey of artificial intelligence applications in finance: Artificial neural networks, expert system and hybrid intelligent systems. *Neural Computing & Applications*, *19*(8), 1165–1195. doi:10.100700521-010-0362-z

Bauer, M., Boussard, M., Bui, N., & Carrez, F. (2013). *Project Deliverable D1.5 Final Architectural Reference Model for IoT.* IoT-A Project, Technical Report.

Bessis, N., & Dobre, C. (Eds.). (2014). *Big data and internet of things: a roadmap for smart environments* (Vol. 546). Springer International Publishing. doi:10.1007/978-3-319-05029-4

Bröring, A., Schmid, S., Schindhelm, C. K., Khelil, A., Käbisch, S., Kramer, D., Le Phouc, D., Mitic, J., Anicic, D., & Teniente, E. (2017). Enabling IoT ecosystems through platform interoperability. *IEEE Software*, *34*(1), 54–61. doi:10.1109/MS.2017.2

Bucherer, E., & Uckelmann, D. (2011). *10 Business Models for the Internet of Things. In Architecting the Internet of Things*. Springer.

Cockburn, I., Henderson, R., & Stern, S. (2018). The Impact of Artificial Intelligence on Innovation: An Exploratory Analysis. In *NBER Chapters*. National Bureau of Economic Research, Inc.

Commission Staff Working Document. (2016). Advancing the Internet of Things in Europe. In Communication from the Commission to the European Parliament, the Council, the European Economic and Social Committee, and the Committee of the Regions, Digitising European Industry Reaping the full benefits of a Digital Single Market, SWD/2016/0110.

Driankov, D., & Saffiotti, A. (Eds.). (2013). *Fuzzy logic techniques for autonomous vehicle navigation* (Vol. 61). Physica.

Duan, Y., Cao, Y., & Sun, X. (2015). Various "aaS" of everything as a service. In *2015 IEEE/ACIS 16th International Conference on Software Engineering, Artificial Intelligence, Networking and Parallel/Distributed Computing (SNPD)* (pp. 1-6). IEEE.

Erevelles, S., Fukawa, N., & Swayne, L. (2016). Big Data Consumer Analytics and the Transformation of Marketing. *Journal of Business Research*, *69*(2), 897–904. doi:10.1016/j.jbusres.2015.07.001

European Commission. (2018). Artificial Intelligence for Europe. In Communication From The Commission To The European Parliament, The European Council, The Council, The European Economic And Social Committee And The Committee Of The Regions, SWD(2018) 137 final.

Fang, X., Misra, S., Xue, G., & Yang, D. (2012). Smart Grid — The New and Improved Power Grid: A Survey. *IEEE Communications Surveys and Tutorials*, *14*(4), 944–980. doi:10.1109/SURV.2011.101911.00087

Fortino, G., Savaglio, C., Palau, C. E., Puga, J. S., Ganzha, M., Paprzycki, M., Montesinos, M., Liotta, A., & Llop, M. (2018). Towards multi-layer interoperability of heterogeneous IoT platforms: the INTER-IoT approach. In R. Gravina, C. Palau, M. Manso, A. Liotta, & G. Fortino (Eds.), *Integration, Interconnection, and Interoperability of IoT Systems. Internet of Things (Technology, Communications and Computing)*. Springer. doi:10.1007/978-3-319-61300-0_10

Gawer, A., & Cusumano, M. A. (2014). Platforms and Innovation. *Journal of Product Innovation Management*, *31*, 417–433. doi:10.1111/jpim.12105

Gottwalt, S., Ketter, W., Block, C., Collins, J., & Weinhardt, C. (2011). Demand side management—A simulation of household behavior under variable prices. *Energy Policy*, *39*(12), 8163–8174. doi:10.1016/j.enpol.2011.10.016

Gundall, M., Schneider, J., Schotten, H. D., Aleksy, M., Schulz, D., Franchi, N., Schwarzenberg, N., Markwart, C., Halfmann, R., Rost, P., & Wübben, D. (2018). 5G as Enabler for Industrie 4.0 Use Cases: Challenges and Concepts. In *2018 IEEE 23rd International Conference on Emerging Technologies and Factory Automation (ETFA)* (Vol. 1, pp. 1401-1408). IEEE.

Hager, G. D., Drobnis, A., Fang, F., Ghani, R., Greenwald, A., Lyons, T., Parkes, D. C., Schultz, J., Saria, S., & Smith, S. F., & Tambe, M. (2019). *Artificial intelligence for social good.* arXiv preprint, arXiv:1901.05406.

Hahanov, V., Gharibi, W., Man, K. L., Iemelianov, I., Liubarskyi, M., Abdullayev, V., Litvinova, E., & Chumachenko, S. (2018). Cyber-Physical Technologies: Hype Cycle 2017. In *Cyber Physical Computing for IoT-driven Services* (pp. 259–272). Springer. doi:10.1007/978-3-319-54825-8_14

Hankel, M., & Rexroth, B. (2015). *The Reference Architectural Model Industrie 4.0 (RAMI 4.0)*. ZVEI.

Hein, A., Schreieck, M., Riasanow, T., Setzke, D. S., Wiesche, M., Böhm, M., & Krcmar, H. (2019). Digital platform ecosystems. *Electronic Markets*.

Hessler, G., & Baringhaus, K. H. (2018). Artificial intelligence in drug design. *Molecules (Basel, Switzerland)*, *23*(10), 2520. doi:10.3390/molecules23102520 PMID:30279331

Holzinger, A. (2018). From Machine Learning to Explainable AI. In *2018 World Symposium on Digital Intelligence for Systems and Machines (DISA)* (pp. 55-66). 10.1109/DISA.2018.8490530

Ibarra-Esquer, J. E., González-Navarro, F. F., Flores-Rios, B. L., Burtseva, L., & Astorga-Vargas, M. A. (2017). Tracking the Evolution of the Internet of Things Concept Across Different Application Domains. *Sensors (Basel)*, *17*(6), 1379. doi:10.339017061379 PMID:28613238

Jackson, D. J. (2011). What is an innovation ecosystem. *National Science Foundation, 1*(2).

Jain, P., & Jain, T. (2014). Impacts of G2V and V2G power on electricity demand profile. In *2014 IEEE International Electric Vehicle Conference (IEVC)* (pp. 1-8). 10.1109/IEVC.2014.7056148

Jarwar, M., Kibria, M., Ali, S., & Chong, I. (2018). Microservices in web objects enabled IoT environment for enhancing reusability. *Sensors (Basel)*, *18*(2), 352. doi:10.339018020352 PMID:29373491

Jeschke, S., Brecher, C., Meisen, T., Özdemir, D., & Eschert, T. (2016). Industrial Internet of Things and Cyber Manufacturing Systems. *Springer Series in Wireless Technology*, 3–19.

Kaplan, A., & Haenlein, M. (2019). Siri, Siri, in my hand: Who's the fairest in the land? On the interpretations, illustrations, and implications of artificial intelligence. *Business Horizons*, *62*(1), 15–25. doi:10.1016/j.bushor.2018.08.004

Kenney, M., & Zysman, J. (2015). Choosing a future in the platform economy: the implications and consequences of digital platforms. In *Kauffman Foundation New Entrepreneurial Growth Conference* (*Vol. 156160*). Academic Press.

Klumpp, M. (2018). Innovation Potentials and Pathways Merging AI, CPS, and IoT. *Applied System Innovation*, *1*(1), 5. doi:10.3390/asi1010005

Kohler, T. (2015). Crowdsourcing-Based Business Models: How to Create and Capture Value. *California Management Review*, *57*(4), 63–84. doi:10.1525/cmr.2015.57.4.63

Komninos, N. (2013). Smart Cities and the Future Internet: Innovation ecosystems of embedded spatial intelligence. In *Proceedings of International Conference for Entrepreneurship, Innovation and Regional Development, ICEIRD* (pp. 1-3). Academic Press.

Kruse, L., Wunderlich, N., & Beck, R. (2019). Artificial Intelligence for the Financial Services Industry: What Challenges Organizations to Succeed. In *Proceedings of the 52nd Hawaii International Conference on System Sciences* (pp. 6408-6417). 10.24251/HICSS.2019.770

Kurzweil, R. (1992). *The Age of Intelligent Machines*. Viking.

Laudien, S. M., & Daxböck, B. (2016). The influence of the industrial internet of things on business model design: A qualitative-empirical analysis. *International Journal of Innovation Management*, *20*(08), 1640014. doi:10.1142/S1363919616400144

Lee, J., Davari, H., Singh, J., & Pandhare, V. (2018). Industrial Artificial Intelligence for industry 4.0-based manufacturing systems. *Manufacturing Letters*, *18*, 20–23. doi:10.1016/j.mfglet.2018.09.002

Li, B. H., Hou, B. C., Yu, W. T., Lu, X. B., & Yang, C. W. (2017). Applications of artificial intelligence in intelligent manufacturing: A review. *Frontiers of Information Technology & Electronic Engineering*, *18*(1), 86–96. doi:10.1631/FITEE.1601885

Lin, S. W., Miller, B., Durand, J., Bleakley, G., Chigani, A., Martin, R., Murhpy, B., & Crawford, M. (2017). The Industrial Internet of Things Volume G1: Reference Architecture. Industrial Internet Consortium, 10-46.

Lindner, M. A., Vaquero, L. M., Rodero-Merino, L., & Caceres, J. (2010). Cloud economics: Dynamic business models for business on demand. *International Journal of Business Information Systems*, *5*(4), 373–392. doi:10.1504/IJBIS.2010.032938

Macaulay, T. (2016). *RIoT control: understanding and managing risks and the internet of things*. Morgan Kaufmann.

Mazhelis, O., Luoma, E., & Warma, H. (2012). Defining an internet-of-things ecosystem. In *Internet of Things, Smart Spaces, and Next Generation Networking* (pp. 1–14). Springer. doi:10.1007/978-3-642-32686-8_1

Morris, M., Schindehutte, M., & Allen, J. (2005). The entrepreneur's business model: Toward a unified perspective. *Journal of Business Research*, *58*(6), 726–735. doi:10.1016/j.jbusres.2003.11.001

Mukherjee, A., Singh, M., & Žaldokas, A. (2017). Do corporate taxes hinder innovation? *Journal of Financial Economics*, *124*(1), 195–221. doi:10.1016/j.jfineco.2017.01.004

Mulas, V., Minges, M., & Applebaum, H. (2016). Boosting tech innovation: Ecosystems in cities: A framework for growth and sustainability of urban tech innovation ecosystems. *Innovations: Technology, Governance, Globalization*, *11*(1-2), 98–125. doi:10.1162/inov_a_00251

Nava Auza, J. M., Boisson de Marca, J., & Lima Siqueira, G. (2019). Design of a Local Information Incentive Mechanism for Mobile Crowdsensing. *Sensors (Basel)*, *19*(11), 2532. doi:10.339019112532 PMID:31163609

Nichols, J. A., Herbert Chan, H. W., & Baker, M. (2019). Machine learning: Applications of artificial intelligence to imaging and diagnosis. *Biophysical Reviews*, *11*(1), 111–118. doi:10.100712551-018-0449-9 PMID:30182201

Nisan, N. (2007). Introduction to mechanism design (for computer scientists). *Algorithmic Game Theory*, *9*, 209-242.

Nisan, N., & Ronen, A. (2001). Algorithmic Mechanism Design. *Games and Economic Behavior*, *35*(1-2), 166–196. doi:10.1006/game.1999.0790

Oh, D.-S., Phillips, F., Park, S., & Lee, E. (2016). Innovation ecosystems: A critical examination. *Technovation*, *54*, 1–6. doi:10.1016/j.technovation.2016.02.004

Pan, Y. (2016). Heading toward artificial intelligence 2.0. *Engineering*, *2*(4), 409–413. doi:10.1016/J.ENG.2016.04.018

Parra-Arnau, J. (2018). Optimized, direct sale of privacy in personal data marketplaces. *Information Sciences*, *424*, 354–384. doi:10.1016/j.ins.2017.10.009

Pierris, G., Kothris, D., Spyrou, E., & Spyropoulos, C. (2015). SYNAISTHISI: An enabling platform for the current internet of things ecosystem. In *Proceedings of the 19th Panhellenic Conference on Informatics* (pp. 438-444). ACM. 10.1145/2801948.2802019

Počuča, S., Maršić, B., & Grgić, A. (2012). Possible scenarios for cloud-based offering by operators. In *2012 Proceedings of the 35th International Convention MIPRO* (pp. 506-511). IEEE.

Quan, X. I., & Sanderson, J. (2018). Understanding the artificial intelligence business ecosystem. *IEEE Engineering Management Review*, *46*(4), 22–25. doi:10.1109/EMR.2018.2882430

Ramchurn, S., Vytelingum, P., Rogers, A., & Jennings, N. R. (2012). Putting the" smarts" into the smart grid: A grand challenge for artificial intelligence. *Communications of the ACM*, *55*(4), 86–97. doi:10.1145/2133806.2133825

Ramos, C. (2007). Ambient Intelligence – A State of the Art from Artificial Intelligence Perspective. In J. Neves, M. F. Santos, & J. M. Machado (Eds.), Lecture Notes in Computer Science: Vol. 4874. *Progress in Artificial Intelligence. EPIA 2007*. Springer. doi:10.1007/978-3-540-77002-2_24

Ray, P., P. (2018). A survey on Internet of Things Architectures. *Journal of King Saud University – Computer and Information Sciences, 30*(3), 291-319.

RendaA. (2019). Artificial Intelligence: Ethics, Governance and Policy Challenge. *CEPS Task Force Report*: SSRN.

Ritala, P., Agouridas, V., Assimakopoulos, D., & Gies, O. (2013). Value creation and capture mechanisms in innovation ecosystems: A comparative case study. *International Journal of Technology Management*, *63*(3/4), 244–267. doi:10.1504/IJTM.2013.056900

Russel, S., & Norvig, P. (2009). *Artificial Intelligence: A Modern Approach* (3rd ed.). Prentice Hall.

Ryman-Tubb, N. F., Krause, P., & Garn, W. (2018). How Artificial Intelligence and machine learning research impacts payment card fraud detection: A survey and industry benchmark. *Engineering Applications of Artificial Intelligence*, *76*, 130–157. doi:10.1016/j.engappai.2018.07.008

Santofimia-Romero, M. J., del Toro-García, X., & López-López, J. C. (2011). Artificial intelligence techniques for smart grid applications. *Green ICT: Trends and Challenges*, 41-44.

Schladofsky, W., Jelena, M., Megner, A. P., Simonato, C., Gioppo, L., Leonardos, D., & Bröring, A. (2017). Business Models for Interoperable IoT Ecosystems. In I. Podnar Žarko, A. Broering, S. Soursos, & M. Serrano (Eds.), Lecture Notes in Computer Science: Vol. 10218. *Interoperability and Open-Source Solutions for the Internet of Things. InterOSS-IoT 2016*. Springer. doi:10.1007/978-3-319-56877-5_6

Schwarting, W., Alonso-Mora, J., & Rus, D. (2018). Planning and decision-making for autonomous vehicles. *Annual Review of Control, Robotics, and Autonomous Systems*, *1*(1), 187–210. doi:10.1146/annurev-control-060117-105157

Smorodinskaya, N., Russell, M., Katukov, D., & Still, K. (2017). Innovation ecosystems vs. innovation systems in terms of collaboration and co-creation of value. In *Proceedings of the 50th Hawaii international conference on system sciences*. 10.24251/HICSS.2017.636

Soursos, S., Žarko, I. P., Zwickl, P., Gojmerac, I., Bianchi, G., & Carrozzo, G. (2016). Towards the cross-domain interoperability of IoT platforms. In *2016 European conference on networks and communications (EuCNC)* (pp. 398-402). IEEE. 10.1109/EuCNC.2016.7561070

Spanoudakis, N., Akasiadis, C., Kechagias, G., & Chalkiadakis, G. (2019). An Open MAS Services Architecture for the V2G/G2V Problem. In *Proceedings of the 18th International Conference on Autonomous Agents and MultiAgent Systems* (pp. 2198-2200). International Foundation for Autonomous Agents and Multiagent Systems.

Thuluva, A. S., Bröring, A., Medagoda, G. P., Don, H., Anicic, D., & Seeger, J. (2017). Recipes for IoT applications. In *Proceedings of the Seventh International Conference on the Internet of Things* (p. 10). ACM.

Tzortzis, G., Akasiadis, C., & Spyrou, E. (2017). *Semantic Complex Service Composition within an IoT Ecosystem. In The Internet of Things: Foundation for Smart Cities, e-Health and Ubiquitous Computing*. Chapman and Hall/CRC.

Venkatraman, N. V., El Sawy, O. A., Pavlou, P. A., & Bharadwaj, A. (2014). *Theorizing digital business innovation: platforms and capabilities in ecosystems.* Fox School of Business Research Paper, (15-080).

Vermesan, O., Bröring, A., Tragos, E., Serrano, M., Bacciu, D., Chessa, S., Gallicchio, C., Micheli, A., Dragone, M., Saffiotti, A., Simoens, P., Cavallo, F., & Bahr, R. (2017). Internet of robotic things : converging sensing/actuating, hypoconnectivity, artificial intelligence and IoT Platforms. In *Cognitive Hyperconnected Digital Transformation: Internet of Things Intelligence Evolution* (pp. 97–155). River Publishers.

Vocke, C., Constantinescu, C., & Popescu, D. (2019). Application potentials of artificial intelligence for the design of innovation processes. *Procedia CIRP*, *84*, 810–813. doi:10.1016/j.procir.2019.04.230

Xia, F., Yang, L. T., Wang, L., & Vinel, A. (2012). Internet of things. *International Journal of Communication Systems*, *25*(9), 1101–1102. doi:10.1002/dac.2417

Yampolskiy, R. (2016). Taxonomy of Pathways to Dangerous Artificial Intelligence. In *AI Ethics and Society*. AAAI.

Yu, K. H., Beam, A. L., & Kohane, I. S. (2018). Artificial intelligence in healthcare. *Nature Biomedical Engineering*, *2*(10), 719–731. doi:10.103841551-018-0305-z PMID:31015651

Zahra, S. A., & Nambisan, S. (2011). Entrepreneurship in global innovation ecosystems. *AMS Review*, *1*(1), 4–17. doi:10.100713162-011-0004-3

ADDITIONAL READING

Dean, J. (2014). *Big data, data mining, and machine learning: value creation for business leaders and practitioners*. John Wiley & Sons. doi:10.1002/9781118691786

Di Martino, B., Li, K. C., Yang, L. T., & Esposito, A. (Eds.). (2017). *Internet of everything: algorithms, methodologies, technologies and perspectives*. Springer.

High-Level Expert Group on Artificial Intelligence. (2019). A Definition Of AI: Main Capabilities And Disciplines. In Deliverables of the High-Level Expert Group on Artificial Intelligence Set Up by the European Commission.

High-Level Expert Group on Artificial Intelligence. (2019). Policy And Investment Recommendations For Trustworthy AI. In Deliverables of the High-Level Expert Group on Artificial Intelligence Set Up by the European Commission.

Lawless, W., Mittu, R., Sofge, D., & Moskowitz, I. S., & Russell, S. (Eds.). (2019). Artificial Intelligence for the Internet of Everything. Academic Press.

Raj, P., & Raman, A. C. (2017). *The Internet of things: Enabling technologies, platforms, and use cases*. CRC Press.

Skilton, M., & Hovsepian, F. (2017). *The 4th Industrial Revolution: Responding to the Impact of Artificial Intelligence on Business*. Springer.

Zdravković, M., Trajanović, M., Sarraipa, J., Jardim-Gonçalves, R., Lezoche, M., Aubry, A., & Panetto, H. (2016). *Survey of Internet-of-Things platforms. In 6th International Conference on Information Society and Technology*, ICIST 2016 (Vol. 1, pp. 216-220).

Chapter 6
An Integrated LoRa-Based IoT Platform Serving Smart Farming and Agro-Logistics

Nikos Tsotsolas
University of West Attica, Greece

Faidon Komisopoulos
University of West Attica, Greece

Philip Papadopoulos
American Farm School, Greece

Eleni Koutsouraki
Green Projects S.A., Greece

ABSTRACT

The value chain of agri-food is radically changed due the fact that consumers, as well as various players in the agro-logistics chain, seek for increased and trustful food safety. Given the specific characteristics of the agri-food supply chain, having numerous origin points, several aggregations hubs at different levels and then again numerous points of sales, the need of a holistic approach in collecting, forwarding and interpreting data in an interoperable way is a dire need. In this chapter, the authors present the architecture of the traceability platform KalaΘos™ and its IoT management module called, GP CoreIoT™. The KalaΘos infrastructure includes a network of sensors devices at farms, equipment, trucks, aggregation, processing, and logistics facilities, connected to a network of LoRa gateways. Its open architecture focuses on semantic and syntactic interoperability approaches for joint exploitation of data collected and managed by other systems with similar aims and scope.

DOI: 10.4018/978-1-7998-4843-1.ch006

INTRODUCTION

There is a great potential for application of Internet-connected technologies in the food and agriculture sector, especially in view of the social and environmental challenges, which the aforementioned sector faces. From the farm to the shelf of a retail store, Internet of Things (IoT) technologies, as an element of the value chain of agri-food, could transform the sector by contributing to food security and to reduction of agricultural inputs and food waste. The data in this kind of supply chains typically initiates from the nurseries and farms, continues at packing, slaughtering and other processing facilities, thereupon reaches the wholesalers' premises and ultimately the retailers' facilities and the points of sale. Fusion of sensors, telecommunication networks, such as LoRAWAN™, and data handling platforms are included in IoT technologies and combined with traceability platforms and decision support systems, aim to provide end-to-end information and knowledge in order to address these specific needs.

The objectives of the chapter are to analyse the current status of agri-food value chain, with the main focus on its nature and on its specific challenges as well as to explore how the IoT technologies may constitute an active part of this value chain. Furthermore, a general overview of the IoT telecommunication networks, of sensors' devices and of data handling platforms is presented. There is also an in-depth discussion about issues related to the IoT approaches and solutions in agri-food value chain for both primary activities and logistics supporting activities.

Business models, such as freemium and sensors as a service, are also discussed, addressing the need of viable ecosystems to be established in which different business actors and stakeholders are actively involved in the collection of the data and the use of the information towards the creation of value.

An extensive description of KalaΘos™ platform and its IoT management module, as well as information about the real-world pilot application of these systems, are also included.

IOT TECHNOLOGIES

IoT and Telecommunication Networks

The Internet of Things (IoT) constitutes the communication network of a variety of devices, home appliances, cars, and any other object that incorporates electronic media, software, sensors, actuators and network connectivity, and allows data connection and exchange. Simply put, the philosophy of IoT is to connect all electronic devices to one another (local area network) and / or to the internet (world wide web) creating Wireless Sensor-Actuator Networks (WSANs). Its operating network layer incorporates a fusion of public and private networks such as Local Area Networks - LAN (Bluetooth, Zigbee, WiFi), Cellular Networks (GSM, 3G, 4G, 5G) and recently Low Power Wide Area Networks - LPWAN (LoRa, Sigfox, NB-IoT) and Satellite Networks (VSAT). The choice of the mixture of various networks intends to achievea communication level of certain quality and reliability taking also into account the security need concerning the transmitted data (Wei & Lv, 2019; The Things Network, 2019).

LPWAN is more suitable for IoT application since each device needs to transfer a very small amount of data in long range, as shown in Fig. 1. The three most popular LPWAN technologies, have arisen at global level are, Sigfox, LoRa, and NB-IoT, which involve many technical and functional differences. The most important of them are the range (up to 40 km for Sigfox, 20 km for LoRa, 10 km for NB-IoT), the power consumption, where LoRa technology is the winning one, and the business model of operation, where LoRa is a public network, Sigfox is a private network, albeit both are using unlicensed bands and NB-IoT is operated by cell carrier companies on licensed bands (21b).As far as the topology is concerned, LoRa and Sigfox technologies need to connect to agateway, which uses high bandwidth networks such as WiFi, Ethernet or Cellular in order to connect to corresponding server, implementing a star-of-stars topology in which gateways relay messages between end-devices and a central network server (The Things Network, 2019;LoRa Alliance, 2019).

Sensors and Technologies Used

The main goal of the IoT approach is to incorporate billions of devices with sensors, which will be acquired by different organizations and people, in order their specific needs to be addressed. These devices will collect vast amount of data. Therefore, the appropriate infrastructure shall be in place to undertake the discovery of the appropriate sensor for each case, the transmitting, processing and integrating of the date towards thc production of knowledge that will support decisions. Given the fact that some of these decisions might be critical and time sensitive for specific applications, solutions that permit the performance of these tasks in real-time, on the move, in the cloud, and securely are needed. Equally important is the ability to evaluate the fidelity and integrity of sensors' data, so it is crucial to be continuously aware of the operation status of each sensor device and detect with high accuracy any faulty sensor (Chakraborty et al., 2018; Georgakopoulos & Jayaraman, 2016).

Figure 1. Required data rate vs. range capacity of radio communication technologies: LPWAN positioning (Mekki, Bajic, Chaxel & Meyer, 2019)

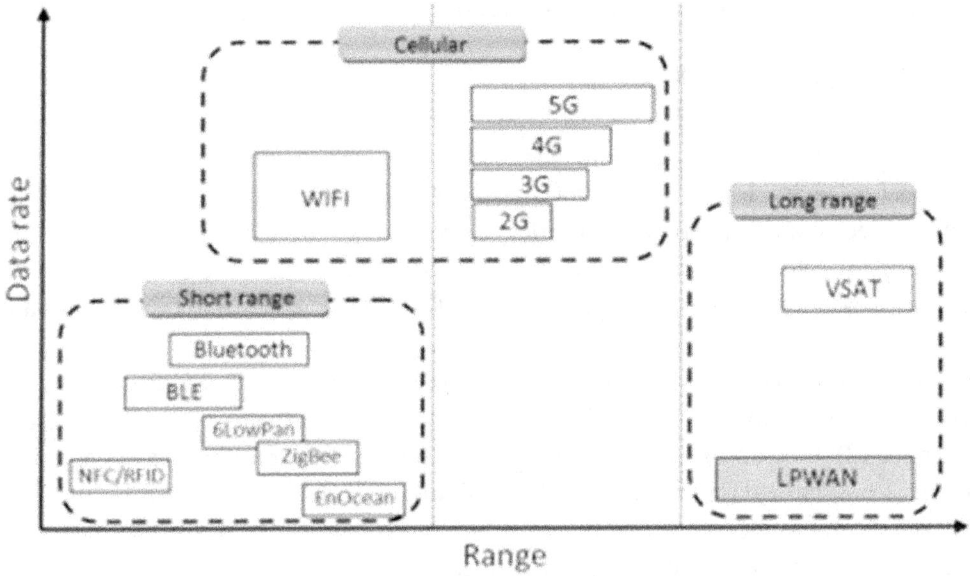

When designing a Wireless Sensors Network (WSN) to support an IoT scenario, one or more architectures shall be chosen in relation to the movement of the devices. Stationary architecture requires sensor devices to be placed at fixed positions for the whole period of the application. Such architecture is chosen for sensors that measure for instance environmental parameters of the air or in the ground at specific places. Mobile architecture requires the sensor nodes to change their position with time. An example of applications based on such architecture is a device attached on a pallet with fruits in order to track the position of the dispatchment and to monitor the conditions of transport. According to mobile architecture, both stationary and mobile nodes are used to provide the necessary information to the users. The latter is used to support for instance precision agriculture applications consisting of mobile farming equipment and stationary field sensors (Wei &Lv, 2019; Srbinovska, Gavrovski, Dimcev, Krkoleva & Borozan, 2015).

There are numerous sensors of different kind, addressing the scope of each application. Sensors that measure the environmental parameters of the air (e.g. temperature, humidity, wind speed and direction, dew point, radiation), the soil (e.g. soil temperature, volumetric water content, salinity), the quality of the air (e.g. concentration of specific air gases, particulate matter), the status of motion (GPS, inertial measurement, vibration) and other elements (light, noise, water flow, electricity parameters) shall be integrated into the same device (node) or into different devices that will collaborate in a seamless way. This is the reason why the integration of multiple technologies in IoT applications necessitates a high-level of interoperability between the various components (GS1, 2016).

IoT Data Handling Platforms

IoT devices that produce big data, characterized by heterogeneity due to the variety of sensors, technologies and protocols that are used. However, this data needs to be handled in an efficient way in order to provide functionality, which need to be exploited towards the creation of novel smart services and products from which enterprises, industries, and society are benefited (Georgakopoulos & Jayaraman, 2016).

IoT applications are developed to support the data handling and they usually cover four main operations: (1) Discover the IoT devices that can provide the data needed, (2) Join and re-join the devices to the gateway, (3) Integrate these IoT devices and their data, and (4) Analyse the integrated data as needed by specific IoT service/product.

Nevertheless, there are two key challenges in enabling the IoT-enabled vision of data-driven cases. Firstly, the ability to receive data from the sensors' nodes, due to the poor internet connectivity in some distant areas, can be mentioned. Secondly the challenge regarding how to make data from different sources actionable by the users of the data. The heterogeneous sensor streams need to be merged and analysed together with other source of data such as satellite data. Moreover, the workload added to the users shall be rational and proportionate to the value, which this data is going to add to the system. More and more efforts towards a more efficient exploitation of IoT data through the development and operation of data handing platforms are made by big companies such as IBM (Watson IoT Platform), Amazon (AWS IoT) and Microsoft (Azure IoT Platform). For instance, FarmBeats, a solution developed by Microsoft, uses new AI & ML algorithms (trained on this data), along with any available remote sensing data, with the aim to provide unique and actionable insights to farmers, which can allow them to improve their productivity (Chandra, 2018; Fountas et al., 2015).

IoT shall be a network of internet connected objects (sensor devices) with the ability to exchange information by using an agreed method and data schema. Unfortunately, several IoT solutions are often in vertical silos with no or little interoperability between them. Thus, this gap of interoperability between IoT platforms is needed to be addressed for a more efficient generation of knowledge based on various sources of IoT data. The most common approach for tackling this issue is the development of API services that can act as integrators of data within the IoT ecosystem (Serrano et al., 2015; Srbinovska, Gavrovski, Dimcev, Krkoleva & Borozan, 2015; Schladofsky et al., 2017).

The communication of various devices and platforms shall be built on an interoperability base, which can be divided into three different levels: (i) Technical Interoperability, which is usually associated with hardware/software components, systems and platforms that enable machine-to-machine communication to take place, (ii) Syntactical Interoperability, which is usually related to data formats, and (iii) Organizational Interoperability, which can be defined as the ability of organizations to effectively communicate and transfer data and information, albeit they may be using a variety of different information systems and different infrastructures (Serrano et al., 2015). Several ontologies have been developed and some of them are being accepted as operational standards, such as the Semantic Sensor Network (SSN) Ontology, which has been developed by World Wide Web Consortium (W3C) Semantic Sensor Networks Incubator Group, and provides a schema that describes sensors, observation, data attributes, and other related concepts (Jayaraman, Yavari, Georgakopoulos, Morshed & Zaslavsky, 2016).

IOT IN AGRI-FOOD VALUE CHAIN

The Value Chain in General

The concept of Supply Chain Management (SCM) has been identified and it is used to highlight the importance of coordination and collaboration of all elements of a company or organization in the value creation process. Researchers have defined the Supply Chain (SC) as a sequence that links every element to the production and supply process, from raw materials to the end user. According to these approaches, SC encompasses the entire value chain and the routing of materials, from the supply of raw materials to the consumption of products by the customer. The purpose of developing the supply chain model is the provision of a complete understanding of the supply chain, both in terms of management and operation (Boonjing et al., 2015).

A typical supply chain is the network of materials, information and services linked to the production of the finished product and its distribution to meet demand. It is the collection and interaction of these elements that affect attributes, functions, behavior, and performance.

Businesses create and deliver products and services through increasingly global and complex chains (Malindretos, 2015). However, the competitive nature of the business environment nowadays, demands businesses to constantly search for ways to reduce operating costs, provide satisfactory customer service, and minimize existing and expected disruption risks by designing and managing efficient supply chains (Bala, 2014).

SCM is an essential part of the value chain of every business and production system. According to the theory introduced by Michael Porter (McGee, 2015), SCM is regarded as one of the core functions of any business producing products or services.

The whole value chain focuses on the business segments that can add value to the product and make that value more visible to the customer, in a way that the business can gain a competitive advantage and if possible, a sustainable competitive advantage. Its functions are divided into two categories: the primary and the support activities.

The goal of the five activities that are classified as the primary activities is the creation of value that exceeds their cost, thus generating profits for the business. This would include: Incoming logistics including receiving, storing, and inventory control of a company's raw materials. Production, that includes the value-added activities used to convert a company's raw materials into finished products. Outbound logistics, which include the activities required to promote a company's final product to its customer for sale. Marketing and sales, which refer to the activities needed to entice a buyer to buy a product and include channel selection, advertising and pricing. Finally, service activities, which are the ones that increase the value of a product, including customer support and repairs (Hugos, 2018).

On the other hand, the support activities include: The firm's infrastructure: including processes and activities such as auditing, public relations, quality assurance, strategic management and operations of business department (eg accounting). Research and development: relating to the equipment, hardware, software, processes and technical knowledge available to convert inputs into output. Human Resource Management: consisting of all activities related to recruitment, training, development, compensation and dismissal. Procurement: relating to processes such as raw materials acquisition, equipment and more.

The Nature of Agri-Food Value Chain

Farmers' products have been traditionally transported to the local market and traded at the highest possible price. With the technological advancement and mass production, market development, standard of living and specialization, nowadays, it is feasible for individual producers to perform all the functions of disposing their products to the end customer, meaning functions such as packaging etc. At the same time, some benefits have been gained by farmers through the improvement of crops and mass production, limited to the production process itself and not to their disposal products on the market, which may now not only be related to the local, but through significant development of logistics, and to the whole world.

The agricultural sector is a key sector that supplies a variety of products and services, of particular importance for the food and beverage industry, which consistently constitutes the driving force behind manufacturing. The contribution of agricultural products to a country's GDP and external trade balance, which presents stability and dynamism even in times of recession in the economy, is very much acknowledged. The supply chains of agricultural products are examined with a particular approach by researchers, due to their relatively short shelf life, their sensitivity, their direct relationship to meet basic household needs, and the public health, (Verdouw, Robbemond, Verwaart, Wolfert, & Beulens, 2015).

The logistics of agricultural products are regarded as one a fast-growing sector, aimed at boosting the agricultural economy and sustainable development and at improving the income of the rural population, and rural development, by the promotion of quality assurance of agricultural products, local products, farm protection and management systems. The transportation and management of agricultural products today is based on the use of modern technology and logistics know-how, including specialized cold rooms, quality controls, legislative restrictions hygiene and safety during transportation and storage, crisis management in cases of cargo alterations, etc.

The goal is to effectively transfer the agricultural products from the field to consumer's shelf or even to consumer houses, with their careful and highly controlled management at all stages of the chain. The agricultural supply chain has now been correlated with greenhouse effect and the extensive development of distribution networks and logistics since there is a great need to ensure a rapid and of high-quality distribution of agricultural products across long supply chains. For instance, in order to make a salad foran English consumer, the imported products in concern (tomatoes, carrots, cucumbers, etc.), need to travel more than 1600 km. Greeks also consume daily pineapples, bananas and other fruits supplied by the Latin market or America and other distant parts of the world (Caro, Ali, Vecchio, & Giaffreda, 2018).

The variety of agricultural products and their availability is one of the stern quality consumer needs that affect directly the rural supply chain products. In particular, the consumers pay great attention to: the variety of agricultural products offered, for wider consumer choice, the quality in relation to 'freshness', nutritional value (production of organic products), their taste, and "Image" (shape, size, color, odor, packaging) of agricultural products, the correlation of packaging in response to actual average consumption.

Hence, many researchers have explored the importance of the relationship and the role of agri-food supply chains in the rural development of an area and especially in the case of 'local' chains. Local development and economy are often cited under the Short Food Supply Chain (SFSC).

With the rapid development of economy, the requirements for food quality are becoming higher and higher, especially the freshness and nutritional value of fresh agricultural products. There is a great need for food safety by various stakeholders, including consumers, which, has led to the design and development of food traceability systems, which can be trusted by the interested parties. These systems shall be able to track and monitor the whole lifespan of food production, including the processes of food raw material cultivation/breeding/fishing, packaging, pre-processing, processing transporting, warehousing, selling, and even recycling. Such systems may increase the level of trust by incorporating IoT systems that may provide data from the whole logistics path, starting from the fields (Wei & Lv, 2019; Lin, Shen, Zhang & Chai, 2018).

IoT and Primary Activities

The agricultural production has specific characteristics that affect the quality and the safety of food as well as various operations of the agro-logistics. One of the key characteristics is that the agriculture production is dependent on the environmental conditions, such as climate (air temperature, air humidity, radiation wind), soil conditions, pests, diseases and weather. The chaotic mix of these conditions results in unpredictable variations in quality, time and quantity of produce. In order to reduce the uncertainty and the consequent impacts, IoT solutions have been developed and applied at the field level (Verdouw, Robbemond, Verwaart, Wolfert & Beulens, 2015).

Moreover, the rapid technological developments of IoT devices and platforms during the last few years, have introduced radical changes in the working environment of the agricultural sector. Agriculture has entered a new era in which the key to success is the access to timely information and elaborated decision making. The farmers need to be skilled and up-to-date informed concerning the latest advancements in research and technology in order to be able to evaluate and choose between various technological options regarding the production. Decision making turns to be an important aspect in farm management and its key point for the development of effective Decision Support Systems (DSS) in the farming sector is to understand why farmers act as they do, using their tacit knowledge. The basis for enhanced decision-making is the availability of timely and of high-quality data (Fountas et al., 2015).

For improving farm productivity, crop performance needs to be understood and forecasted under a wide variety of environmental, soil, fertilisation, and irrigation conditions. The productivity of a farm can be improved by determining which crop variety has produced the greatest yield under similar soil, climate, fertilisation, and irrigation conditions. The same data-driven approach to crop selection can also address climate change, resource constraints (water, labour, and energy shortages), and societal concerns around issues such as animal welfare, fertilizers, and environment that often have impact on the agricultural production(Jayaraman, Yavari, Georgakopoulos, Morshed & Zaslavsky, 2016).

Sophisticated ICT approaches are introduced during the last years into the agriculture business processes towards more efficient production processes, which include the notions of smart farming and precision agriculture. These approaches focus on data monitoring, data processing, knowledge inference and finally knowledge transfer back to the farm or greenhouse (Barmpounakis et al., 2015). In this context, WSN solutions are playing a significant role to the implementation of precision agriculture practices. The advances in WSNs have enabled the development and production of low-cost, low-power and multi-functional sensors, which are small in size and communicate in short distances with very low energy consumption. Low-cost devices with one or most of the times more, smart sensors, networked through wireless links and deployed in large numbers, whereas they provide enormous opportunities for monitoring and controlling farms and greenhouses (Srbinovska, Gavrovski, Dimcev, Krkoleva & Borozan, 2015).

IoT and Supporting Activities

The agri-food sector faces many challenges regarding its specific needs concerning the logistics approach that shall be adopted. Issues such as temperature, humidity and ethylene concentration play a significant role to the quality status of the product and its expected self-life, given their intense perishability. Order-to-delivery lead times of vast quantities of products are expected to be really short for most of the fresh fruits, and supply chains have to tackle unpredictable variations in the quality and quantity of supply (Lin, Shen, Zhang & Chai, 2018).

Given the need for an efficient management of agro-logistics processes, several IT applications and electronic platforms have been developed to handle different sources of information occurring at various stages of the supply chain between and within various actors. Key information concerning ICT for agri-food logistics includes timely and flexible announcement of products availability and of their underlying quality (Verdouw, Robbemond, Verwaart, Wolfert & Beulens, 2015).

IoT solutions can effectively collaborate with ICT systems in the agri-food sector so as to provide real-time monitoring, by using sensors, and control, by using actuators, of temperature and humidity in the process of agricultural product distribution. Sensor devices can also provide almost real-time information about the actual position of its shipment supporting the credible planning of transportation routes. The timely feedback and connection of information are important factors that could increase the efficiency of agricultural product cold chain logistics by improving the transportation speed of agricultural products, and by reducing the damage rate of products (Wei &Lv, 2019).

Real-time information from the supply chain processes is critical for the safety and quality of perishable food. In some cases, even small temperature and humidity deviations during the storing, the loading and the transportation of fresh fruits and vegetables may result in quality decay, which may lead to significant loss of products. Other conditions such as the vibration of the trucks or the occurrence of light for a long time, may lead to the damage of the perishable products. In traditional cold chain management systems, thermometers and humidity sensors are installed in vehicles and warehouses. However, these methods cannot always be considered as fully/completely reliable since the owner and the provider of the corresponding information might be the one that could forge the information or the one that does not want to share the real-time data with remote users. Furthermore, these methods cannot record the environmental conditions during truck loading, vehicle switching or temporary storage, etc. Thus, IoT devices attached on pallets or placed in the boxes can fill this gap by providing real-time and continuous environmental information about perishable food (Ojha, Misra & Raghuwanshi, 2015).

Wireless sensor networks may be used for the collection and the transmission of data relating to temperature, relative humidity, carbon dioxide concentration, vibration, light and GPS location in a periodical mode. As such, real time environmental information can be provided about the perishable food with good performance and affordable cost; small enough sensor nodes can be manufactured in order to be installed in the boxes containing perishable food or attached on the pallets and go through the whole supply chain. Moreover, the states of motion, including illegal opening, abnormal vibration, excessive tilt and unexpected fall of the container, are detected by sensors and transmitted in an event-driven mode (Wang et al., 2015).

Within this framework, the last few years various integrated solutions have been developed and tested. Several of them are using LoRa technology, which makes it easy and affordable for smart supply chain and logistics to track highly valued assets that are in transit. Due to LoRa Technology's long range and low power consumption qualities and GPS-free geolocation abilities, cargo, vehicles and other assets can be easily monitored over large geographic regions and within harsh environments (SEMTECH, 2019; Jedermann et al., 2018).

THE PILOT CASE

As already mentioned, the importance of traceability and food safety is acknowledged by the food industry globally. The case, being discussed in the following paragraphs, confronts the challenges of meeting regulatory requirements and satisfying agro-logistics stakeholders and consumers expectations for safe foods. This holistic approach focuses on unique identification of products and the standardized exchange of product data at critical tracking events through the supply chain, and it contributes to food safety whereas also establishes cost-efficient business processes for information linkages to all participants in the supply chain.

The Platform Architecture

The solution is based on the traceability platform KalaΘos™ and its IoT management module called, GP CoreIoT™. The KalaΘos infrastructure includes a network of sensors at farms, equipment, trucks, aggregation, processing and logistics facilities, connected to a network of LoRa gateways stations. Its open architecture focuses on semantic and syntactic interoperability approaches for joint exploitation of data collected and managed by other systems with similar aims and scope.

Through IoT devices, web, smartphones and tablets, real-time information is provided by KalaΘos Main Platform and its complementary modules, which can operate independently or in conjunction with other information systems. The SOA approach is applied and more specifically JSON implementation is adopted. This open architecture overall approach furthers modularity within KalaΘos and total operability with external systems.

The entire range of production and distribution of fresh fruit and vegetables from the farm to the wholesaler is covered by KalaΘos platform together with its individual modules. Fig. 2 schematically depicts the information entry points along the supply chain at the level of the different entrances.

Figure 2. Data flow in KalaΘos platform

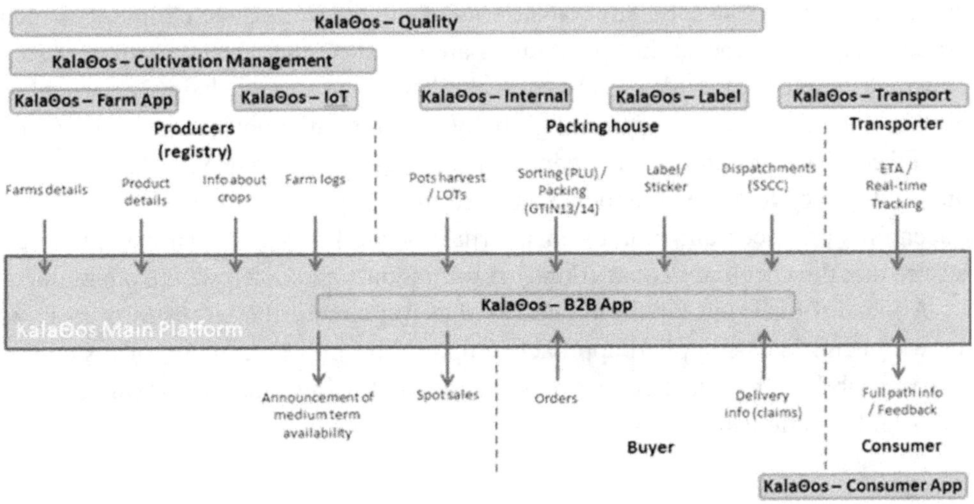

The individual modules of KalaΘos support the following functions:

- KalaΘos - Farm App: Detailed information concerning the farms (crop history, soil analysis, fertilization applications, plant protection, crops, photos, etc.).
- KalaΘos – IoT Module: Farm sensors system and interfaces for connection with KalaΘos - Farm App.
- KalaΘos – Quality Module: Quality monitoring tool, which supports established quality systems such as GLOBALG.A.P.
- KalaΘos – Cultivation Management: A tool for importing and managing data of soil analysis, of irrigation water and of waste or compost to use.
- KalaΘos – Internal Module: Internal tracing tool at the packing-house level using GS1 global standards.
- KalaΘos – Label Module: Information selection tool for labelling with connection interfaces with label creation and printing programs.
- KalaΘos – Transport Module: Transport scheduling and tracking of each shipment in real-time by focusing on ETA (Estimated Time of Arrival) and check-in, check-out events.

The platform beside its logistics focus, addresses the needs of consumer for food safety through the provision of rich and credible information. The KalaΘos Consumer App, provides to the consumers detailed product information from ground to mouth, by using KalaΘos TraceID, a unique identification number at the level of batch unit.

The ability to provide the above information to the consumer is feasible due to the "end-to-end" traceability processes of the supply chain of fresh produce, which is followed by combining internal and external tracing procedures, so that each operator is able to locate the immediate source and the immediate recipient of each product. KalaΘos traceability procedures are based on the "one step up, one step down" principle to provide effective traceability in the supply chain. In particular, each distinct product is recognized globally and in a unique way, so that it can be identified upstream and downstream of the supply chain. All participants in the distribution network are able to use the system to implement internal and external traceability practices, and in addition, internal traceability is applied in a way that can ensure that the necessary connections between inputs and outflows are maintained.

A general overview of the processes that implement the traceability tasks is shown in fig. 3. The applied approach supports the implementation of a step-by-step traceability procedure concerning the tracing, tracking and monitoring of fresh fruits and vegetables.

Figure 3. General overview of the processes involved in KalaΘos platform

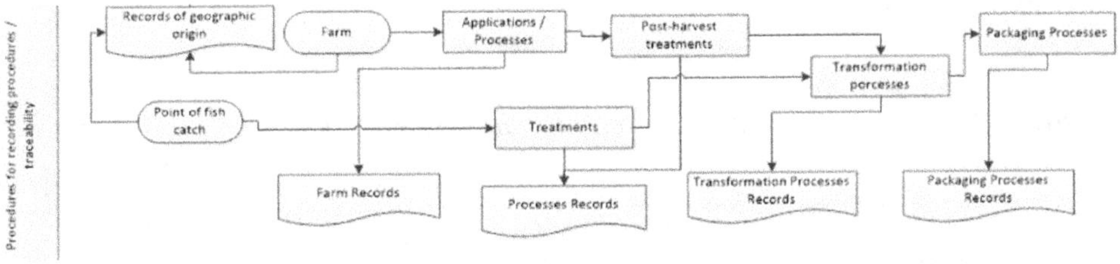

Platform Traceability Approach

Implementing traceability across a supply chain, relies on distribution channel participants collecting, recording, storing, and sharing minimum pieces of information for traceability. The main focus of KalaΘos is to effectively support this implementation following a 4-stages process:

1. Identification: By following GS1 Standards (GS1, 2016), KalaΘos begins with GS1 Identification Numbers used to uniquely distinguish all fresh products (trade items), logistic units, locations, assets, and relationships across the supply chain from grower to consumer. These numbers provide the linkages between the fresh product and the information pertaining to the product.
2. Capturing: GS1 System Data Carriers are used for holding varying amounts of data to accommodate different supply chain process needs for different products.
3. Evaluating: The captured information may be evaluated against targets that will have been set. A blind benchmarking approach could be also considered by using KalaΘos.
4. Sharing: The interoperability of KalaΘos Platform and its Modules facilitate the seamless exchange of information during commerce transactions.

The adoption of the use of EPICS, which support full-path traceability across the whole supply chain, constitutes a core element in KalaΘos platform. More specifically EPCIS enables visibility from farm to all various links of the supply chain. The provided visibility improves business processes, complies also with regulations and increases consumer safety. This is due to the fact that EPCIS can be utilised to capture and share information on all relevant business processes of the fresh produce value chain such as cultivation, harvesting, processing, packing and receiving – batch or lot number. EPCIS defines interfaces for sharing visibility event data - with other supply chain stakeholders. In Fig. 4 the tracing of the information among the various locations (external traceability) and within locations (internal traceability) are shown.

Figure 4. Internal and external traceability in KalaΘos based on EPCIS approach

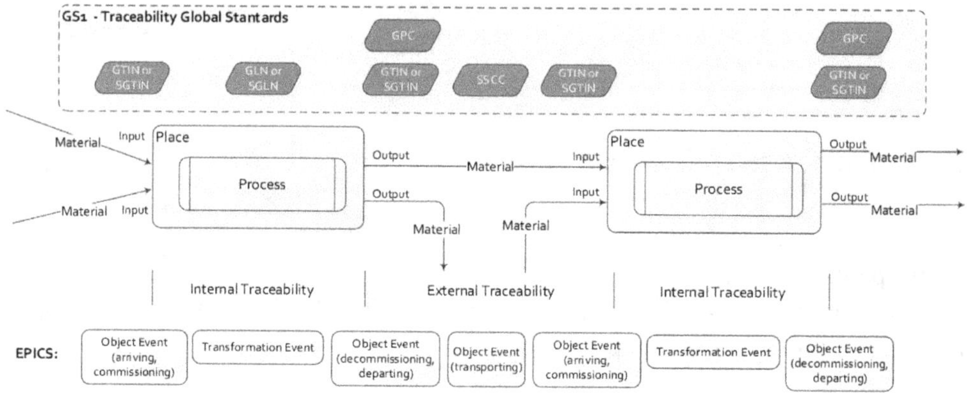

Platform IoT Approach

Towards an approach of automatic capturing of "big data" directly from the farm, but also from other points of the fresh produce supply chain, KalaΘos infrastructure is consisted of open APIs, which have been developed using JSON and REST services as part of a telemetry system. This system uses the libraries, which are provided by the manufactures of the sensor devices. The team of KalaΘos has developed an effective telemetric system, which meets the need for seamless collection and transfer of data from different sources in an effective manner. Its effectiveness could be evaluated against the criteria of: (i) easy to be installed, (ii) easy to use, (iii)minimum requirements for maintenance, (iv) extensibility and connectivity, (v) interoperability, and (vi) cost of operation.

The main element of IoT infrastructure is GP IoT Core module, which supports data reception and management (on cloud), visualization of data and reporting generation. It also includes a web App and a mobile App for interfacing with the users.

An integrated telemetric network has been implemented using KalaΘos infrastructure, bringing together IoT technologies, namely meteorological and other sensor devices, as well as devices attached on farm equipment. The telemetry network is the point of gathering, pre-processing and transmitting data and events from all connected devices through the usage of the appropriate APIs. Another essential element in this telemetric network is the KalaΘos Data Logger, which operates as the middle-tier for data management system. The structure of the KalaΘos telematics network is shown in Fig. 5.

Figure 5. KalaΘos IoT infrastructure architecture (Adapted from LoRa Alliance, 2015)

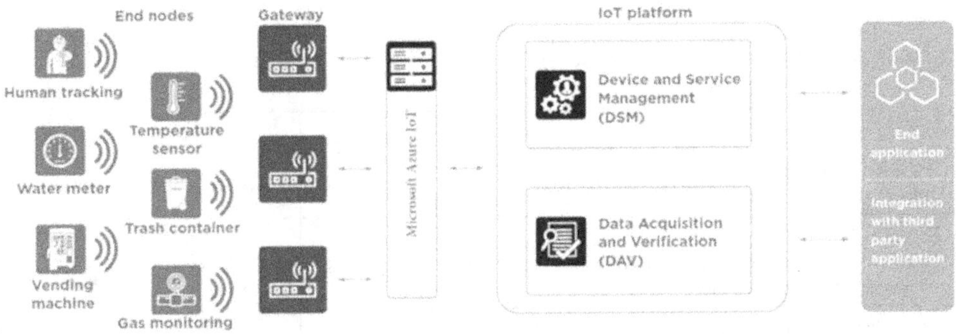

For the communication and management of the devices through platform, several open APIs have been built (or extended when open APIs are provided by the manufacturers). These APIs play a dual role. Firstly, they provide access to data, which is acquired by the devices and secondly, they manage the devices and support simultaneously the monitoring, the configuration and the updating (firmware and software) of devices connected. The latter role is the key for the maintenance of their efficiency and responsive performance.

The IoT devices communicate through a LoRaWAN network using the Low Power Wide Area Network protocol at 863 to 870 MHz for Europe, with its main feature to be the wide range of coverage (signal transmission at a distance from 20 km to 100 Km in rural areas) with very low power consumption and with no operational costs. Next to the Data Logger system, a LoRa Gateway is set up for receiving the data from the LoRa nodes (IoT devices) using MQTT (Message Queuing Telemetry Transport) protocol. Currently, nine different devices types have been developed by Green Projects SA, the company that has developed the KalaΘos platform, using three types of PCBs, as shown in Table 1.

The Pilots Running

In 2019, several small-scale pilots started in Greece at the region of Central Macedonia and at the region of Crete for the evaluation of KalaΘos and GP CoreIoT systems focusing on two products, table grapes and kiwis. Before the selection of the exact placing position of each gateway, a simulation procedure had been implemented, concerning the signal intensity for a range of 100 km around the alternative mounting points. The CloudRF software had been used for the simulation. CloudRF is an open source, an online service for radio signal propagation modelling, taking into account the terrain of each area. Thus, through this process we were able to know in advance where we will be communicating with each gateway and the corresponding signal strength.

Table 1. IoT devices for KalaΘos platform

Device	PCB Type	Energy
GP LoRa Node Air Atmospheric temperature, humidity & pressure sensor, GPS	GP LoRa Node	Battery
GP LoRa Node Soil Atmospheric temperature, humidity & pressure sensor, GPS, soil moisture & temperature sensor		
GP LoRa Node Air + Gas Atmospheric temperature, humidity & pressure sensor, GPS, gas sensor (e.g. CO_2, NO_2, CH_4)		
GP Mini LoRa Node Pallet Atmospheric temperature, humidity & pressure sensor, GPS, inertial measurement sensor, luminosity sensor, vibration sensor, SD Card	GP LoRa Mini Node	USB charging / Battery
GP Mini LoRa Node Truck GPS, inertial measurement sensor		
GP Mini LoRa Node Tractor GPS, inertial measurement sensor, vibration sensor		
GP LoRa Hub Meteo Atmospheric temperature, humidity & pressure sensor, GPS, Wind speed sensor, wind direction sensor, tipping bucket rain gauge, solar radiation sensor	GP LoRa Hub	Autonomous (PV panel)
GP LoRa Hub Farm The same as GP LoRa Hub Meteo + soil moisture & temperature sensor		

By using the aforementioned simulation procedure,16 places were selected for placing the LoRa gateways in order to cover the farms and the packing houses, where the pilots would run. In addition, a set of 52 LoRa sensor devices (nodes) was used to implement the LoRa pilot network, namely: 28 *GP LoRa Node Air + Soil*, 8 *GP Mini LoRa Node Pallet*, 10 *GP Mini LoRa Node Truck*, 6 *GP Mini LoRa Node Tractor*, 5GP LoRa Node Air + Gas and two *GP LoRa Hub Farm*.

Through the GP Core IoT information system, the devices and the received information were managed as part of the pilot setup of the LoRa network. More specifically, through the GP Core IoT the following procedures were implemented:

1. Registration and management of gateways

2. Registration and management of devices - nodes
3. Display of spatial information about the devices
4. Display of metering data from LoRa devices
5. Display metering data from third-party apps using APIs.

Figure 6. GP CorreIot™ platform screenshot

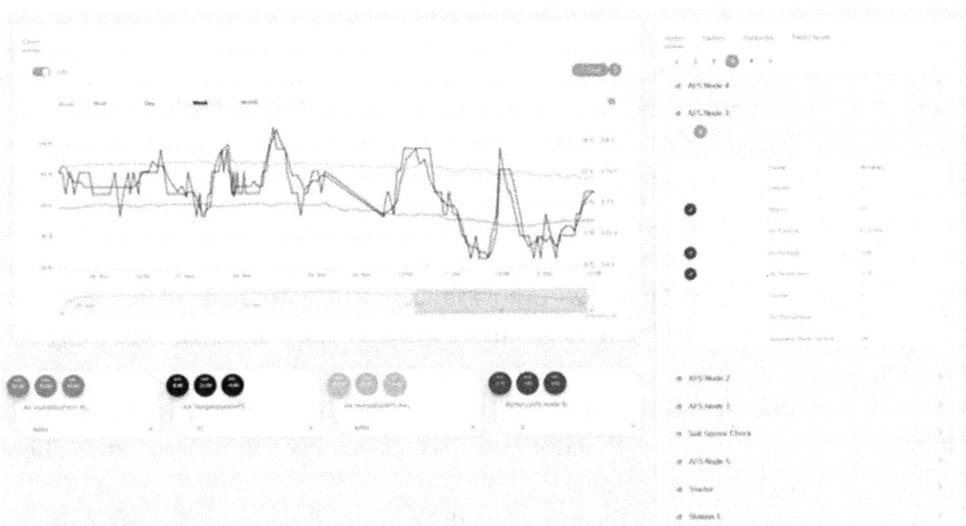

Figure 7. KalaΘos™ platform screenshot

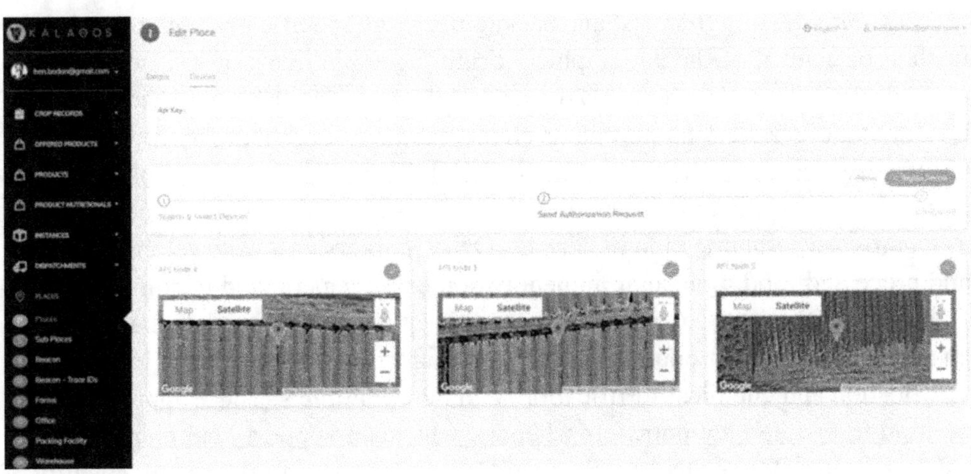

In Fig. 6 a screenshot of GP Core IoT module is shown, while in Fig. 7 a screenshot of KalaΘos platform is presented, showing information about the exact location of the connected sensors devices.

FUTURE RESEARCH DIRECTIONS

Technology issues

The next steps for KalaΘos platform is the development and incorporation of a Common Authentication and Quality Assurance Protocol, which will be developed and operate additionally to established quality systems (e.g. GLOBALG.A.P., HACCP, etc.) and authentication schemes (e.g. PDO, PGI, TSG) in order further assurance to traders and consumers concerning the products and the processes to be provided. The proposed Authentication and Quality Assurance Protocol will determine specific steps covering all products: (i) Pre-evaluation of farms based on soil, water, plant and livestock analysis, (ii) Intense consulting towards more sustainable farming and breeding, (iii) Full records of fertiliser and pesticide applications, of nutrition and of use of antibiotics (iv) Biochemical analysis of samples, (v) Genetic and genomic analysis along for variety verification, (vi) Isotope analysis for origin verification, (vii) Nutritional profile of products.

A key feature of the common protocol will be the integrated process of certifying a series of critical characteristics of freshproducts in terms of the authentication of species, their proven geographical origin (avoidance of fraud), their nutritional value (actual per product) the cultivation process (residual measurement) and the process of processing (recipes) and packaging. More specifically, with regard to the method of control of the geographical origin, isotopic maps of selected products will be developed. For the analysis, an IRMS device will be used, connected to a sampling element. This particular elemental analyser has the ability to operate either with a combustion system for N, C and S analysis, or with pyrolysis for the H and C analysis, enabling the collection of isotopic data for all elements. As far as regards the authentication of species, DNA Markers will be developed for fresh and processed food molecular authentication using genetic and genomic analysis. Additionally, the protocol will include specific guidelines concerning the nutritional analysis of the fresh products through the use fortification technologies (i.e., bio-fortification and chemical fortification) and nutrigenomics. These approaches will be used to enable new nutrition schemas, whichcan support healthier and better wellness states. These DNA markers will be used to monitor the genetic identity of food components in fresh fruits and vegetables. The isotopic profiles of the products along with the DNA markers and the nutritional profiles, will be stored in a data base, which will be available through KalaΘos platform.

A general overview of the processes, which will support the implementation of the common protocol concerning the authentication of geographic origin and of species, as well as the quality assurance of fresh products following a step-by-step traceability procedure, is shown in Fig. 8.

Figure 8. General overview of the future extended version of KalaΘos platform

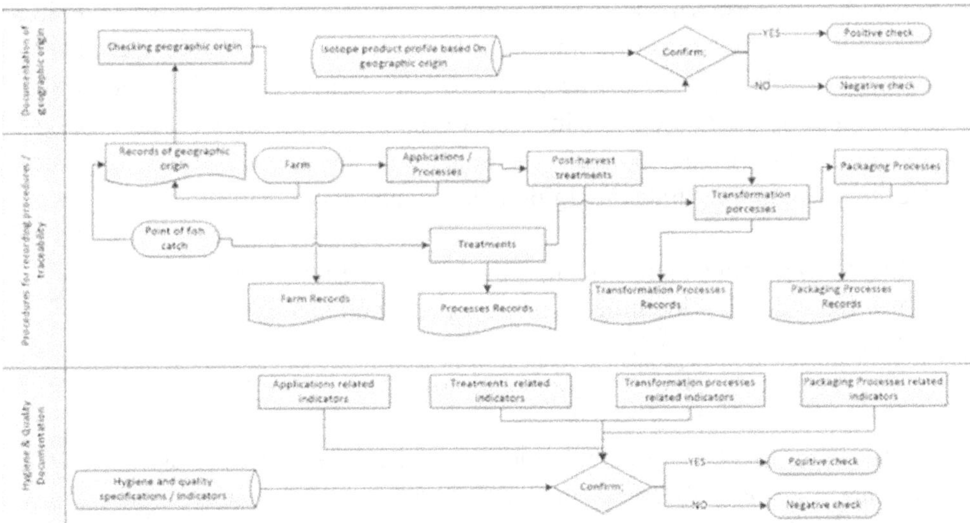

IoT and Business Models

Beside the pure technological aspect of the IoT systems, its business aspects shall also be studied given the fact that the sustainability of such complex ecosystems depends on the success of the exploitation strategy that will be adopted. As many analysts state, IoT revenues are expected to reach 7 trillion $ by the end of 2020. Given this tremendous revenue potential, the industry invests in research and development of innovative business models as well as in improvement of the already existing ones. Many sectors are currently investing in IoT business models such as energy, healthcare, telecommunications and transport technologies.

In its traditional form, a business model seeks to explain what a company offers and promises to the customer, namely what we call Value Proposition. The business model describes and explains how a company will actually generate revenue, in other words its revenue model. On top of that, the business model analyses/ describes how a company will create value for the customer, who similarly brings in revenue for the company. In fact, we are discussing about the value chain, as a central pointof every business model and the value creation processes coordinated by the entrepreneur (Chan, 2015).

The academic discussion on business models has been conducted since the 1990s. As a result, since then many models were suggested by the academia. However, no commonly accepted definition for the term 'business model' has been adopted (Zott, Amit and Massa, 2011). The IoT philosophy developed novel applications and business models. But designing realistic business models requires more than a variety of data collected form sensors. The promise of solving realistic business problems is the one that enables the development of IoT services and IoT revenue models.

Notwithstanding the wide acceptance of the importance of developing IoT business models, researchers and industry experts focus on different problems and application, making the adoption of a common IoT business model almost impossible.

Hence, there are separate emerging IoT business models for:

- Identifying value chains in various computing environments
- IoT value drivers' identification and value chain analysis
- Methodology approaches
- Multipath design and deployment approaches,

On the other hand, IoT Business models are deployed on a per-use case, which means that a separate business model is developed on a use-case scenario, on application in the following sectors:

Health care & health services: Considering that smart devices are already used by many people for health monitoring, it is expected that in the near future hospitals will widely adopt e-health initiatives using the IoT, which will reduce patient care costs.

Transportation: Many big companies have developed autonomous cars. Cars are connected to the internet gathering through their sensors on route, traffic, road condition, etc. The sensors gather data and the decision on the appropriate speed and optimal route will be taken after the appropriate analysis.

Retail: Consumers and stores will benefit from IoT deployment in commerce. The inventory will be monitored automatically and there will be a real-time monitor of the business processes. Furthermore, the company will be able to process information about their consumers' preferences based on their behavior. Ultimately, product advertising and promotion will become more effective. From the consumer's side, information about products and the purchases will be safer and faster (Leminen, Westerlund, Rajahonka & Siuruainen, 2012).

A business model can be defined as a structure of components and the relationship between these components. The business model as stated previously, describes how companies generate revenue and the overall structures of process such as channels, resources, value proposition, capabilities and more. The goal is to minimize the cost while maximizing the revenue.

There have been several literature approaches on the IoT business model, that could be applied generally or are industry specific. Here is a short list of the literature review:

- Li & Xu, in 2013, using the MOP business model, suggested a multidimensional structure with elements of strategy, technology and policy for each industry.
- Sun et al. in 2012, using the DNA Model especially in Smart Logistic, suggested the visual structure and relationships with the DNA blocks.
- Qin & Yu in2015, using the Value Net Model, focusing in the telecommunication sector, suggested the customer centered strategy.
- Leminen et al. in 2012 used the 2x2 matrix dimension business model in automobile sector, suggested B2C solutions using IOT.
- Bucherer & Uckelmann in 2011 used the Business model canvas in the Information Systems, asserted the importance of information.
- Chan in 2015 suggested the three-dimensional model (collaborators, networks and benefits)
- Dijkman et al, in 2015, used the Business model canvas, and combines it with the use of building blocks.

In most cases, the business model canvas, the framework proposed by Osterwalder and Pigneur, is adopted in order to analyse different types of IoT business models. This is a visual way to present and understand the value proposition of the proposed solution, the needed infrastructure, the customer segments and financial elements. The business model canvas, as expected, since it was widely adopted, was furtherly developed, while some other variations were also proposed (Ju, Kim &Ahn, 2016).

Following the business model canvas methodology, the key blocks of the model for IoT applications would contain the following elements (Dijkman, Sprenkels, Peeters& Janssen, 2015):

Key Partners: Software developer, Data analytics companies, Hardware manufacturers, Service Distributors and other suppliers and Logistics

Key Activities: Product and Software development, Customer and Market development, Platform development, Sales, Marketing

Key Resources: Software, Employee capabilities, Relations, Physical resources, Intellectual property, financial resources

Value Propositions: Convenience/usability, getting the job done, Performance, Comfort, Accessibility, Cost reduction, Risk reduction, Design,

Cost Structure: Product development, IT cost, Hardware/production cost, Personnel cost, Marketing & sales cost, Logistics

Customer Relationships: Personal assistance, Dedicated assistance, Automated service, Co-creation

Customer Segments: Mass market, Niche market, Self-service, Diversified Communities, Multi-sided platforms

Channels: Sales force, Web sales, Own stores, Partner stores, Wholesaler

Revenue Streams: Asset sale, Usage fee, Subscription fees, Lending/leasing, Licensing, Brokerage fees, Advertising, Installation fees (Fleisch, Weinberger & Wortmann, 2020).

CONCLUSION

The present study aimed to explore the current situation in IoT approaches in agro-logistics sector and their connection with traceability needs. The challenges and limitations associated with IoT technologies for the agri-food sector were discussed through the presentation of the traceability platform KalaΘos, its IoT management module called, GP CoreIoT and their application in several pilot projects in Greece. It should be highlighted that there is aneed for implementation of large-scale pilot projects in agriculture based on IoT technologies. An articulated architectural approach is proposed, focusing on the interoperability aspects that are critical to the adoption of IoT technologies in the agri-food sector.

The core business model for KalaΘos and its modules would probably be a mix of three general business models for IoT and digital products. These are: (i) physical freemium (a business model based on the Internet, where basic services are provided for free and more advanced services are provided on a charge), (ii) digital add-ons (product as point of sales and installation of additional options for products during the post-sale/usage period), (iii) sensors as a service (when the customer pays only for the operation of the infrastructure for getting the data).

The above business models should be evaluated in terms of the extent to which they will address the challenges that will arise in the adoption and implementation of integrated IoT solutions at the operational level along the entire length of the agro-food supply chain.Besides the positive implications that are expected at different points and for various stakeholders, which are related to improved processes for tacking, tracing and monitoring, several issues were raised during the pilots that need to be tackled. These issues are related to the devices, the network and the data handling. More specifically, as far as the devices is concerned, we are facing novel technology with no sufficient experience concerning the aging of the devices in 2-3 years from now. Furthermore, robustness issues concerning the operation of the devices and the accuracy of the measurements are also faced. The direct link between devices and LPWAN network for data transmission is another issue that should concern us given the need for viable networks worldwide, a viability that is certainly not obvious till now.

Finally, the business models that will be implemented should be adapted to the perspective that IoT ecosystems shall be more data-driven than device-centred. And when it comes to data, we also refer to their processing processes with the aim of producing information and knowledge of the field. These models should focus on procedures for providing information services and providing specialized high-level consulting services in terms of reliability and continuous and rapid evolution.

REFERENCES

Bala, K. (2014). Supply Chain Management: Some Issues and Challenges - A Review. *International Journal of Current Engineering and Technology*. http://inpressco.com/category/ijcet

Barmpounakis, S., Kaloxylos, A., Groumas, A., Katsikas, L., Sarris, V., Dimtsa, K., Fournier, F., Antoniou, E., Alonistioti, N., & Wolfert, S. (2015). Management and control applications in Agriculture domain via a Future Internet Business-to-Business platform. *Information Processing in Agriculture*, *2*(1), 51–63. doi:10.1016/j.inpa.2015.04.002

Boonjing, V., Chanvarasuth, P., & Lertwongsatien, C. (2015). An Impact of Supply Chain Management Components on Firm Performance. *Proceedings of the 2015 (6th) International Conference on Engineering, Project, and Production Management*. 10.32738/CEPPM.201509.0054

Caro, M., Ali, M., Vecchio, M., & Giaffreda, R. (2018). *Blockchain-based traceability in Agri-Food supply chain management: A practical implementation. In 2018 Iot Vertical And Topical Summit On Agriculture - Tuscany*. IOT Tuscany. doi:10.1109/IOT-TUSCANY.2018.8373021

Chakraborty, T., Nambi, A., Chandra, R., Sharma, R., Swaminathan, M., Kapetanovic, Z., & Appavoo, J. (2018). *Fall-curve: A novel primitive for IoT Fault Detection and Isolation*. Retrieved 1 January 2020, from https://www.microsoft.com/en-us/research/publication/fall-curve-a-novel-primitive-for-iot-fault-detection-and-isolation/

Chan, H. (2015). Internet of Things Business Models. *Journal of Service Science and Management*, *08*(04), 552–568. doi:10.4236/jssm.2015.84056

Chandra, R. (2018). *FarmBeats: Automating Data Aggregation*. Microsoft Research. Available at: https://www.microsoft.com/en-us/research/publication/farmbeats-automating-data-aggregation/

Dijkman, R., Sprenkels, B., Peeters, T., & Janssen, A. (2015). Business models for the Internet of Things. *International Journal of Information Management*, *35*(6), 672–678. doi:10.1016/j.ijinfomgt.2015.07.008

Fleisch, E., Weinberger, M., & Wortmann, F. (2020). *Business Models and the Internet of Things*. Retrieved 3 January 2020, from https://cocoa.ethz.ch/downloads/2014/10/2090_EN_Bosch%20Lab%20White%20Paper%20GM%20im%20IOT%201_2.pdf

Fountas, S., Carli, G., Sørensen, C., Tsiropoulos, Z., Cavalaris, C., Vatsanidou, A., Liakos, B., Canavari, M., Wiebensohn, J., & Tisserye, B. (2015). Farm management information systems: Current situation and future perspectives. *Computers and Electronics in Agriculture*, *115*, 40–50. doi:10.1016/j.compag.2015.05.011

GS1. (2016). *GS1 and the Internet of Things*. GS1 AISBL. Retrieved from https://www.gs1.org/sites/default/files/images/standards/internet-of-things/gs1-and-the-internet-of-things-iot.pdf

Georgakopoulos, D., & Jayaraman, P. (2016). Internet of things: From internet scale sensing to smart services. *Computing*, *98*(10), 1041–1058. doi:10.100700607-016-0510-0

Hugos, M. (2018). *Essentials of supply chain management* (4th ed.). Wiley. doi:10.1002/9781119464495

Jayaraman, P., Yavari, A., Georgakopoulos, D., Morshed, A., & Zaslavsky, A. (2016). Internet of Things Platform for Smart Farming: Experiences and Lessons Learnt. *Sensors (Basel)*, *16*(11), 1884. doi:10.339016111884 PMID:27834862

Jedermann, R., Borysov, M., Hartgenbusch, N., Jaeger, S., Sellwig, M., & Lang, W. (2018). Testing Lora for food applications - Example application for airflow measurements inside cooled warehouses with apples. *Procedia Manufacturing*, *24*, 284–289. doi:10.1016/j.promfg.2018.06.026

Ju, J., Kim, M., & Ahn, J. (2016). Prototyping Business Models for IoT Service. *Procedia Computer Science*, *91*, 882–890. doi:10.1016/j.procs.2016.07.106

Leminen, S., Westerlund, M., Rajahonka, M., & Siuruainen, R. (2012). Towards IOT Ecosystems and Business Models. *Internet Of Things, Smart Spaces, And Next Generation Networking*, 15-26. doi:10.1007/978-3-642-32686-8_2

Lin, J., Shen, Z., Zhang, A., & Chai, Y. (2018). Blockchain and IoT based Food Traceability for Smart Agriculture. *Proceedings Of The 3Rd International Conference On Crowd Science And Engineering - ICCSE'18*. 10.1145/3265689.3265692

LoRa Alliance. (2015). *A technical overview of LoRa® and LoRaWAN™*. Retrieved 8 January 2020, from https://lora-alliance.org/sites/default/files/2018-04/what-is-lorawan.pdf

LoRa Alliance. (2019). *About LoRaWAN® | LoRa Alliance®*. Retrieved 14 December 2019, from https://lora-alliance.org/about-lorawan

Malindretos, G. (2015). *Supply Chain, Logistics and Customer Service*. Hellenic Academic Libraries Link. http://hdl.handle.net/11419/5391

McGee, J. (2015). Value Chain. *Wiley Encyclopedia of Management, 1-5*. Advance online publication. doi:10.1002/9781118785317.weom120081

Mekki, K., Bajic, E., Chaxel, F., & Meyer, F. (2019). A comparative study of LPWAN technologies for large-scale IoT deployment. *ICT Express*, *5*(1), 1–7. doi:10.1016/j.icte.2017.12.005

Ojha, T., Misra, S., & Raghuwanshi, N. (2015). Wireless sensor networks for agriculture: The state-of-the-art in practice and future challenges. *Computers and Electronics in Agriculture*, *118*, 66–84. doi:10.1016/j.compag.2015.08.011

Schladofsky, W., Mitic, J., Megner, A., Simonato, C., Gioppo, L., Leonardos, D., & Bröring, A. (2017). Business Models for Interoperable IoT Ecosystems. In *Interoperability and Open-Source Solutions for the Internet of Things* (1st ed., pp. 91–106). Springer. doi:10.1007/978-3-319-56877-5_6

SEMTECH. (2019). *Semtech LoRa Technology Overview | Semtech*. Retrieved 8 January 2020, from https://www.semtech.com/lora

Serrano, M., Payam, P., Carrez, F., Cousin, P., Vermesan, O., & Friess, P. (2015). *IoT Semantic Interoperability: Research Challenges, Best Practices, Recommendations and Next Steps*. European Research Cluster on the Internet of Things.

Srbinovska, M., Gavrovski, C., Dimcev, V., Krkoleva, A., & Borozan, V. (2015). Environmental parameters monitoring in precision agriculture using wireless sensor networks. *Journal of Cleaner Production*, *88*, 297–307. doi:10.1016/j.jclepro.2014.04.036

The Things Network. (2019). *The Things Network.* Retrieved 8 December 2019, from https://www.thethingsnetwork.org/

Verdouw, C., Robbemond, R., Verwaart, T., Wolfert, J., & Beulens, A. (2015). A reference architecture for IoT-based logistic information systems in agri-food supply chains. *Enterprise Information Systems*, *12*(7), 755–779. doi:10.1080/17517575.2015.1072643

Wang, J., Wang, H., He, J., Li, L., Shen, M., Tan, X., Min, H., & Zheng, L. (2015). Wireless sensor network for real-time perishable food supply chain management. *Computers and Electronics in Agriculture*, *110*, 196–207. doi:10.1016/j.compag.2014.11.009

Wei, J., & Lv, S. (2019). Research on the Distribution System of Agricultural Products Cold Chain Logistics Based on Internet of Things. *IOP Conference Series. Earth and Environmental Science*, *237*, 052036. doi:10.1088/1755-1315/237/5/052036

Zott, C., Amit, R., & Massa, L. (2011). The Business Model: Recent Developments and Future Research. *Journal of Management*, *37*(4), 1019–1042. doi:10.1177/0149206311406265

Chapter 7
Financial Technology Ecosystem in Promoting a Healthy Lifestyle

Muhammad Anshari
https://orcid.org/0000-0002-8160-6682
Universiti Brunei Darussalam, Brunei

Mohammad Nabil Almunawar
https://orcid.org/0000-0001-5296-2576
Universiti Brunei Darussalam, Brunei

Masairol Masri
Universiti Brunei Darussalam, Brunei

ABSTRACT

Financial technology (FinTech) is new innovation to create a better financial ecosystem for both consumers and business. The research proposes a modeling framework on how to connect public and business to promote social work activities and at the same time financially reward through a FinTech as a platform. The study deployed a mixed methods to assess public perspectives on FinTech's ecosystem in promoting a healthy lifestyle. It is expected to encourage people who are physically active to participate in raising funds for social work activities and at the same time generate income for the participants. The ecosystem provides people more meaning to collect their distance in kilometers by either walking, running, or cycling that will impact physically, socially, and financially to promote a healthy society.

DOI: 10.4018/978-1-7998-4843-1.ch007

INTRODUCTION

Many countries have moved from physical cash and have evolved into a cashless society to make payments in their daily lives. With the input of a couple of numbers, a transaction can be made and a bill settled without the individual even stepping out of the comfort of their homes. In addition, the latest generation consisting mostly of Generation Y, the 'millennials' and the future Generation Z who are smart, tech savvy and exposed with technology during their younger age (Mulyani et al., 2019a). With Internet of things, processes are becoming easier, faster, thus increasing the efficiency and effectiveness of a system. This is where almost everything can be done within the reach of one fingertip using the smartphones and tablets (Ahad et al., 2017; Razzaq et al., 2018; Anshari et al., 2020a).

It is on the feasibility of an application (Apps) that encourages someone who are physically active to participate in raising funds for charities and at the same time get income from their physical exercise (Mulyani et al., 2019b; Anshari et al., 2020a). The platform promotes a channel for charities to consistently receive public funding that are approved by the government. Additionally, it also creates an opportunity for corporations to have a joint effort as part of their corporate social responsibility (CSR) and will be acknowledged as supporters of the cause. It connects public, sponsors (corporations and marketing organizations), merchants, and charity organizations together into a single platform. People can make donations based on the distance they have covered (collect their distance in kilometers by either walking, running or cycling). The distance is converted into points of rewards. On the other hand, the sponsors will fund the user's donations according to the collected points in kilometers. The funds raised will be channeled to the charities organization. In addition, some portions of collected points can be converted into reward bonus that can be cashed in or vouchers for commerce transactions at partnering merchants. Partnering merchants will share benefits from any transactions made to the platform for funding.

Financial Technology (FinTech) ecosystem with digital payment enabled will connects public, sponsors (corporations and marketing organizations), merchants, and charity organizations together into a single platform (Lee & Shin, 2018; Leong et al., 2017). Since there are not many research have been conducted in the domain of social work, health activities coined with FinTech development, then this research might fill the gap of each domain of knowledge. The aim of the research is to look into the feasibility of developing a platform that will help ease the process of making a donation. The study was developed using mixed methods by collecting and analyzing data from the potential stakeholders and to develop its prototype. The model promises an effective means to engage corporation for corporate social responsibility (CSR) and be acknowledged supporters of the cause, charity organization to gain the funding easier, general public to promote healthy lifestyle as well as financial benefits (Al-mudimigh & Anshari, 2020; Hamdan & Anshari, 2020; Still et al., 2016). The platform develops FinTech's ecosystem that encourages general public a healthy lifestyle allowing people to collect and convert their distance in kilometers by either walking, running or cycling and record their daily movement hence, giving them more meaning to every distance they have covered physically and socially impact to the society (Almunawar et al., 2015). The research can fill the gap of each domain of knowledge.

Social Work and Financial Technology

Non-governmental organizations which claimed to be private organizations as defined by Iriye (1999) are voluntary and open associations of individuals outside the formal setting, where profit and engaging in political activities are not their primary objectives. Marten (2002) characterized NGOs as 'formal (professionalized) independent societal organizations whose primary aim is to promote common goals at the national or the international level'.

IoT, and growth of mobile and communication had accelerate the changes in volunteering platform giving the rises in online volunteering. An online volunteering model can be seen from two aspects where the first aspect is utilizing the internet as a medium to assist partly in volunteering activities. Whereby, the Internet serves to organize the creation of the volunteer project and act as a medium to run it, while the volunteering activities itself takes place offline (Amichai-Hamburger, 2008).

The existence of the Internet has influenced a lot of change in people's lives and in relation to the ever growing, ever advancement of technologies, it forces people to move forward with it. The Internet brings about positive and negative impacts where, in this report, will talk about its positive impacts. Few of the positive impacts are such that it made sources or information to be easily accessed and it made transactions a lot easier such as mobile banking (Jocevski et al., 2020). There is a constant change in technology in this day and age where these changes bring economic and social consequences on a daily basis (Rajani & Chandio, 2004). In the future, there will come a time in the future where people will have less time to prepare themselves for the fast-changing pace of technologies.

With the growth of the Internet, a wide range of ICT have transformed social relationships and social work, and the dissemination of information (Brian, 2017). It is argued that online relationships can have properties of intimacy, richness, and liberation that rival or exceed offline relationships, as online relationships tend to be based more on mutual interest rather than physical proximity (Bargh, McKenna, & Fitzsimons, 2002). It has been suggested that information and communication technologies (ICT) can and do play a number of roles in social work activities.

Furthermore, FinTech is one of the most cutting edge technology ever created in the 21st century. The scope of FinTech is very broad where it covers many financial activities. There are new capabilities and modes in insurance, e-payment, money transaction, digital security, investment, data analysis, Peer-to-Peer lending, crowdfunding and etc (Kohler, 2015). These product provide a positive customer experience and all user friendly while also reducing costs. FinTech has existed for many years and there is an enormous gap from when our society started establishing the system. Many organizations are investing in FinTech can deliver additional value or even disruptive to the existing financial institution. Utilizing FinTech for social and financial empowerment for expanding network to ensure good access of potential customers to the e-financial services and also ensuring high quality of services in terms of safety with reasonable cost to gain more trusts and satisfactions of customers.

Charity Organization Perspective

In the interview, the representative was first introduced to social charity App and were later on asked regarding its feasibility and how it will be able to help NGOs. According to respondent, it will help charity organization to cut their costs in terms of fundraising events. Hence, through this Apps, it will help them to reduce the frequency of their fundraising events which usually have high overhead costs. Additionally, respondent mentioned regarding charity organization opening an account in local banks to make donations made easier, however, the donations through the account is very unstable as banks charged the person processing fee or transfer charges when they make donations through bank transfer and that made it inefficient. Another reason as to why cutting costs are important due to the unstable monthly donations they receive that they had experience "dry season" where they did not get any monetary support for a few months. Charity organization was very enthusiastic about the idea of a social charity app to actually be realized as she mentioned that majority of the charity organizations in the country have not been able to penetrate the mass public thus, they are lacking in publicity though they are one of the most recognized charity organizations in the country. Respondent mentioned that with the existence of such app, it will also help charity organization to reduce their fundraising events.

Corporate Perspective

The other objectives of the research was to understand the standpoint of stakeholders, who are the potential users, charity organizations and prospective corporate sponsors. Among the companies that were approached for this study, only one corporation responded. According to the correspondent, the organization carries out CSR activities on the basis of three core pillars; Community, Education and Entrepreneurship. Activities revolving around this three topics have the opportunity to be chosen as part of their CSR activity. When asked about the frequency and whether the organization has allocated budget for CSR activities, it was revealed that the company does have annual budget allocated and that CSR activities are done mainly on a quarterly basis, with some CSR requirements that need to be achieved annually.

General Public Perspective

We asked to the respondents' respond on "*how* often *do you walk, jog, run or cycle?*" and majority mentioned that it is as frequent as once a week, followed by daily and on the weekdays only whereas the rest is lower than 15% such as once every few months, weekends only, a few times a week and when they have free time. This indicates that majority people are somehow active in doing physical activities and are interested in living a healthy lifestyle. Furthermore, the question asks "*how* active *are you in a charity walk, jog, run or cycle?*" and more than 75% of the total respondents are active while about 22% have never participated yet.

Furthermore, the question reads *"how often do you donate to charity organizations as an individual?"*.The keyword to this question is *as an individual* where only 9% of the respondents have never donated before and this actually supports the statement that majority of people are philanthropic either due to the culture of helping others when an opportunity comes. The survey asked the respondents to list out the charities that they support and these are the names of NGOs that were mentioned.

Easy of making donation - *"Do you think it is difficult to make donations here?"* is the fifth question and about 70% mentioned that it is not as difficult. Though it may not be difficult, charity organizations still struggle from time to time as did not receive stable donations hence, the more reasons to develop Apps as what the respondent from charity organization mentioned, not all charity organizations have enough publicity to create awareness.

Motivation to donate - The respondents were then asked, *"if you were able to make donations just by walking, jogging, running or cycling, would you be interested to participate?"* most of the participants are most likely to do physical activities if the motivation is to donate.

Feasibility of Apps - When asked *"do you think that an app that allows you to make donations by doing healthy activities is feasible? Explain"*,about 70% voted yes, 21.7% are unsure and about 9% mentioned that it is not workable. Their explanations as to why it will succeed are; public are active and philanthropist, a similar concept has been done however, without using any Apps, Apps is in trend, it is convenient, exercising is currently in trend and that this app is an interesting concept to some

(Anshari et al., 2013a). On the other hand, the reason as to why they think it will not succeed are; they have doubts about the Apps as it is something new, they are unable to see how the platform will be able to retain its user and that these type of platform requires attractiveness as well.

As for the final question, the respondents were asked: *"what are your expectations if you were to register on a social charity app mentioned above?"*.The respondent's answers are divided into three categories; Platform (User-friendly, Easy accessibility, e-Payment features, Redeemable rewards -- this will be Apps' customer retention strategy, Varieties of device compatibility, Regular updates and troubleshooting), Transparency (Activity and donation tracking, Notified when donations are received by NGOs, How the donations are used by the NGOs -- however, it would be difficult for anyone outside of the NGOs to get information or have control over this issue thus, this point is considered invalid), and Commitment (Makes people want to commit to using the app) (Anshari et al., 2013b; Almunawar & Anshari, 2014).

Prototype

A prototype is a platform draft design that combine the user's expectations where in this case, it is specially made for design and testing. The prototype is in the second section of the survey where firstly, it shows the public the paper prototype and then followed up with a few questions on its user-friendliness and color scheme. As for the user-friendliness, 59% of the respondents say it is good while 30% says it is fair and 13% mentioned that it is excellent. On the other hand, for the color scheme; 48% of the respondents think it is good, 48% think it is fair and 4% think it has a poor color scheme. Overall, 87% of the respondents are likely to register and will use it.

After analyzing the findings from the survey as well as from the interviews, there are a few recommendations that can help in making Apps attractive to its intended users. Below are Apps' prototype. Figure 1 shows login page, homepage, goals page and challenge page. Login page differ between users, charity organization, and corporations depending upon their role. Users are general public that takes part in physical exercise activities. Charity organizations require login to officially register into the platform to get funding. Corporations are sponsor that support program from their CSR. However, the platform also allows general publics to become sponsor from their personal charities. Homepage is the welcoming page once the user successfully login into the system. Goal page is personal page for each user that they can set and customize accordingly about their physical activities that they want to achieve. Challenge page is alert page containing physical events. It is push messaging services from provider. It has more choices of challenges where Apps can even organize or create challenges that are attractive.

Figure 1.

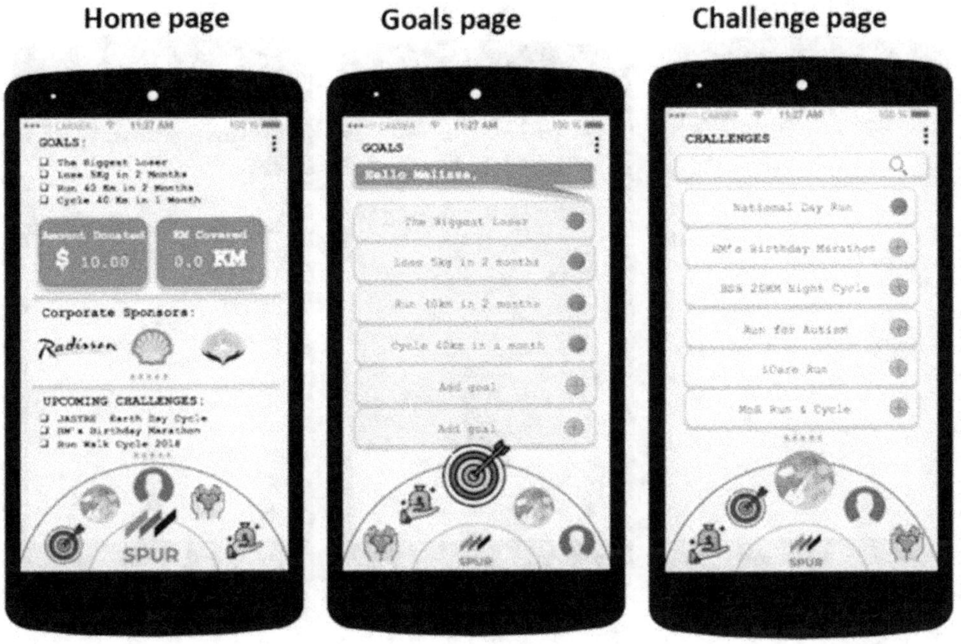

While, Figure 2 consists of profile page, menu page, charity page, and sponsor page. Charity page includes clips from the charity organization, where members of each organization could pitch their plans for its organization thoroughly in order to gain the trust and support of users or clips of what has been achieved with the donations they received. Profile page has social media enabled feature connecting the App to social media. Profile page also includes other activities/sports to the activity that can be detected, instead of just activities that calculate distance, perhaps it can be improved to detect calories burnt or energy consumption for particular activities. Sponsor page is where sponsors can donate and recognition and appreciation of the sponsors are displayed throughout push messaging services and social media promotion. Menu page is where the users are able to sync/connect with multiple smart devices such as a smartwatch or fitness band (i.e Fitbit, Jawbone). Finally, the menu page consist of rewards that can be expected by users because it is also having Financial Technology (FinTech) feature where the physical activities are also converted to the points of rewards. Adding on the FinTech's features as a customer retention where the users can claim points or cash in the point or prizes such as vouchers or discounts in collaborating merchants. These rewards can converted from the distance they have achieved or when they have achieved their goals.

Figure 2.

CONCLUSION

In conclusion, the Apps promises the potential to transform the social and physical activities into gain competitive advantage for all actors that it can improve the overall quality of the society. The research idea of developing a social charity platform is welcomed and might be the way forward for charity organizations, corporations that are looking into diversifying their CSR as well as for health enthusiast people that are trying to add more value to their daily routine. Apps with FinTech enabled will simplify lives and streamline all connecting entities and that is exactly where FinTech pursue and delivers.

REFERENCES

Ahad, A. D., Anshari, M., & Razzaq, A. (2017). Domestication of smartphones among adolescents in Brunei darussalam. *International Journal of Cyber Behavior, Psychology and Learning*, *7*(4), 26–39. doi:10.4018/IJCBPL.2017100103

Al-Mudimigh, A., & Anshari, M. (2020). Financial technology and innovative financial inclusion. In *Financial technology and disruptive innovation in ASEAN* (pp. 119–129). IGI Global.

Almunawar, M. N., & Anshari, M. (2014). Empowering customers in electronic health (e–health) through social customer relationship management. *International Journal of Electronic Customer Relationship Management*, *8*(1-3), 87–100. doi:10.1504/IJECRM.2014.066887

Almunawar, M. N., Anshari, M., & Younis, M. Z. (2015). Incorporating customer empowerment in mobile health. *Health Policy and Technology*, *4*(4), 312–319. doi:10.1016/j.hlpt.2015.08.008

Amichai-Hamburger, Y. (2008). Potential and promise of online volunteering. *Computers in Human Behavior*, *24*(2), 544–562. doi:10.1016/j.chb.2007.02.004

Anshari, M., Almunawar, M. N., Low, P. K. C., & Al-Mudimigh, A. S. (2013). Empowering clients through e-health in healthcare services: Case Brunei. *International Quarterly of Community Health Education*, *33*(2), 189–219. doi:10.2190/IQ.33.2.g PMID:23661419

Anshari, M., Almunawar, M. N., Low, P. K. C., Wint, Z., & Younis, M. Z. (2013). Adopting customers' empowerment and social networks to encourage participations in e-health services. *Journal of Health Care Finance*, *40*(2), 17–41. PMID:24551960

Anshari, M., Almunawar, M. N., & Masri, M. (2020a). An overview of financial technology in Indonesia. *Financial technology and disruptive innovation in ASEAN*, 216-224.

Anshari, M., Almunawar, M. N., & Masri, M. (2020b). Financial Technology and Disruptive Innovation in Business: Concept and Application. *International Journal of Asian Business and Information Management*, *11*(4), 29–43. doi:10.4018/IJABIM.2020100103

Anshari, M., Almunawar, M. N., Masri, M., & Hamdan, M. (2019). Digital marketplace and FinTech to support agriculture sustainability. *Energy Procedia*, *156*, 234–238. doi:10.1016/j.egypro.2018.11.134

Azaraimy, A. (2018). *Cardiovascular disease leading cause of death in Brunei.* Retrieved from https://borneobulletin.com.bn/cardiovascular-disease-leading-cause-of-death-in-brunei/

Bargh, J. A., McKenna, K., & Fitzsimons, G. M. (2002). Can you see the real me? Activation and expression of the "true self" on the internet. *The Journal of Social Issues*, *58*(1), 33–48. doi:10.1111/1540-4560.00247

Brian, E., & Perron, J. (2011). *Information and Communication Technologies in Social Work*. Retrieved 3 April 2017, from https://www.ncbi.nlm.nih.gov/pmc/articles/PMC3117433/

Hamdan, M., & Anshari, M. (2020). Paving the Way for the Development of FinTech Initiatives in ASEAN. In *Financial technology and disruptive innovation in ASEAN* (pp. 80–107). IGI Global. doi:10.4018/978-1-5225-9183-2.ch004

Hasmawati, F., Samiha, Y. T., Razzaq, A., & Anshari, M. (2020). Understanding Nomophobia Among Digital Natives: Characteristics And Challenges. *Journal of Critical Reviews*, *7*(13), 122–131.

Iriye, A. (1999). A Century of NGOs. *Diplomatic History*, *23*(3), 421–435. doi:10.1111/0145-2096.00175

Jocevski, M., Ghezzi, A., & Arvidsson, N. (2020). Exploring the growth challenge of mobile payment platforms: A business model perspective. *Electronic Commerce Research and Applications*, *40*, 100908. doi:10.1016/j.elerap.2019.100908

Kohler, T. (2015). Crowdsourcing-based business models: How to create and capture value. *California Management Review*, *57*(4), 63–84. doi:10.1525/cmr.2015.57.4.63

Lee, I., & Shin, Y. J. (2018). Fintech: Ecosystem, business models, investment decisions, and challenges. *Business Horizons*, *61*(1), 35–46. doi:10.1016/j.bushor.2017.09.003

Leong, C., Tan, B., Xiao, X., Tan, F. T. C., & Sun, Y. (2017). Nurturing a FinTech ecosystem: The case of a youth microloan startup in China. *International Journal of Information Management*, *37*(2), 92–97. doi:10.1016/j.ijinfomgt.2016.11.006

Martens, K. (2002). Article. *Voluntas*, *13*(3), 271–285. doi:10.1023/A:1020341526691

Morris, J., Heady, J., Raffle, P., Roberts, C., & Parks, J. (1953). Coronary heart disease and physical activity of work. *Lancet*, *262*(6795), 1053–1057. doi:10.1016/S0140-6736(53)90665-5 PMID:13110049

Mulyani, M. A., Razzaq, A., Ridho, S. L. Z., & Anshari, M. (2019a, October). Smartphone and Mobile Learning to Support Experiential Learning. In *2019 International Conference on Electrical Engineering and Computer Science (ICECOS)* (pp. 6-9). IEEE. 10.1109/ICECOS47637.2019.8984501

Mulyani, M. A., Razzaq, A., Sumardi, W. H., & Anshari, M. (2019b, August). Smartphone Adoption in Mobile Learning Scenario. In *2019 International Conference on Information Management and Technology (ICIMTech)* (Vol. 1, pp. 208-211). IEEE. 10.1109/ICIMTech.2019.8843755

Rajani, M. K., & Chandio, M. S. (2004). Use of Internet and its effects on our Society. *National Conference On Emerging Technologies,* 157 - 161. Retrieved from http://www.szabist.edu.pk/Publications/Session%20VIII%20Paper%20No%20 2%20(P%2015 7-161).pdf

Razzaq, A., Samiha, Y. T., & Anshari, M. (2018). Smartphone Habits and Behaviors in Supporting Students Self-Efficacy. *International Journal of Emerging Technologies in Learning, 13*(2), 94. doi:10.3991/ijet.v13i02.7685

Shiroma, E., & Lee, I. (2010). Physical Activity and Cardiovascular Health. *Circulation, 122*(7), 743–752. doi:10.1161/CIRCULATIONAHA.109.914721 PMID:20713909

Still, K., Huhtala, T., & Saraniemi, S. (2016). FinTech as business and innovation ecosystems. Paper presented at ISPIM Summit, Kuala Lumpur, Malaysia.

Top 50 Countries with Highest Internet Penetration Rates - Country Literacy Rates. (2018). Retrieved from https://www.internetworldstats.com/top25.htm

Compilation of References

Adner, R. (2006). Match your innovation strategy to your innovation ecosystem. *Harvard Business Review, 84*(4), 98–107.

Adner, R., & Kapoor, R. (2010). Value creation in innovation ecosystems: How the structure of technological interdependence affects firm performance in new technology generations. *Strategic Management Journal, 31*(3), 306–333.

Afgan, E., Baker, D., van den Beek, M., Blankenberg, D., Bouvier, D., Čech, M., Chilton, J., Clements, D., Coraor, N., Eberhard, C., Grüning, B., Guerler, A., Hillman-Jackson, J., Von Kuster, G., Rasche, E., Soranzo, N., Turaga, N., Taylor, J., Nekrutenko, A., & Goecks, J. (2016). The Galaxy platform for accessible, reproducible and collaborative biomedical analyses: 2016 update. *Nucleic Acids Research, 44*(W1), W3–W10. doi:10.1093/nar/gkw343 PMID:27137889

Aggarwal, P., & Basu, A. K. (2014). Value co-creation: Factors affecting discretionary effort exertion. *Services Marketing Quarterly, 35*(4), 321–336. doi:10.1080/15332969.2014.946876

Ahad, A. D., Anshari, M., & Razzaq, A. (2017). Domestication of smartphones among adolescents in Brunei darussalam. *International Journal of Cyber Behavior, Psychology and Learning, 7*(4), 26–39. doi:10.4018/IJCBPL.2017100103

Ahokangas, P., Boter, H., & Iivari, M. (2018). Ecosystems Perspective on Entrepreneurship. In R. Turcan & N. M. Fraser (Eds.), *The Palgrave Handbook of Multidisciplinary Perspectives on Entrepreneurship* (pp. 387–407). Palgrave Macmillan.

Ahokangas, P., Matinmikko-Blue, M., Yrjölä, S., Seppänen, V., Hämmäinen, H., Jurva, R., & Latva-aho, M. (2019). Generic Business Models for Local 5G Micro Operators. *IEEE Transactions on Cognitive Communications and Networking, 5*(3), 730–740.

Ajzen, I. (1991). The theory of planned behavior. *Organizational Behavior and Human Decision Processes, 50*(2), 179–211. doi:10.1016/0749-5978(91)90020-T

Akaka, M. A., Schau, H. J., & Vargo, S. L. (2013). The Co-Creation of Value-in-Cultural-Context. In Consumer Culture Theory. Emerald Group Publishing Limited.

Akasiadis, C., & Chalkiadakis, G. (2017). Mechanism Design for Demand-Side Management. *IEEE Intelligent Systems, 32*(1), 24–31. doi:10.1109/MIS.2017.6

Akasiadis, C., & Chalkiadakis, G. (2017b). Cooperative electricity consumption shifting. *Sustainable Energy. Grids and Networks*, *9*, 38–58.

Akasiadis, C., Pitsilis, V., & Spyropoulos, C. D. (2019). A Multi-Protocol IoT Platform Based on Open-Source Frameworks. *Sensors (Basel)*, *19*(19), E4217. doi:10.339019194217 PMID:31569338

Albrecht, M., Donnelly, P., Bui, P., & Thain, D. (2012). Makeflow: A Portable Abstraction for Data Intensive Computing on Clusters, Clouds, and Grids. *Proceedings of the 1st ACM SIGMOD Workshop on Scalable Workflow Execution Engines and Technologies - SWEET '12*. 10.1145/2443416.2443417

Al-Mudimigh, A., & Anshari, M. (2020). Financial technology and innovative financial inclusion. In *Financial technology and disruptive innovation in ASEAN* (pp. 119–129). IGI Global.

Almunawar, M. N., & Anshari, M. (2014). Empowering customers in electronic health (e–health) through social customer relationship management. *International Journal of Electronic Customer Relationship Management*, *8*(1-3), 87–100. doi:10.1504/IJECRM.2014.066887

Almunawar, M. N., Anshari, M., & Younis, M. Z. (2015). Incorporating customer empowerment in mobile health. *Health Policy and Technology*, *4*(4), 312–319. doi:10.1016/j.hlpt.2015.08.008

Alves, H., Fernandes, C., & Raposo, M. (2016). Value co-creation: Concept and contexts of application and study. *Journal of Business Research*, *69*(5), 1626–1633. doi:10.1016/j.jbusres.2015.10.029

Amichai-Hamburger, Y. (2008). Potential and promise of online volunteering. *Computers in Human Behavior*, *24*(2), 544–562. doi:10.1016/j.chb.2007.02.004

Amit, R., & Zott, C. (2001). Value creation in E-business. *Strategic Management Journal*, *22*(6-7), 493–520.

Amshoff, B., Dülme, C., Echterfeld, J., & Gausemeier, J. (2015). Business Model Patterns for Disruptive Technologies. *International Journal of Innovation Management*, *19*(03), 1540002. doi:10.1142/S1363919615400022

Andersson, P., & Mattsson, L. G. (2015). Service Innovations Enabled by the "Internet of Things". *IMP Journal*, *9*(1), 85–106. doi:10.1108/IMP-01-2015-0002

Andrade, A. D. (2009). Interpretive Research Aiming at Theory Building: Adopting and Adapting the Case Study Design. *Qualitative Report*, *14*(1), 42–60.

Anh, P. N. T., & Thuy, P. N. (2017). The effects of interaction behaviors of service frontliners on customer participation in the value co-creation: A study of health care service. *Service Business*, *11*(2), 253–277. doi:10.100711628-016-0307-4

Anshari, M., Almunawar, M. N., & Masri, M. (2020a). An overview of financial technology in Indonesia. *Financial technology and disruptive innovation in ASEAN*, 216-224.

Anshari, M., Almunawar, M. N., Low, P. K. C., & Al-Mudimigh, A. S. (2013). Empowering clients through e-health in healthcare services: Case Brunei. *International Quarterly of Community Health Education, 33*(2), 189–219. doi:10.2190/IQ.33.2.g PMID:23661419

Anshari, M., Almunawar, M. N., Low, P. K. C., Wint, Z., & Younis, M. Z. (2013). Adopting customers' empowerment and social networks to encourage participations in e-health services. *Journal of Health Care Finance, 40*(2), 17–41. PMID:24551960

Anshari, M., Almunawar, M. N., & Masri, M. (2020b). Financial Technology and Disruptive Innovation in Business: Concept and Application. *International Journal of Asian Business and Information Management, 11*(4), 29–43. doi:10.4018/IJABIM.2020100103

Anshari, M., Almunawar, M. N., Masri, M., & Hamdan, M. (2019). Digital marketplace and FinTech to support agriculture sustainability. *Energy Procedia, 156*, 234–238. doi:10.1016/j.egypro.2018.11.134

Arnould, Price, & Malshe. (2006). Toward a Cultural Resource-Based Theory of the Customer. *The Service-Dominant Logic of Marketing: Dialog, Debate, and Directions*, 91-104.

Arnould, E. (2005). Animating the big middle. *Journal of Retailing, 81*(2), 89–96. doi:10.1016/j.jretai.2005.03.001

Arnould, E. J. (2007). Service-dominant logic and consumer culture theory: Natural allies in an emerging paradigm. In *Consumer culture theory* (pp. 57–76). Emerald Group Publishing Limited.

Arnould, E. J., & Thompson, C. J. (2005). Consumer culture theory (CCT): Twenty years of research. *The Journal of Consumer Research, 31*(4), 868–882. doi:10.1086/426626

Aspara, J., Hietanen, J., & Tikkanen, H. (2010). Business model innovation vs replication: Financial performance implications of strategic emphases. *Journal of Strategic Marketing, 18*(1), 39–56.

Autio, E., & Thomas, L. (2014). Innovation ecosystems. The Oxford handbook of innovation management, 204-288.

Autio, E., Thomas, L., & Gann, D. (2016). *Ecosystem value co-creation*. Innovation & Entrepreneurship Department Working Papers: 28. London, UK: Imperial College Business School.

Autio, E., Nambisan, S., Thomas, L. D., & Wright, M. (2018). Digital affordances, spatial affordances, and the genesis of entrepreneurial ecosystems. *Strategic Entrepreneurship Journal, 12*(1), 72–95.

Autio, E., & Thomas, L. D. (2020). Value co-creation in ecosystems: Insights and research promise from three disciplinary perspectives. In *Handbook of Digital Innovation*. Edward Elgar Publishing. doi:10.4337/9781788119986.00017

Azaraimy, A. (2018). *Cardiovascular disease leading cause of death in Brunei*. Retrieved from https://borneobulletin.com.bn/cardiovascular-disease-leading-cause-of-death-in-brunei/

Bahrammirzaee, A. (2010). A comparative survey of artificial intelligence applications in finance: Artificial neural networks, expert system and hybrid intelligent systems. *Neural Computing & Applications*, *19*(8), 1165–1195. doi:10.100700521-010-0362-z

Bala, K. (2014). Supply Chain Management: Some Issues and Challenges - A Review. *International Journal of Current Engineering and Technology*. http://inpressco.com/category/ijcet

Baldwin, C. (2008). Where Do Transactions Come From? Modularity, Transactions, and the Boundaries of Firms. *Industrial and Corporate Change*, *17*(1), 155–195.

Baldwin, C., & Clark, K. (2000). *Design Rules: The Power of Modularity*. MIT Press.

Baldwin, C., & Woodard, J. (2009). The Architecture of Platforms: A Unified View. InPlatforms, Riding in the Open Source Development Model? *Management Science*, *52*(7), 1116–1127.

Banati, A., Kacsuk, P., & Kozlovszky, M. (2015). Four level provenance support to achieve portable reproducibility of scientific workflows. *2015 38th International Convention on Information and Communication Technology, Electronics and Microelectronics (MIPRO)*. 10.1109/MIPRO.2015.7160272

Bandura, A. (1991). Social cognitive theory of self-regulation. *Organizational Behavior and Human Decision Processes*, *50*(2), 248–287. doi:10.1016/0749-5978(91)90022-L

Bargh, J. A., McKenna, K., & Fitzsimons, G. M. (2002). Can you see the real me? Activation and expression of the "true self" on the internet. *The Journal of Social Issues*, *58*(1), 33–48. doi:10.1111/1540-4560.00247

Barmpounakis, S., Kaloxylos, A., Groumas, A., Katsikas, L., Sarris, V., Dimtsa, K., Fournier, F., Antoniou, E., Alonistioti, N., & Wolfert, S. (2015). Management and control applications in Agriculture domain via a Future Internet Business-to-Business platform. *Information Processing in Agriculture*, *2*(1), 51–63. doi:10.1016/j.inpa.2015.04.002

Baron, S., & Warnaby, G. (2011). Individual customers' use and integration of resources: Empirical findings and organizational implications in the context of value co-creation. *Industrial Marketing Management*, *40*(2), 211–218. doi:10.1016/j.indmarman.2010.06.033

Barrutia, J. M., Paredes, M. R., & Echebarria, C. (2016). Value co-creation in e-commerce contexts: Does product type matter? *European Journal of Marketing*, *50*(3–4), 442–463. doi:10.1108/EJM-10-2014-0603

Bauer, M., Boussard, M., Bui, N., & Carrez, F. (2013). *Project Deliverable D1.5 Final Architectural Reference Model for IoT.* IoT-A Project, Technical Report.

Beaulieu-Jones, B. K., & Greene, C. S. (2017). Reproducibility of computational workflows is automated using continuous analysis. *Nature Biotechnology*, *35*(4), 342–346. doi:10.1038/nbt.3780 PMID:28288103

Belk, R. W., Price, L., & Peñaloza, L. (Eds.). (2013). *Consumer culture theory*. Emerald Group Publishing. doi:10.1108/S0885-2111(2013)15

Benet-Martínez, V. (2012). Multiculturalism: Cultural, social, and personality processes. In K. Deaux & M. Snyder (Eds.), *Handbook of personality and social psychology*. Oxford University Press.

Bengtsson, M., & Kock, S. (2000). "Coopetition" in business networks—To cooperate and compete simultaneously. *Industrial Marketing Management*, (29), 411–426.

Bessis, N., & Dobre, C. (Eds.). (2014). *Big data and internet of things: a roadmap for smart environments* (Vol. 546). Springer International Publishing. doi:10.1007/978-3-319-05029-4

Bettiga, D., Lamberti, L., & Noci, G. (2018). Investigating social motivations, opportunity and ability to participate in communities of virtual co-creation. *International Journal of Consumer Studies*, *42*(1), 155–163. doi:10.1111/ijcs.12409

Betz, C., & Jung, R. (2021). Conceptualizing and Analyzing Business Ecosystem Service Offerings. *Proceedings of the 54th Hawaii International Conference on System Sciences*, 1-10.

Bharadwaj, A., El Sawy, O., Pavlou, P., & Venkataraman, N. (2013). Digital business strategy: Toward a next generation of insights. *Management Information Systems Quarterly*, *37*(2), 471–482.

Bharti, K., Agrawal, R., & Sharma, V. (2015). Literature review and proposed conceptual framework. *International Journal of Market Research*, *57*(4), 571–604. doi:10.2501/IJMR-2015-012

Bhattacharya, H. (2012). Interpretive Research. In L. M. Given (Ed.), *The SAGE Encyclopedia of Qualitative Research Methods* (pp. 465–467). SAGE Publications.

Birenham, A., & Sagarin, E. (1976). *Norms and human behavior*. Praeger.

Black, H. G., & Gallan, A. S. (2015). Transformative service networks: Cocreated value as well-being. *Service Industries Journal*, *35*(15-16), 826–845. doi:10.1080/02642069.2015.1090978

Bocken, N. M., Rana, P., & Short, S. W. (2015). Value mapping for sustainable business thinking. *Journal of Industrial and Production Engineering*, *32*(1), 67–81.

Boley, H. & Chang, E. (2007). *Digital Ecosystems: Principles and Semantics*. Academic Press.

Bolton, R. N., McColl-Kennedy, J. R., Cheung, L., Gallan, A., Orsingher, C., Witell, L., & Zaki, M. (2018). Customer experience challenges: Bringing together digital, physical and social realms. *Journal of Service Management*, *29*(5), 776–808. Advance online publication. doi:10.1108/JOSM-04-2018-0113

Boonjing, V., Chanvarasuth, P., & Lertwongsatien, C. (2015). An Impact of Supply Chain Management Components on Firm Performance. *Proceedings of the 2015 (6th) International Conference on Engineering, Project, and Production Management*. 10.32738/CEPPM.201509.0054

Börger, E. (2011). Approaches to modeling business processes: A critical analysis of BPMN, workflow patterns and YAWL. *Software & Systems Modeling*, *11*(3), 305–318. doi:10.100710270-011-0214-z

Brian, E., & Perron, J. (2011). *Information and Communication Technologies in Social Work.* Retrieved 3 April 2017, from https://www.ncbi.nlm.nih.gov/pmc/articles/PMC3117433/

Brodie, R. J., Hollebeek, L. D., Jurić, B., & Ilić, A. (2011). Customer engagement: Conceptual domain, fundamental propositions, and implications for research. *Journal of Service Research, 14*(3), 252–271. doi:10.1177/1094670511411703

Bröring, A., Schmid, S., Schindhelm, C. K., Khelil, A., Käbisch, S., Kramer, D., Le Phouc, D., Mitic, J., Anicic, D., & Teniente, E. (2017). Enabling IoT ecosystems through platform interoperability. *IEEE Software, 34*(1), 54–61. doi:10.1109/MS.2017.2

Bucherer, E., & Uckelmann, D. (2011). *10 Business Models for the Internet of Things. In Architecting the Internet of Things.* Springer.

Buhalis, D., Harwood, T., Bogicevic, V., Viglia, G., Beldona, S., & Hofacker, C. (2019). Technological disruptions in services: Lessons from tourism and hospitality. *Journal of Service Management, 30*(4), 484–506. Advance online publication. doi:10.1108/JOSM-12-2018-0398

Caridà, A., Edvardsson, B., & Colurcio, M. (2019). Conceptualizing resource integration as an embedded process: Matching, resourcing and valuing. *Marketing Theory, 19*(1), 65–84. doi:10.1177/1470593118772215

Caro, M., Ali, M., Vecchio, M., & Giaffreda, R. (2018). *Blockchain-based traceability in Agri-Food supply chain management: A practical implementation. In 2018 Iot Vertical And Topical Summit On Agriculture - Tuscany.* IOT Tuscany. doi:10.1109/IOT-TUSCANY.2018.8373021

Carvalho, L. A. M. C., Essawy, B. T., & Garijo, D. (2017). Requirements for supporting the iterative exploration of scientific workflow variants. *Proceedings of the Workshop on Capturing Scientific Knowledge (SciKnow).*

Casadesus-Masanell, R., & Llanes, G. (2011). Mixed source. *Management Science, 57*(7), 1212–1230.

Cennamo, C. (2019). Competing in digital markets: A platform-based perspective. *The Academy of Management Perspectives.*

Chakraborty, T., Nambi, A., Chandra, R., Sharma, R., Swaminathan, M., Kapetanovic, Z., & Appavoo, J. (2018). *Fall-curve: A novel primitive for IoT Fault Detection and Isolation.* Retrieved 1 January 2020, from https://www.microsoft.com/en-us/research/publication/fall-curve-a-novel-primitive-for-iot-fault-detection-and-isolation/

Chandler, J. D., & Vargo, S. L. (2011). Contextualization and value-in-context: How context frames exchange. *Marketing Theory, 11*(1), 35–49. doi:10.1177/1470593110393713

Chandra, R. (2018). *FarmBeats: Automating Data Aggregation.* Microsoft Research. Available at: https://www.microsoft.com/en-us/research/publication/farmbeats-automating-data-aggregation/

Chan, H. (2015). Internet of Things Business Models. *Journal of Service Science and Management, 08*(04), 552–568. doi:10.4236/jssm.2015.84056

Chan, H. C. (2015). Internet of things business models. *Journal of Service Science and Management*, *8*(4), 552.

Chen, S. C., Raab, C., & Tanford, S. (2015). Antecedents of mandatory customer participation in service encounters: An empirical study. *International Journal of Hospitality Management*, *46*, 65–75. doi:10.1016/j.ijhm.2015.01.012

Chesbrough, H. (2012). Open innovation: Where we've been and where we're going. *Research Technology Management*, *55*(4), 20–27.

Chirigati, C. F., Shasha, D., & Freire, J. (2013). ReproZip: using provenance to support computational reproducibility. *Proceedings of the 5th USENIX Workshop on the Theory and Practice of Provenance*.

Choi, L., & Lotz, S. (2016). Motivations leading to customer citizenship behavior in services: Scale development and validation. *Journal of Consumer Marketing*, *33*(7), 539–551. doi:10.1108/JCM-01-2016-1683

Chou, E. Y., Lin, C. Y., & Huang, H. C. (2016). Fairness and devotion go far: Integrating online justice and value co-creation in virtual communities. *International Journal of Information Management*, *36*(1), 60–72. doi:10.1016/j.ijinfomgt.2015.09.009

Chow, W. S., & Chan, L. S. (2008). Social network, social trust and shared goals in organizational knowledge sharing. *Information & Management*, *45*(7), 458–465. doi:10.1016/j.im.2008.06.007

Cockburn, I., Henderson, R., & Stern, S. (2018). The Impact of Artificial Intelligence on Innovation: An Exploratory Analysis. In *NBER Chapters*. National Bureau of Economic Research, Inc.

Coghlan, D., & Brannick, T. (2010). *Doing Action Research in your own organization* (3rd ed.). Sage.

Commission Staff Working Document. (2016). Advancing the Internet of Things in Europe. In Communication from the Commission to the European Parliament, the Council, the European Economic and Social Committee, and the Committee of the Regions, Digitising European Industry Reaping the full benefits of a Digital Single Market, SWD/2016/0110.

Csaba, F. F. (2017). Commentary on "Co-creating stakeholder and brand identities: A cross-cultural consumer perspective". *Journal of Business Research*, *70*, 411–413. doi:10.1016/j.jbusres.2016.06.018

Cusumano, M., & Gawer, A. (2002). The elements of platform leadership. *MIT Sloan Management Review*, *43*(3), 51–58.

Dahl, A. J., Peltier, J. W., & Milne, G. R. (2018). Development of a value Co-creation wellness model: The role of physicians and digital information seeking on health behaviors and health outcomes. *The Journal of Consumer Affairs*, *52*(3), 562–594. doi:10.1111/joca.12176

Damkuviene, M., Tijunaitiene, R., Petukiene, E., & Bersenaite, J. (2012). Customer perceived co-creation value: Synthesis of the extant literature. *Social Research*, *4*(29), 59–68.

Davey, J., & Grönroos, C. (2019). Health service literacy: Complementary actor roles for transformative value co-creation. *Journal of Services Marketing*, *33*(6), 687–701. doi:10.1108/JSM-09-2018-0272

Davis, J. P. (2016). The Group Dynamics of Interorganizational Relationships: Collaborating with Multiple Partners in Innovation Ecosystems. *Administrative Science Quarterly*, *61*(4), 621–661.

De Langen, P. W. (2006). Stakeholders, conflicting interests and governance in port clusters. *Research in Transportation Economics*, *17*, 457–477.

de Reuver, M., Sørensen, C., & Basole, R. C. (2017). The digital platform: A research agenda. *Journal of Information Technology*, *33*(2), 124–135.

Dedehayir, O., Mäkinen, S. J., & Ortt, J. R. (2018). Roles during innovation ecosystem genesis: A literature review. *Technological Forecasting and Social Change*, *136*, 18–29.

Deelman, E., Gannon, D., Shields, M., & Taylor, I. (2009). Workflows and e-Science: An overview of workflow system features and capabilities. *Future Generation Computer Systems*, *25*(5), 528–540. doi:10.1016/j.future.2008.06.012

Deelman, E., Vahi, K., Juve, G., Rynge, M., Callaghan, S., Maechling, P. J., Mayani, R., Chen, W., Ferreira da Silva, R., Livny, M., & Wenger, K. (2015). Pegasus, a workflow management system for science automation. *Future Generation Computer Systems*, *46*, 17–35. doi:10.1016/j.future.2014.10.008

Demil, B., Lecocq, X., & Warnier, V. (2018). Business model thinking, business ecosystems and platforms: the new perspective on the environment of the organization. *M@n@gement*, *21*(4).

Devereux, M. T., & Gallarza, M. G. G. (2019). Social value co-creation: Insights from consumers, employees, and managers. In *Corporate social responsibility: Concepts, methodologies, tools, and applications* (pp. 55–79). IGI Global. doi:10.4018/978-1-5225-6192-7.ch004

Dholakia, U. M., Bagozzi, R. P., & Pearo, L. K. (2004). A social influence model of consumer participation in network-and small-group-based virtual communities. *International Journal of Research in Marketing*, *21*(3), 241–263. doi:10.1016/j.ijresmar.2003.12.004

Dijkman, R., Sprenkels, B., Peeters, T., & Janssen, A. (2015). Business models for the Internet of Things. *International Journal of Information Management*, *35*(6), 672–678. doi:10.1016/j.ijinfomgt.2015.07.008

Doganova, L., & Eyquem-Renault, M. (2009). What do business models do? Innovation devices in technology entrepreneurship. *Research Policy*, *38*(10), 1559–1570.

Donoho, D. L., Maleki, A., Rahman, I. U., Shahram, M., & Stodden, V. (2009). Reproducible Research in Computational Harmonic Analysis. *Computing in Science & Engineering*, *11*(1), 8–18. doi:10.1109/MCSE.2009.15

Driankov, D., & Saffiotti, A. (Eds.). (2013). *Fuzzy logic techniques for autonomous vehicle navigation* (Vol. 61). Physica.

Duan, Y., Cao, Y., & Sun, X. (2015). Various "aaS" of everything as a service. In *2015 IEEE/ACIS 16th International Conference on Software Engineering, Artificial Intelligence, Networking and Parallel/Distributed Computing (SNPD)* (pp. 1-6). IEEE.

Eden, C., & Huxham, C. (2006). Researching organizations using action research. In S. R. Clegg, C. Hardy, T. B. Lawrence, & W. R. Nord (Eds.), *The Sage handbook of organization studies* (pp. 389–408). Sage Publications.

Edvardsson, B., Tronvoll, B., & Gruber, T. (2011). Expanding understanding of service exchange and value co-creation: A social construction approach. *Journal of the Academy of Marketing Science*, *39*(2), 327–339. doi:10.100711747-010-0200-y

Ekman, P., Raggio, R. D., & Thompson, S. M. (2016). Service network value co-creation: Defining the roles of the generic actor. *Industrial Marketing Management*, *56*, 51–62. doi:10.1016/j.indmarman.2016.03.002

Eletxigerra, A., Barrutia, J. M., & Echebarria, C. (2018). Place marketing examined through a service-dominant logic lens: A review. *Journal of Destination Marketing & Management*, *9*, 72–84. doi:10.1016/j.jdmm.2017.11.002

Engeström, Y. (2015). *Learning by Expanding*. Cambridge University Press.

Erevelles, S., Fukawa, N., & Swayne, L. (2016). Big Data Consumer Analytics and the Transformation of Marketing. *Journal of Business Research*, *69*(2), 897–904. doi:10.1016/j.jbusres.2015.07.001

European Commission. (2018). Artificial Intelligence for Europe. In Communication From The Commission To The European Parliament, The European Council, The Council, The European Economic And Social Committee And The Committee Of The Regions, SWD(2018) 137 final.

Fang, X., Misra, S., Xue, G., & Yang, D. (2012). Smart Grid — The New and Improved Power Grid: A Survey. *IEEE Communications Surveys and Tutorials*, *14*(4), 944–980. doi:10.1109/SURV.2011.101911.00087

Faraj, S. A., Kolker, E., Bevilacqua, L., & Özdemir, V. (2012). Collective theranostics and postgenomics entrepreneurship: Rethinking innovations as knowledge ecosystems built by complex collaboration. *Expert Review of Molecular Diagnostics*, *12*(8), 787–790. doi:10.1586/erm.12.124 PMID:23249193

Ferenhof, H. A., & Fernandes, R. F. (2016). Demystifying the Literature Review as basis for Scientific Writing: SSF Method. *Revista ACB*, *21*(3), 550–563.

Findsrud, R., Tronvoll, B., & Edvardsson, B. (2018). Motivation: The missing driver for theorizing about resource integration. *Marketing Theory*, *18*(4), 493–519. doi:10.1177/1470593118764590

Fleisch, E., Weinberger, M., & Wortmann, F. (2020). *Business Models and the Internet of Things*. Retrieved 3 January 2020, from https://cocoa.ethz.ch/downloads/2014/10/2090_EN_Bosch%20Lab%20White%20Paper%20GM%20im%20IOT%201_2.pdf

Floyd, J. (2012). Action research and integral futures studies: A path to embodied foresight. *Futures*, *44*(10), 870–882.

Fortino, G., Savaglio, C., Palau, C. E., Puga, J. S., Ganzha, M., Paprzycki, M., Montesinos, M., Liotta, A., & Llop, M. (2018). Towards multi-layer interoperability of heterogeneous IoT platforms: the INTER-IoT approach. In R. Gravina, C. Palau, M. Manso, A. Liotta, & G. Fortino (Eds.), *Integration, Interconnection, and Interoperability of IoT Systems. Internet of Things (Technology, Communications and Computing)*. Springer. doi:10.1007/978-3-319-61300-0_10

Fountas, S., Carli, G., Sørensen, C., Tsiropoulos, Z., Cavalaris, C., Vatsanidou, A., Liakos, B., Canavari, M., Wiebensohn, J., & Tisserye, B. (2015). Farm management information systems: Current situation and future perspectives. *Computers and Electronics in Agriculture*, *115*, 40–50. doi:10.1016/j.compag.2015.05.011

Frankenberger, K., Weiblen, T., & Gassmann, O. (2014). The antecedents of open business models: An exploratory study of incumbent firms. *R & D Management*, *44*(2), 173–188.

Frosch, R. A., & Gallopoulos, N. E. (1989). Strategies for Manufacturing. *Scientific American*, *261*(3), 144–152.

Fulmer, A., & Dirks, K. (2018). Multilevel trust: A theoretical and practical imperative. *Journal of Trust Research*, *8*(2), 137–141. doi:10.1080/21515581.2018.1531657

Fyrberg Yngfalk, A. (2013). 'It's not us, it's them!'–Rethinking value co-creation among multiple actors. *Journal of Marketing Management*, *29*(9-10), 1163–1181. doi:10.1080/0267257X.2013.796318

Galateanu, E., & Avasilcai, S. (2013). Business ecosystems architecture. *Annals of the Oradea University*, *1*(May), 79–84.

Galateanu, E., & Avasilcai, S. (2013). Business ecosystems architecture. *Annals of the Oradea University*, *22*(1), 79–84.

Gawer, A. (2014). Bridging differing perspectives on technological platforms: Toward an integrative framework. *Research Policy*, *43*(7), 1239–1249.

Gawer, A., & Cusumano, M. A. (2014). Industry platforms and ecosystem innovation. *Journal of Product Innovation Management*, *31*(3), 417–433.

Gawer, A., & Cusumano, M. A. (2014). Platforms and Innovation. *Journal of Product Innovation Management*, *31*, 417–433. doi:10.1111/jpim.12105

Gebauer, J., Füller, J., & Pezzei, R. (2013). The dark and the bright side of co-creation: Triggers of member behavior in online innovation communities. *Journal of Business Research*, *66*(9), 1516–1527. doi:10.1016/j.jbusres.2012.09.013

Gelfand, M. (2019, Sep 9). *Understanding Cultural Differences Around Social Norms*. Retrieved from https://behavioralscientist.org/understanding-cultural-differences-around-social-norms/

Georgakopoulos, D., & Jayaraman, P. (2016). Internet of things: From internet scale sensing to smart services. *Computing*, *98*(10), 1041–1058. doi:10.100700607-016-0510-0

Goecks, J., Nekrutenko, A., Taylor, J., & Galaxy Team, T. (2010). Galaxy: A comprehensive approach for supporting accessible, reproducible, and transparent computational research in the life sciences. *Genome Biology*, *11*(8), R86. doi:10.1186/gb-2010-11-8-r86 PMID:20738864

Gomes, J. F., Iivari, M., Pikkarainen, M., & Ahokangas, P. (2018). Business Models as Enablers of Ecosystemic Interaction: A Dynamic Capability Perspective. *International Journal of Social Ecology and Sustainable Development*, *9*(3), 1–13.

Gottwalt, S., Ketter, W., Block, C., Collins, J., & Weinhardt, C. (2011). Demand side management—A simulation of household behavior under variable prices. *Energy Policy*, *39*(12), 8163–8174. doi:10.1016/j.enpol.2011.10.016

Granovetter, M. (1983). The strength of weak ties: A network theory revisited. *Sociological Theory*, *1*, 201–233. doi:10.2307/202051

Grissemann, U. S., & Stokburger-Sauer, N. E. (2012). Customer co-creation of travel services: The role of company support and customer satisfaction with the co-creation performance. *Tourism Management*, *33*(6), 1483–1492. doi:10.1016/j.tourman.2012.02.002

Grönroos, C., & Gummerus, J. (2014). The service revolution and its marketing implications: Service logic vs service-dominant logic. *Managing Service Quality*, *24*(3), 206–229. doi:10.1108/MSQ-03-2014-0042

Grüning, B., Chilton, J., Köster, J., Dale, R., Soranzo, N., van den Beek, M., Goecks, J., Backofen, R., Nekrutenko, A., & Taylor, J. (2018). Practical Computational Reproducibility in the Life Sciences. *Cell Systems*, *6*(6), 631–635. doi:10.1016/j.cels.2018.03.014 PMID:29953862

GS1. (2016). *GS1 and the Internet of Things*. GS1 AISBL. Retrieved from https://www.gs1.org/sites/default/files/images/standards/internet-of-things/gs1-and-the-internet-of-things-iot.pdf

Gundall, M., Schneider, J., Schotten, H. D., Aleksy, M., Schulz, D., Franchi, N., Schwarzenberg, N., Markwart, C., Halfmann, R., Rost, P., & Wübben, D. (2018). 5G as Enabler for Industrie 4.0 Use Cases: Challenges and Concepts. In *2018 IEEE 23rd International Conference on Emerging Technologies and Factory Automation (ETFA)* (Vol. 1, pp. 1401-1408). IEEE.

Hager, G. D., Drobnis, A., Fang, F., Ghani, R., Greenwald, A., Lyons, T., Parkes, D. C., Schultz, J., Saria, S., & Smith, S. F., & Tambe, M. (2019). *Artificial intelligence for social good*. arXiv preprint, arXiv:1901.05406.

Hahanov, V., Gharibi, W., Man, K. L., Iemelianov, I., Liubarskyi, M., Abdullayev, V., Litvinova, E., & Chumachenko, S. (2018). Cyber-Physical Technologies: Hype Cycle 2017. In *Cyber Physical Computing for IoT-driven Services* (pp. 259–272). Springer. doi:10.1007/978-3-319-54825-8_14

Hamdan, M., & Anshari, M. (2020). Paving the Way for the Development of FinTech Initiatives in ASEAN. In *Financial technology and disruptive innovation in ASEAN* (pp. 80–107). IGI Global. doi:10.4018/978-1-5225-9183-2.ch004

Hankel, M., & Rexroth, B. (2015). *The Reference Architectural Model Industrie 4.0 (RAMI 4.0)*. ZVEI.

Hardwicke, T. E., Mathur, M. B., MacDonald, K., Nilsonne, G., Banks, G. C., Kidwell, M. C., Hofelich Mohr, A., Clayton, E., Yoon, E. J., Henry Tessler, M., Lenne, R. L., Altman, S., Long, B., & Frank, M. C. (2018). Data availability, reusability, and analytic reproducibility: Evaluating the impact of a mandatory open data policy at the journalCognition. *Royal Society Open Science*, *5*(8), 180448. doi:10.1098/rsos.180448 PMID:30225032

Haslam, S. A., Oakes, P. J., Turner, J. C., & McGarty, C. (1996). Social identity, self-categorization and the perceived homogeneity of in groups and outgroups: The interaction between social motivation and cognition. In R. M. Sorrentino & E. T. Higgins (Eds.), *Handbook of motivation and cognition* (Vol. 3, pp. 182–222). Guilford.

Hasmawati, F., Samiha, Y. T., Razzaq, A., & Anshari, M. (2020). Understanding Nomophobia Among Digital Natives: Characteristics And Challenges. *Journal of Critical Reviews*, *7*(13), 122–131.

Hein, A., Schreieck, M., Riasanow, T., Setzke, D. S., Wiesche, M., Böhm, M., & Krcmar, H. (2019). Digital platform ecosystems. *Electronic Markets*.

Helkkula, A., Dube, A., & Arnould, E. (2018). The contextual nature of value and value co-creation. The SAGE handbook of service-dominant logic, 118-132.

Hepi, M., Foote, J., Finsterwalder, J., Carswell, S., & Baker, V. (2017). An integrative transformative service framework to improve engagement in a social service ecosystem: The case of He Waka Tapu. *Journal of Services Marketing*, *31*(4/5), 423–437. doi:10.1108/JSM-06-2016-0222

Hernández-López, L., & Del Barrio-García, S. (2018). Value Co-Creation in Ecotourism: Finding Solutions in a Digital Era. Journal of Business. *Universidad del Pacífico (Lima, Peru)*, *10*(1), 38–51.

Hessler, G., & Baringhaus, K. H. (2018). Artificial intelligence in drug design. *Molecules (Basel, Switzerland)*, *23*(10), 2520. doi:10.3390/molecules23102520 PMID:30279331

Hettrick, S. J. (2014). UK Research Software Survey 2014 [Data set]. doi:10.5281/zenodo.14809

Holzinger, A. (2018). From Machine Learning to Explainable AI. In *2018 World Symposium on Digital Intelligence for Systems and Machines (DISA)* (pp. 55-66). 10.1109/DISA.2018.8490530

Hothorn, T., & Leisch, F. (2011). Case studies in reproducibility. [PubMed]. *Briefings in Bioinformatics*, *12*(3), 288–300. doi:10.1093/bib/bbq084

Hugos, M. (2018). *Essentials of supply chain management* (4th ed.). Wiley. doi:10.1002/9781119464495

Iansiti, M., & Levien, R. (2004). *The Keystone Advantage: What the New Dynamics of Business Ecosystems Mean for Strategy, Innovation and Sustainability*. Harvard Business Press.

Iansiti, M., & Richards, G. L. (2006). The Information Technology Ecosystem: Structure, Health, and Performance. *The Antitrust Bulletin*, *51*(1), 77–110.

Ibarra-Esquer, J. E., González-Navarro, F. F., Flores-Rios, B. L., Burtseva, L., & Astorga-Vargas, M. A. (2017). Tracking the Evolution of the Internet of Things Concept Across Different Application Domains. *Sensors (Basel)*, *17*(6), 1379. doi:10.339017061379 PMID:28613238

Iivari, M. (2015). Dynamics of Openness in SMEs: A business model and innovation strategy perspective. *Journal of Business Models*, *3*(2), 30–50.

Iivari, M., Ahokangas, P., Komi, M., Tihinen, M., & Valtanen, K. (2016). Toward ecosystemic business models in the context of industrial internet. *Journal of Business Models*, *4*(2), 42–59.

Inayatullah, S. (2006). Anticipatory action learning: Theory and practice. *Futures*, *38*, 656–666.

Ind, N., Coates, N., & Lerman, K. (2019). The gift of co-creation: What motivates customers to participate. *Journal of Brand Management*. Advance online publication. doi:10.105741262-019-00173-7

Iriye, A. (1999). A Century of NGOs. *Diplomatic History*, *23*(3), 421–435. doi:10.1111/0145-2096.00175

Isenberg, D. J. (2010). How to Start an Entrepreneurial Revolution. *Harvard Business Review*, *88*(6), 41–50.

Jaakkola, E., & Alexander, M. (2014). The role of customer engagement behavior in value co-creation: A service system perspective. *Journal of Service Research*, *17*(3), 247–261. doi:10.1177/1094670514529187

Jaakkola, E., Helkkula, A., & Aarikka-Stenroos, L. (2015). Service experience co-creation: Conceptualization, implications, and future research directions. *Journal of Service Management*, *26*(2), 182–205. doi:10.1108/JOSM-12-2014-0323

Jackson, D. J. (2011). What is an innovation ecosystem. *National Science Foundation, 1*(2).

Jacobides, M. G., Cennamo, C., & Gawer, A. (2018). Towards a theory of ecosystems. *Strategic Management Journal*, *39*(8), 2255–2276.

Jain, P., & Jain, T. (2014). Impacts of G2V and V2G power on electricity demand profile. In *2014 IEEE International Electric Vehicle Conference (IEVC)* (pp. 1-8). 10.1109/IEVC.2014.7056148

Jansson, N., Ahokangas, P., Iivari, M., Perälä-Heape, M., & Salo, S. (2014). The competitive advantage of an ecosystemic business model: The Case of OuluHealth. *Interdisciplinary Studies Journal*, *3*(4), 282–294.

Järvinen, P. (2008). On developing and evaluating of the literature review. *The 31st Information Systems Research Seminar*.

Jarwar, M., Kibria, M., Ali, S., & Chong, I. (2018). Microservices in web objects enabled IoT environment for enhancing reusability. *Sensors (Basel), 18*(2), 352. doi:10.339018020352 PMID:29373491

Jayaraman, P., Yavari, A., Georgakopoulos, D., Morshed, A., & Zaslavsky, A. (2016). Internet of Things Platform for Smart Farming: Experiences and Lessons Learnt. *Sensors (Basel), 16*(11), 1884. doi:10.339016111884 PMID:27834862

Jeble, S., Kumari, S., & Patil, Y. (2018). Role of Big Data in Decision Making. *Operations and Supply Chain Management, 11*(1), 36–44.

Jedermann, R., Borysov, M., Hartgenbusch, N., Jaeger, S., Sellwig, M., & Lang, W. (2018). Testing Lora for food applications - Example application for airflow measurements inside cooled warehouses with apples. *Procedia Manufacturing, 24*, 284–289. doi:10.1016/j.promfg.2018.06.026

Jeschke, S., Brecher, C., Meisen, T., Özdemir, D., & Eschert, T. (2016). Industrial Internet of Things and Cyber Manufacturing Systems. *Springer Series in Wireless Technology*, 3–19.

Jocevski, M., Ghezzi, A., & Arvidsson, N. (2020). Exploring the growth challenge of mobile payment platforms: A business model perspective. *Electronic Commerce Research and Applications, 40*, 100908. doi:10.1016/j.elerap.2019.100908

Johnson, A. G., & Neuhofer, B. (2017). Airbnb–an exploration of value co-creation experiences in Jamaica. *International Journal of Contemporary Hospitality Management, 29*(9), 2361–2376. doi:10.1108/IJCHM-08-2016-0482

Ju, J., Kim, M., & Ahn, J. (2016). Prototyping Business Models for IoT Service. *Procedia Computer Science, 91*, 882–890. doi:10.1016/j.procs.2016.07.106

Juve, G., Chervenak, A., Deelman, E., Bharathi, S., Mehta, G., & Vahi, K. (2013). Characterizing and profiling scientific workflows. *Future Generation Computer Systems, 29*(3), 682–692. doi:10.1016/j.future.2012.08.015

Kanterakis, A., Potamias, G., Swertz, M. A., & Patrinos, G. P. (2018). Creating Transparent and Reproducible Pipelines: Best Practices for Tools, Data, and Workflow Management Systems. *Human Genome Informatics*, 15–43. doi:10.1016/B978-0-12-809414-3.00002-4

Kaplan, A., & Haenlein, M. (2019). Siri, Siri, in my hand: Who's the fairest in the land? On the interpretations, illustrations, and implications of artificial intelligence. *Business Horizons, 62*(1), 15–25. doi:10.1016/j.bushor.2018.08.004

Karim, M., Michel, A., Zappa, A., Baranov, P., Sahay, R., & Rebholz-Schuhmann, D. (2017). *Improving data workflow systems with cloud services and use of open data for bioinformatics research*. Briefings Bioinf.

Kasnakoglu, B. T. (2016). Antecedents and consequences of cocreation in credence-based service contexts. *Service Industries Journal, 36*(1-2), 1–20. doi:10.1080/02642069.2016.1138472

Katz, M., & Shapiro, C. (1994). Systems Competition and Network Effects. *The Journal of Economic Perspectives, 8*(2), 93–115.

Kenney, M., & Zysman, J. (2015). Choosing a future in the platform economy: the implications and consequences of digital platforms. In *Kauffman Foundation New Entrepreneurial Growth Conference* (*Vol. 156160*). Academic Press.

Klumpp, M. (2018). Innovation Potentials and Pathways Merging AI, CPS, and IoT. *Applied System Innovation, 1*(1), 5. doi:10.3390/asi1010005

Kluyver, T., Ragan-Kelley, B., Perez, F., Granger, B., & Bussonnier. (2016). Jupyter Notebooks-A Publishing Format for Reproducible Computational Workflows (ELPUB). Academic Press.

Knuth, D. E. (1984). Literate programming. *The Computer Journal, 27*(2), 97–111. doi:10.1093/comjnl/27.2.97

Kohler, T. (2015). Crowdsourcing-Based Business Models: How to Create and Capture Value. *California Management Review, 57*(4), 63–84. doi:10.1525/cmr.2015.57.4.63

Komninos, N. (2013). Smart Cities and the Future Internet: Innovation ecosystems of embedded spatial intelligence. In *Proceedings of International Conference for Entrepreneurship, Innovation and Regional Development, ICEIRD* (pp. 1-3). Academic Press.

Krčo, S., von Kranenburg, R., Lončar, M., Ziouvelou, X., & McGroarty, F. (2019). Digitalization of Value Chains and Ecosystems. In A. Aagaard (Ed.), *Digital Business Models* (pp. 81–116). Palgrave MacMillan.

Kruse, L., Wunderlich, N., & Beck, R. (2019). Artificial Intelligence for the Financial Services Industry: What Challenges Organizations to Succeed. In *Proceedings of the 52nd Hawaii International Conference on System Sciences* (pp. 6408-6417). 10.24251/HICSS.2019.770

Kurzweil, R. (1992). *The Age of Intelligent Machines*. Viking.

Laamanen, M., & Skålén, P. (2015). Collective–conflictual value co-creation: A strategic action field approach. *Marketing Theory, 15*(3), 381–400. doi:10.1177/1470593114564905

Lan, J., Ma, Y., Zhu, D., Mangalagiu, D., & Thornton, T. (2017). Enabling value co-creation in the sharing economy: The case of mobike. *Sustainability, 9*(9), 1504. doi:10.3390u9091504

Lanzolla, G., Pesce, D., & Tucci, C. L. (forthcoming). The digital transformation of search and recombination in the innovation function: Tensions and an integrative framework. *Journal of Product Innovation Management*.

Laud, G., & Karpen, I. O. (2017). Value co-creation behaviour–Role of embeddedness and outcome considerations. *Journal of Service Theory and Practice, 27*(4), 778–807. doi:10.1108/JSTP-04-2016-0069

Laudien, S. M., & Daxböck, B. (2016). The influence of the industrial internet of things on business model design: A qualitative-empirical analysis. *International Journal of Innovation Management*, *20*(08), 1640014. doi:10.1142/S1363919616400144

Lee, I., & Shin, Y. J. (2018). Fintech: Ecosystem, business models, investment decisions, and challenges. *Business Horizons*, *61*(1), 35–46. doi:10.1016/j.bushor.2017.09.003

Lee, J., Davari, H., Singh, J., & Pandhare, V. (2018). Industrial Artificial Intelligence for industry 4.0-based manufacturing systems. *Manufacturing Letters*, *18*, 20–23. doi:10.1016/j.mfglet.2018.09.002

Lee, Y. L., Pan, L. Y., Hsu, C. H., & Lee, D. C. (2019). Exploring the sustainability correlation of value Co-creation and customer loyalty-A case study of fitness clubs. *Sustainability*, *11*(1), 97. doi:10.3390u11010097

Leipzig, J. (2016). A review of bioinformatic pipeline frameworks. *Brief. Bioinf.*. doi:10.1093/bib/bbw020

Leminen, S., Westerlund, M., Rajahonka, M., & Siuruainen, R. (2012). Towards IOT Ecosystems and Business Models. *Internet Of Things, Smart Spaces, And Next Generation Networking*, 15-26. doi:10.1007/978-3-642-32686-8_2

Leong, C., Tan, B., Xiao, X., Tan, F. T. C., & Sun, Y. (2017). Nurturing a FinTech ecosystem: The case of a youth microloan startup in China. *International Journal of Information Management*, *37*(2), 92–97. doi:10.1016/j.ijinfomgt.2016.11.006

Lepore, D., Nambisan, S., Tucci, C. L., & Zahra, S. A. (2019, July). Digital Transformation & Firms' Innovative Strategies: Capabilities, Ecosystems, and Business Models. In Academy of Management Proceedings (Vol. 2019, No. 1, p. 14623). Briarcliff Manor, NY: Academy of Management.

Li, B. H., Hou, B. C., Yu, W. T., Lu, X. B., & Yang, C. W. (2017). Applications of artificial intelligence in intelligent manufacturing: A review. *Frontiers of Information Technology & Electronic Engineering*, *18*(1), 86–96. doi:10.1631/FITEE.1601885

Lin, J., Shen, Z., Zhang, A., & Chai, Y. (2018). Blockchain and IoT based Food Traceability for Smart Agriculture. *Proceedings Of The 3Rd International Conference On Crowd Science And Engineering - ICCSE'18*. 10.1145/3265689.3265692

Lin, S. W., Miller, B., Durand, J., Bleakley, G., Chigani, A., Martin, R., Murhpy, B., & Crawford, M. (2017). The Industrial Internet of Things Volume G1: Reference Architecture. Industrial Internet Consortium, 10-46.

Lin, C., Lu, S., Fei, X., & Chebotko, A. (2009). A Reference Architecture for Scientific Workflow Management Systems and the VIEW SOA Solution. *IEEE Transactions on Services Computing*, *2*(1), 79–92. doi:10.1109/TSC.2009.4

Lincoln, Y. S., & Guba, E. G. (1985). *Naturalistic inquiry* (vol. 75). Academic Press.

Lindner, M. A., Vaquero, L. M., Rodero-Merino, L., & Caceres, J. (2010). Cloud economics: Dynamic business models for business on demand. *International Journal of Business Information Systems*, *5*(4), 373–392. doi:10.1504/IJBIS.2010.032938

Lin, X., Sarker, S., & Featherman, M. (2019). Users' psychological perceptions of information sharing in the context of social media: A comprehensive model. *International Journal of Electronic Commerce*, *23*(4), 453–491. doi:10.1080/10864415.2019.1655210

Liu, W., Fan, X., Ji, R., & Jiang, Y. (2020). Perceived Community Support, Users' Interactions, and Value Co-Creation in Online Health Community: The Moderating Effect of Social Exclusion. *International Journal of Environmental Research and Public Health*, *17*(1), 204. doi:10.3390/ijerph17010204 PMID:31892188

Li, Y.-R. (2009). The technological roadmap of Cisco's business ecosystem. *Technovation*, *29*(5), 379–386. doi:10.1016/j.technovation.2009.01.007

Loannidis, J. P. A. (2009). Repeatability of published microarray gene expression analyses. *Nature Genetics*, *41*(2), 149–155. doi:10.1038/ng.295 PMID:19174838

LoRa Alliance. (2015). *A technical overview of LoRa® and LoRaWAN™*. Retrieved 8 January 2020, from https://lora-alliance.org/sites/default/files/2018-04/what-is-lorawan.pdf

LoRa Alliance. (2019). *About LoRaWAN® | LoRa Alliance®*. Retrieved 14 December 2019, from https://lora-alliance.org/about-lorawan

Lorenzo-Romero, C., Constantinides, E., & Brünink, L. A. (2014). Co-creation: Customer integration in social media based product and service development. *Procedia: Social and Behavioral Sciences*, *148*, 383–396. doi:10.1016/j.sbspro.2014.07.057

Luk, S. T., Liu, B. S., & Li, E. L. (2018). Effect of multilevel trust on effort-in-use and service co-design behaviour. *Journal of Services Marketing*, *32*(4), 505519. doi:10.1108/JSM-08-2015-0261

Macaulay, T. (2016). *RIoT control: understanding and managing risks and the internet of things*. Morgan Kaufmann.

Mackewn, J. (2008). *Facilitation as action research in the moment. The Sage Handbook of Action Research. Participative Inquiry and Practice*. Sage Publications.

Maechling, P. (2006). SCEC CyberShake workflows—automating probabilistic seismic hazard analysis calculations. In E. D. I. Taylor, D. Gannon, & M. Shields (Eds.), *Workflows for e-Science*. Springer.

Malindretos, G. (2015). *Supply Chain, Logistics and Customer Service*. Hellenic Academic Libraries Link. http://hdl.handle.net/11419/5391

Mangone, E. (2018). The Cultural System and the Social Problems. In *Social and Cultural Dynamics* (pp. 53–62). Springer. doi:10.1007/978-3-319-68309-6_5

Martens, K. (2002). Article. *Voluntas*, *13*(3), 271–285. doi:10.1023/A:1020341526691

Martins, L., Rindova, V., & Greenbaum, B. (2015). Unlocking the hidden value of concepts: A cognitive approach to business model innovation. *Strategic Entrepreneurship Journal*, *9*(1), 99–117.

Mazhelis, O., Luoma, E., & Warma, H. (2012). Defining an internet-of-things ecosystem. In *Internet of Things, Smart Spaces, and Next Generation Networking* (pp. 1–14). Springer. doi:10.1007/978-3-642-32686-8_1

McAfee, A., Brynjolfsson, E., Davenport, T. H., Patil, D. J., & Barton, D. (2012). Big data: The management revolution. *Harvard Business Review*, *90*(10), 60–68.

McColl-Kennedy, J. R., Vargo, S. L., Dagger, T. S., Sweeney, J. C., & Kasteren, Y. V. (2012). Health care customer value cocreation practice styles. *Journal of Service Research*, *15*(4), 370–389. doi:10.1177/1094670512442806

McDonald, H., & Karg, A. J. (2014). Managing co-creation in professional sports: The antecedents and consequences of ritualized spectator behavior. *Sport Management Review*, *17*(3), 292–309. doi:10.1016/j.smr.2013.07.004

McGee, J. (2015). Value Chain. *Wiley Encyclopedia of Management*, *1-5*. Advance online publication. doi:10.1002/9781118785317.weom120081

McGrath, R. (2010). Business models: A discovery driven approach. *Long Range Planning*, *43*(2–3), 247–261.

Mekki, K., Bajic, E., Chaxel, F., & Meyer, F. (2019). A comparative study of LPWAN technologies for large-scale IoT deployment. *ICT Express*, *5*(1), 1–7. doi:10.1016/j.icte.2017.12.005

Merrilees, B. (2016). Interactive brand experience pathways to customer-brand engagement and value co-creation. *Journal of Product and Brand Management*, *25*(5), 402–408. doi:10.1108/JPBM-04-2016-1151

Merz, M. Y., Czerwinski, D., & Merz, M. A. (2013). Exploring the antecedents for value co-creation during healthcare service provision. *Journal of Business and Behavioral Sciences*, *25*(2), 152.

Meynhardt, T., Chandler, J. D., & Strathoff, P. (2016). Systemic principles of value co-creation: Synergetics of value and service ecosystems. *Journal of Business Research*, *69*(8), 2981–2989. doi:10.1016/j.jbusres.2016.02.031

Miles, M. B., & Huberman, A. M. (1994). *Qualitative data analysis*. Sage publications.

Moore, J. (1993). Predators and Prey: The New Ecology of Competition. *Harvard Business Review*, *71*(3), 75–86.

Moore, J. F. (1996). *The Death of Competition: Leadership and Strategy in the Age of Business Ecosystems*. Harper Collins Publishers.

Morris, J., Heady, J., Raffle, P., Roberts, C., & Parks, J. (1953). Coronary heart disease and physical activity of work. *Lancet*, *262*(6795), 1053–1057. doi:10.1016/S0140-6736(53)90665-5 PMID:13110049

Morris, M., Schindehutte, M., & Allen, J. (2005). The entrepreneur's business model: Toward a unified perspective. *Journal of Business Research, 58*(6), 726–735.

Mukherjee, A., Singh, M., & Žaldokas, A. (2017). Do corporate taxes hinder innovation? *Journal of Financial Economics, 124*(1), 195–221. doi:10.1016/j.jfineco.2017.01.004

Mulas, V., Minges, M., & Applebaum, H. (2016). Boosting tech innovation: Ecosystems in cities: A framework for growth and sustainability of urban tech innovation ecosystems. *Innovations: Technology, Governance, Globalization, 11*(1-2), 98–125. doi:10.1162/inov_a_00251

Mulyani, M. A., Razzaq, A., Ridho, S. L. Z., & Anshari, M. (2019a, October). Smartphone and Mobile Learning to Support Experiential Learning. In *2019 International Conference on Electrical Engineering and Computer Science (ICECOS)* (pp. 6-9). IEEE. 10.1109/ICECOS47637.2019.8984501

Mulyani, M. A., Razzaq, A., Sumardi, W. H., & Anshari, M. (2019b, August). Smartphone Adoption in Mobile Learning Scenario. In *2019 International Conference on Information Management and Technology (ICIMTech)* (Vol. 1, pp. 208-211). IEEE. 10.1109/ICIMTech.2019.8843755

Munafò, M. R., Nosek, B. A., Bishop, D. V. M., & Button, K. S. (2017). A manifesto for reproducible science. *Nature Human Behaviour, 1*(1), 21. . doi:10.103841562-016-0021

Nachira, F., Dini, P. & Nicolai, A. (2007). *A network for digital business ecosystems in Europe: Roots, processes and perspectives*. European Commission, Information Society and Media.

Nadeem, W., Juntunen, M., Shirazi, F., & Hajli, N. (2020). Consumers' value co-creation in sharing economy: The role of social support, consumers' ethical perceptions and relationship quality. *Technological Forecasting and Social Change, 151*, 119786. doi:10.1016/j.techfore.2019.119786

NangiaU.KatzD. S. (2017). *Track 1 Paper: Surveying the US National Postdoctoral Association Regarding Software Use and Training in Research*. doi:10.6084/m9.figshare.5328442.v3

Nava Auza, J. M., Boisson de Marca, J., & Lima Siqueira, G. (2019). Design of a Local Information Incentive Mechanism for Mobile Crowdsensing. *Sensors (Basel), 19*(11), 2532. doi:10.339019112532 PMID:31163609

Neghina, C., Caniëls, M. C., Bloemer, J. M., & van Birgelen, M. J. (2015). Value cocreation in service interactions: Dimensions and antecedents. *Marketing Theory, 15*(2), 221–242. doi:10.1177/1470593114552580

Nekrutenko, A., & Taylor, J. (2012). Next-generation sequencing data interpretation: Enhancing reproducibility and accessibility. *Nature Reviews. Genetics, 13*(9), 667–672. doi:10.1038/nrg3305 PMID:22898652

Nichols, J. A., Herbert Chan, H. W., & Baker, M. (2019). Machine learning: Applications of artificial intelligence to imaging and diagnosis. *Biophysical Reviews, 11*(1), 111–118. doi:10.100712551-018-0449-9 PMID:30182201

Nielsen, C., & Lund, M. (2018). Building scalable business models. *MIT Sloan Management Review*, *59*(2), 65–69.

Nisan, N. (2007). Introduction to mechanism design (for computer scientists). *Algorithmic Game Theory*, *9*, 209-242.

Nisan, N., & Ronen, A. (2001). Algorithmic Mechanism Design. *Games and Economic Behavior*, *35*(1-2), 166–196. doi:10.1006/game.1999.0790

Occhiocupo, N., & Friess, M. (2013, June). Exploring what motivates consumers to co-create value in virtual fashion communities. In Lucrare prezentată la Forumul Naples Forum on Service, Ischia (Vol. 13). Academic Press.

Oh, D.-S., Phillips, F., Park, S., & Lee, E. (2016). Innovation ecosystems: A critical examination. *Technovation*, *54*, 1–6. doi:10.1016/j.technovation.2016.02.004

Ojha, T., Misra, S., & Raghuwanshi, N. (2015). Wireless sensor networks for agriculture: The state-of-the-art in practice and future challenges. *Computers and Electronics in Agriculture*, *118*, 66–84. doi:10.1016/j.compag.2015.08.011

Onetti, A., Zucchella, A., Jones, M., & McDougal-Covin, P. (2012). Internationalization, innovation and entrepreneurship: Business models for new technology-based firms. *The Journal of Management and Governance*, *16*(3), 337–368.

Ophof, S. (2013). *Motives for customers to engage in co-creation activities* (Bachelor's thesis). University of Twente.

Osei-Frimpong, K., Wilson, A., & Owusu-Frimpong, N. (2015). Service experiences and dyadic value co-creation in healthcare service delivery: A CIT approach. *Journal of Service Theory and Practice*, *25*(4), 443–462. doi:10.1108/JSTP-03-2014-0062

Osterwalder, A., & Pigneur, Y. (2010). *Business Model Generation: A Handbook for Visionaries, Game Changers, and Challengers*. John Wiley & Sons.

Palma, F. C., Trimi, S., & Hong, S. G. (2019). Motivation triggers for customer participation in value co-creation. *Service Business*, *13*(3), 557–580. doi:10.100711628-018-00395-w

Pan, Y. (2016). Heading toward artificial intelligence 2.0. *Engineering*, *2*(4), 409–413. doi:10.1016/J.ENG.2016.04.018

Pappas, I. O., Mikalef, P., Giannakos, M. N., & Pavlou, P. A. (2017). Value co-creation and trust in social commerce: An fsQCA approach. *Proceedings of the 25th European Conference on Information Systems (ECIS)*, 2153–2168.

Parra-Arnau, J. (2018). Optimized, direct sale of privacy in personal data marketplaces. *Information Sciences*, *424*, 354–384. doi:10.1016/j.ins.2017.10.009

Paulus-Rohmer, D., Schatton, H., & Bauernhansl, T. (2016). Ecosystems, strategy and business models in the age of digitization - How the manufacturing industry is going to change its logic. *Procedia CIRP*, *57*, 8–13.

Payne, A. F., Storbacka, K., & Frow, P. (2008). Managing the co-creation of value. *Journal of the Academy of Marketing Science*, *36*(1), 83–96. doi:10.100711747-007-0070-0

Peltoniemi, M., & Vuori, E. (2004). Business ecosystem as the new approach to complex adaptive business environments. *Proceedings of eBusiness Research Forum*, 18, 267-281.

Peng, R. D. (2011). Reproducible research in computational science. *Science*, *334*(6060), 1226–1227. doi:10.1126cience.1213847 PMID:22144613

Perkel, J. M. (2018). A toolkit for data transparency takes shape. *Nature*, *560*(7719), 513–515. doi:10.1038/d41586-018-05990-5 PMID:30127481

Phillips, M. A., & Ritala, P. (2019). A complex adaptive systems agenda for ecosystem research methodology. *Technological Forecasting and Social Change*, *148*, 119739.

Piccolo, S. R., & Frampton, M. B. (2016). Tools and techniques for computational reproducibility. *GigaScience*, *5*(1), 30. Advance online publication. doi:10.118613742-016-0135-4 PMID:27401684

Pierris, G., Kothris, D., Spyrou, E., & Spyropoulos, C. (2015). SYNAISTHISI: An enabling platform for the current internet of things ecosystem. In *Proceedings of the 19th Panhellenic Conference on Informatics* (pp. 438-444). ACM. 10.1145/2801948.2802019

Pikkarainen, M., Ervasti, M., Hurmelinna-Laukkanen, P., & Nätti, S. (2017). Orchestration Roles to Facilitate Networked Innovation in a Healthcare Ecosystem. *Technology Innovation Management Review*, *7*(9), 30–43.

Pilinkienė, V., & Maciulis, P. (2014). Comparison of different ecosystem analogies: The main economic determinants and levels of impact. *Procedia: Social and Behavioral Sciences*, *156*, 365–370.

Plé, L. (2016). Studying customers' resource integration by service employees in interactional value co-creation. *Journal of Services Marketing*, *30*(2), 152–164. doi:10.1108/JSM-02-2015-0065

Počuča, S., Maršić, B., & Grgić, A. (2012). Possible scenarios for cloud-based offering by operators. In *2012 Proceedings of the 35th International Convention MIPRO* (pp. 506-511). IEEE.

Polo Peña, A. I., Frías Jamilena, D. M., & Rodríguez Molina, M. Á. (2014). Value co-creation via information and communications technology. *Service Industries Journal*, *34*(13), 1043–1059. doi:10.1080/02642069.2014.939641

Ponsignon, F., & Derbaix, M. (2020). The impact of interactive technologies on the social experience: An empirical study in a cultural tourism context. *Tourism Management Perspectives*, *35*, 100723. doi:10.1016/j.tmp.2020.100723

Pop, O. M., Leroi-Werelds, S., Roijakkers, N., & Andreassen, T. W. (2018). Institutional types and institutional change in healthcare ecosystems. *Journal of Service Management, 29*(4), 593–614. doi:10.1108/JOSM-02-2017-0041

Prahalad, C. K., & Ramaswamy, V. (2004). *The future of competition: Co-creating unique value with customers.* Harvard Business Press.

Priem, R. L., Wenzel, M., & Koch, J. (2018). Demand-side strategy and business models: Putting value creation for consumers center stage. *Long Range Planning, 51*(1), 22–31.

Qasha, R., Cala, J., & Watson, P. (2016). A framework for scientific workflow reproducibility in the cloud. *2016 IEEE 12th International Conference on e-Science (e-Science).* 10.1109/eScience.2016.7870888

Qazi, A. A., & Ali, F. (2017). The antecedents and consequents of customer value co-creation among small and medium enterprises. *Pakistan Journal of Commerce and Social Sciences, 11*(3), 934–958.

Quan, X. I., & Sanderson, J. (2018). Understanding the artificial intelligence business ecosystem. *IEEE Engineering Management Review, 46*(4), 22–25. doi:10.1109/EMR.2018.2882430

Rajani, M. K., & Chandio, M. S. (2004). Use of Internet and its effects on our Society. *National Conference On Emerging Technologies,* 157 - 161. Retrieved from http://www.szabist.edu.pk/Publications/Session%20VIII%20Paper%20No%202%20(P%2015 7-161).pdf

Ramaswamy, V., & Ozcan, K. (2018). What is co-creation? An interactional creation framework and its implications for value creation. *Journal of Business Research, 84,* 196–205. doi:10.1016/j.jbusres.2017.11.027

Ramchurn, S., Vytelingum, P., Rogers, A., & Jennings, N. R. (2012). Putting the" smarts" into the smart grid: A grand challenge for artificial intelligence. *Communications of the ACM, 55*(4), 86–97. doi:10.1145/2133806.2133825

Ramos, C. (2007). Ambient Intelligence – A State of the Art from Artificial Intelligence Perspective. In J. Neves, M. F. Santos, & J. M. Machado (Eds.), Lecture Notes in Computer Science: Vol. 4874. *Progress in Artificial Intelligence. EPIA 2007.* Springer. doi:10.1007/978-3-540-77002-2_24

Randles, B. M., Pasquetto, I. V., Golshan, M. S., & Borgman, C. L. (2017). Using the Jupyter Notebook as a Tool for Open Science: An Empirical Study. *2017 ACM/IEEE Joint Conference on Digital Libraries (JCDL).* 10.1109/JCDL.2017.7991618

Ray, P., P. (2018). A survey on Internet of Things Architectures. *Journal of King Saud University – Computer and Information Sciences, 30*(3), 291-319.

Razzaq, A., Samiha, Y. T., & Anshari, M. (2018). Smartphone Habits and Behaviors in Supporting Students Self-Efficacy. *International Journal of Emerging Technologies in Learning, 13*(2), 94. doi:10.3991/ijet.v13i02.7685

Reason, P., & Bradbury, H. (2008). *The SAGE Handbook of Action Research* (2nd ed.). SAGE.

RendaA. (2019). Artificial Intelligence: Ethics, Governance and Policy Challenge. *CEPS Task Force Report*: SSRN.

Rihova, I., Buhalis, D., Moital, M., & Gouthro, M. B. (2013). Social layers of customer-to-customer value co-creation. *Journal of Service Management, 24*(5), 553–566. doi:10.1108/JOSM-04-2013-0092

Ritala, P., Agouridas, V., Assimakopoulos, D., & Gies, O. (2013). Value creation and capture mechanisms in innovation ecosystems: A comparative case study. *International Journal of Technology Management, 63*(3/4), 244–267. doi:10.1504/IJTM.2013.056900

Roberts, D., Hughes, M., & Kertbo, K. (2014). Exploring consumers' motivations to engage in innovation through co-creation activities. *European Journal of Marketing, 48*(1/2), 147–169. doi:10.1108/EJM-12-2010-0637

Romero, J. (2017). Customer engagement behaviors in hospitality: Customer-based antecedents. *Journal of Hospitality Marketing & Management, 26*(6), 565–584. doi:10.1080/19368623.2017.1288192

Roy, S. K., Balaji, M. S., Soutar, G., & Jiang, Y. (2020). The antecedents and consequences of value co-creation behaviors in a hotel setting: A two-country study. *Cornell Hospitality Quarterly, 61*(3), 353–368. doi:10.1177/1938965519890572

Rule, A., Birmingham, A., Zuniga, C., Altintas, I., Huang, S.-C., Knight, R., Moshiri, N., Nguyen, M. H., Rosenthal, S. B., Pérez, F., & Rose, P. W. (2019). Ten simple rules for writing and sharing computational analyses in Jupyter Notebooks. *PLoS Computational Biology, 15*(7), e1007007. doi:10.1371/journal.pcbi.1007007 PMID:31344036

Russel, S., & Norvig, P. (2009). *Artificial Intelligence: A Modern Approach* (3rd ed.). Prentice Hall.

Ryman-Tubb, N. F., Krause, P., & Garn, W. (2018). How Artificial Intelligence and machine learning research impacts payment card fraud detection: A survey and industry benchmark. *Engineering Applications of Artificial Intelligence, 76*, 130–157. doi:10.1016/j.engappai.2018.07.008

Saarijärvi, H. (2012). The mechanisms of value co-creation. *Journal of Strategic Marketing, 20*(5), 381–391. doi:10.1080/0965254X.2012.671339

Saarijärvi, H., Kannan, P. K., & Kuusela, H. (2013). Value co-creation: Theoretical approaches and practical implications. *European Business Review, 25*(1), 6–19. doi:10.1108/09555341311287718

Sanchez, R., & Mahoney, J. (1996). Modularity, Flexibility, and Knowledge Management in Product Contingencies. *Management Information Systems Quarterly, 23*(2), 261–290.

Santofimia-Romero, M. J., del Toro-García, X., & López-López, J. C. (2011). Artificial intelligence techniques for smart grid applications. *Green ICT: Trends and Challenges*, 41-44.

Sarmah, B., & Rahman, Z. (2018). Antecedents of co-creation intention and their role in developing technology-based new services via customer involvement: A conceptual analysis. *International Journal of Business Excellence, 15*(2), 239–255. doi:10.1504/IJBEX.2018.091921

Scaringella, L., & Radziwon, A. (2018). Innovation, entrepreneurial, knowledge, and business ecosystems: Old wine in new bottles? *Technological Forecasting and Social Change*, *136*, 59–87.

Schaltegger, S., Hansen, E., & Lüdeke-Freund, F. (2016). Business models for sustainability: Origins, present research, and future avenues. *Organization & Environment*, *29*(1), 3–10.

Schilling, M. (2000). Toward a General Modular Systems Theory and Its Application to Interfirm Product Organization and Design. *Strategic Management Journal*, *17*(1), 63–76.

Schladofsky, W., Jelena, M., Megner, A. P., Simonato, C., Gioppo, L., Leonardos, D., & Bröring, A. (2017). Business Models for Interoperable IoT Ecosystems. In I. Podnar Žarko, A. Broering, S. Soursos, & M. Serrano (Eds.), Lecture Notes in Computer Science: Vol. 10218. *Interoperability and Open-Source Solutions for the Internet of Things. InterOSS-IoT 2016*. Springer. doi:10.1007/978-3-319-56877-5_6

Schwarting, W., Alonso-Mora, J., & Rus, D. (2018). Planning and decision-making for autonomous vehicles. *Annual Review of Control, Robotics, and Autonomous Systems*, *1*(1), 187–210. doi:10.1146/annurev-control-060117-105157

See-To, E. W., & Ho, K. K. (2014). Value co-creation and purchase intention in social network sites: The role of electronic Word-of-Mouth and trust–A theoretical analysis. *Computers in Human Behavior*, *31*, 182–189. doi:10.1016/j.chb.2013.10.013

SEMTECH. (2019). *Semtech LoRa Technology Overview | Semtech*. Retrieved 8 January 2020, from https://www.semtech.com/lora

Serrano, M., Payam, P., Carrez, F., Cousin, P., Vermesan, O., & Friess, P. (2015). *IoT Semantic Interoperability: Research Challenges, Best Practices, Recommendations and Next Steps*. European Research Cluster on the Internet of Things.

Shamim, A., & Ghazali, Z. (2015). The role of self-construals in developing customer value co-creation behavior. *Global Business and Management Research*, *7*(2), 19–27.

Shamim, A., Ghazali, Z., & Albinsson, P. A. (2017). Construction and validation of customer value co-creation attitude scale. *Journal of Consumer Marketing*, *34*(7), 591–602. doi:10.1108/JCM-01-2016-1664

Shin, H., Perdue, R. R., & Pandelaere, M. (2020). Managing customer reviews for value co-creation: An empowerment theory perspective. *Journal of Travel Research*, *59*(5), 792–810. doi:10.1177/0047287519867138

Shiroma, E., & Lee, I. (2010). Physical Activity and Cardiovascular Health. *Circulation*, *122*(7), 743–752. doi:10.1161/CIRCULATIONAHA.109.914721 PMID:20713909

Smorodinskaya, N., Russell, M., Katukov, D., & Still, K. (2017). Innovation ecosystems vs. innovation systems in terms of collaboration and co-creation of value. In *Proceedings of the 50th Hawaii international conference on system sciences*. 10.24251/HICSS.2017.636

Soltani, M., Jandaghi, G., & Forouzandeh Shahraki, P. (2017). Co-Creation Intention; Presenting a Model of Antecedents and its Impact on Attitude Toward the Product (Case Study in Shatel Company). *Iranian Journal of Management Studies*, *10*(1), 143–174.

Soursos, S., Žarko, I. P., Zwickl, P., Gojmerac, I., Bianchi, G., & Carrozzo, G. (2016). Towards the cross-domain interoperability of IoT platforms. In *2016 European conference on networks and communications (EuCNC)* (pp. 398-402). IEEE. 10.1109/EuCNC.2016.7561070

Spadaro, G., Gangl, K., Van Prooijen, J. W., Van Lange, P. A., & Mosso, C. O. (2020). Enhancing feelings of security: How institutional trust promotes interpersonal trust. *PLoS One*, *15*(9), e0237934. doi:10.1371/journal.pone.0237934 PMID:32916694

Spanoudakis, N., Akasiadis, C., Kechagias, G., & Chalkiadakis, G. (2019). An Open MAS Services Architecture for the V2G/G2V Problem. In *Proceedings of the 18th International Conference on Autonomous Agents and MultiAgent Systems* (pp. 2198-2200). International Foundation for Autonomous Agents and Multiagent Systems.

Srbinovska, M., Gavrovski, C., Dimcev, V., Krkoleva, A., & Borozan, V. (2015). Environmental parameters monitoring in precision agriculture using wireless sensor networks. *Journal of Cleaner Production*, *88*, 297–307. doi:10.1016/j.jclepro.2014.04.036

Stampfl, G., Prügl, R., & Osterloh, V. (2013). An explorative model of business model scalability. *International Journal of Product Development*, *18*(3-4), 226–248.

Stevenson, T. (2002). Anticipatory action learning: Conversations about the future. *Futures*, *34*(5), 417–425.

Stevenson, T. (2006). From vision into action. *Futures*, *38*(6), 667–672.

Still, K., Huhtala, T., & Saraniemi, S. (2016). FinTech as business and innovation ecosystems. Paper presented at ISPIM Summit, Kuala Lumpur, Malaysia.

Stodden, V., McNutt, M., Bailey, D. H., Deelman, E., Gil, Y., Hanson, B., Heroux, M. A., Ioannidis, J. P. A., & Taufer, M. (2016). Enhancing reproducibility for computational methods. *Science*, *354*(6317), 1240–1241. doi:10.1126cience.aah6168 PMID:27940837

Taghizadeh, S. K., Rahman, S. A., & Marimuthu, M. (2019). Idea generation leveraged from value co-creation process enhances new service development performance. *Journal of Strategic Marketing*, *27*(6), 483–504. doi:10.1080/0965254X.2018.1430052

Talmar, M., Walrave, B., Podoynitsyna, X., Holmström, J., & Romme, G. L. (2018). (in press). Mapping, analyzing and designing innovation ecosystems: The Ecosystem pie model. *Long Range Planning*.

Teece, D. (2010). Business models, business strategy and innovation. *Long Range Planning*, *43*(2-3), 172–194.

Teece, D. J. (2018). Profiting from innovation in the digital economy: Enabling technologies, standards, and licensing models in the wireless world. *Research Policy*, *47*, 1367–1387.

The Things Network. (2019). *The Things Network.* Retrieved 8 December 2019, from https://www.thethingsnetwork.org/

Thomas, L.D.W. & Autio, E. (2019) *Innovation ecosystems*. Academic Press.

Thuluva, A. S., Bröring, A., Medagoda, G. P., Don, H., Anicic, D., & Seeger, J. (2017). Recipes for IoT applications. In *Proceedings of the Seventh International Conference on the Internet of Things* (p. 10). ACM.

Top 50 Countries with Highest Internet Penetration Rates - Country Literacy Rates. (2018). Retrieved from https://www.internetworldstats.com/top25.htm

Tóth, Z., Peters, L. D., Pressey, A., & Johnston, W. J. (2018). Tension in a value co-creation context: A network case study. *Industrial Marketing Management*, *70*, 34–45. doi:10.1016/j.indmarman.2017.08.015

Tranfield, D., Denyer, D., & Smart, P. (2003). Towards a methodology for developing evidence-informed management knowledge by means of systematic review. *British Journal of Management*, *14*(3), 207–222. doi:10.1111/1467-8551.00375

Tregua, M., Russo-Spena, T., & Casbarra, C. (2015). Being social for social: A co-creation perspective. *Journal of Service Theory and Practice*, *25*(2), 198–219. doi:10.1108/JSTP-09-2013-0183

Tsujimoto, M., Kajikawa, Y., Tomita, J., & Matsumoto, Y. (2018). A review of the ecosystem concept—Towards coherent ecosystem design. *Technological Forecasting and Social Change*, *136*, 49–58.

Tzortzis, G., Akasiadis, C., & Spyrou, E. (2017). *Semantic Complex Service Composition within an IoT Ecosystem. In The Internet of Things: Foundation for Smart Cities, e-Health and Ubiquitous Computing*. Chapman and Hall/CRC.

Van Alstyne, M. W., Parker, G. G., & Choudary, S. P. (2016). Pipelines, platforms, and the new rules of strategy. *Harvard Business Review*, *94*(4), 54–62.

Van der Borgh, M., Cloodt, M., & Romme, A. G. L. (2012). Value-creation by knowledge-based ecosystems: Evidence from a field study. *R & D Management*, *42*(2), 150–169.

Vargo, S. L., & Lusch, R. F. (2016). Service-dominant logic. Marketing Theory: A Student Text. Sage Publications.

Vargo, S. L., & Akaka, M. A. (2012). Value cocreation and service systems (re) formation: A service ecosystems view. *Service Science*, *4*(3), 207–217. doi:10.1287erv.1120.0019

Vargo, S. L., & Lusch, R. F. (2004). Evolving To a New Dominant Logic For Marketing. *Journal of Marketing*, *68*(1), 1–17. doi:10.1509/jmkg.68.1.1.24036

Vargo, S. L., & Lusch, R. F. (2017). Service-dominant logic 2025. *International Journal of Research in Marketing*, *34*(1), 46–67. doi:10.1016/j.ijresmar.2016.11.001

Vargo, S. L., Maglio, P. P., & Akaka, M. A. (2008). On value and value co-creation: A service systems and service logic perspective. *European Management Journal*, *26*(3), 145–152. doi:10.1016/j.emj.2008.04.003

Venkatesh, A., & Penaloza, L. (2014). The value of value in CCT. *Marketing Theory*, *14*(1), 135–138. doi:10.1177/1470593113500386

Venkatraman, N. V., El Sawy, O. A., Pavlou, P. A., & Bharadwaj, A. (2014). *Theorizing digital business innovation: platforms and capabilities in ecosystems.* Fox School of Business Research Paper, (15-080).

Verdouw, C., Robbemond, R., Verwaart, T., Wolfert, J., & Beulens, A. (2015). A reference architecture for IoT-based logistic information systems in agri-food supply chains. *Enterprise Information Systems*, *12*(7), 755–779. doi:10.1080/17517575.2015.1072643

Verleye, K. (2015). The co-creation experience from the customer perspective: Its measurement and determinants. *Journal of Service Management*, *26*(2), 321–342. doi:10.1108/JOSM-09-2014-0254

Verleye, K., Jaakkola, E., Hodgkinson, I. R., Jun, G. T., Odekerken-Schröder, G., & Quist, J. (2017). What causes imbalance in complex service networks? Evidence from a public health service. *Journal of Service Management*, *28*(1), 34–56. doi:10.1108/JOSM-03-2016-0077

Vermesan, O., Bröring, A., Tragos, E., Serrano, M., Bacciu, D., Chessa, S., Gallicchio, C., Micheli, A., Dragone, M., Saffiotti, A., Simoens, P., Cavallo, F., & Bahr, R. (2017). Internet of robotic things : converging sensing/actuating, hypoconnectivity, artificial intelligence and IoT Platforms. In *Cognitive Hyperconnected Digital Transformation: Internet of Things Intelligence Evolution* (pp. 97–155). River Publishers.

Verstraete, T., & Jouison-Laffitte, E. (2011). A conventionalist theory of the business model in the context of business creation for understanding organizational impetus. *Management International*, *15*(2), 109–124.

Vocke, C., Constantinescu, C., & Popescu, D. (2019). Application potentials of artificial intelligence for the design of innovation processes. *Procedia CIRP*, *84*, 810–813. doi:10.1016/j.procir.2019.04.230

Voros, J. (2008). Integral futures: An approach to futures inquiry. *Futures*, *40*(2), 190–201.

Voyer, B. G., Kastanakis, M. N., & Rhode, A. K. (2017). Co-creating stakeholder and brand identities: A cross-cultural consumer perspective. *Journal of Business Research*, *70*, 399–410. doi:10.1016/j.jbusres.2016.07.010

Wajid, A., Raziq, M. M., Malik, O. F., Malik, S. A., & Khurshid, N. (2019). Value co-creation through actor embeddedness and actor engagement. *Marketing Intelligence & Planning*, *37*(3), 271–283. doi:10.1108/MIP-07-2018-0241

Walrave, B., Talmar, M., Podoynitsyna, K. S., Romme, A. G. L., & Verbong, G. P. (2018). A multi-level perspective on innovation ecosystems for path-breaking innovation. *Technological Forecasting and Social Change*, *136*, 103–113.

Wang, H. K., Tseng, J. F., & Yen, Y. F. (2014). How do institutional norms and trust influence knowledge sharing? An institutional theory. *Innovation*, *16*(3), 374–391. doi:10.1080/14479338.2014.11081994

Wang, J., Wang, H., He, J., Li, L., Shen, M., Tan, X., Min, H., & Zheng, L. (2015). Wireless sensor network for real-time perishable food supply chain management. *Computers and Electronics in Agriculture*, *110*, 196–207. doi:10.1016/j.compag.2014.11.009

Wang, W., Hsieh, P., & Yen, H. R. (2011, May). Engaging customers in value co-creation: The emergence of customer readiness. In *2011 International Joint Conference on Service Sciences* (pp. 135-139). IEEE. 10.1109/IJCSS.2011.34

Wei, J., & Lv, S. (2019). Research on the Distribution System of Agricultural Products Cold Chain Logistics Based on Internet of Things. *IOP Conference Series. Earth and Environmental Science*, *237*, 052036. doi:10.1088/1755-1315/237/5/052036

Weill, P., & Woerner, S. L. (2015). Thriving in an increasingly digital ecosystem. *MIT Sloan Management Review*, *56*(4), 27.

Wirtz, B. W., Schilke, O., & Ullrich, S. (2010). Strategic development of business models: Implications of the Web 2.0 for creating value on the internet. *Long Range Planning*, *43*(2), 272–290.

Wise, S., Paton, R. A., & Gegenhuber, T. (2012). Value co-creation through collective intelligence in the public sector: A review of US and European initiatives. *VINE Journal of Information and Knowledge Management Systems*, *42*(2), 251–276.

Wolstencroft, K., Haines, R., Fellows, D., Williams, A., Withers, D., Owen, S., Soiland-Reyes, S., Dunlop, I., Nenadic, A., Fisher, P., Bhagat, J., Belhajjame, K., Bacall, F., Hardisty, A., Nieva de la Hidalga, A., Balcazar Vargas, M. P., Sufi, S., & Goble, C. (2013). The Taverna workflow suite: Designing and executing workflows of Web Services on the desktop, web or in the cloud. *Nucleic Acids Research*, *41*(W1), W557–W561. doi:10.1093/nar/gkt328 PMID:23640334

Xia, F., Yang, L. T., Wang, L., & Vinel, A. (2012). Internet of things. *International Journal of Communication Systems*, *25*(9), 1101–1102. doi:10.1002/dac.2417

Yampolskiy, R. (2016). Taxonomy of Pathways to Dangerous Artificial Intelligence. In *AI Ethics and Society*. AAAI.

Yang, X., & Li, G. (2016). Factors influencing the popularity of customer-generated content in a company-hosted online co-creation community: A social capital perspective. *Computers in Human Behavior*, *64*, 760–768. doi:10.1016/j.chb.2016.08.002

Yenni, G. M., Christensen, E. M., Bledsoe, E. K., Supp, S. R., Diaz, R. M., White, E. P., & Ernest, S. K. M. (2019). Developing a modern data workflow for regularly updated data. *PLoS Biology*, *17*(1), e3000125. doi:10.1371/journal.pbio.3000125 PMID:30695030

Yi, Y., & Gong, T. (2013). Customer value co-creation behavior: Scale development and validation. *Journal of Business Research*, *66*(9), 1279–1284. doi:10.1016/j.jbusres.2012.02.026

Yousefian, J. (2015). *The Effect of Self-efficacy, Role Clarity, and Trust on Customer Well-being and Loyalty Through Value Co-creation: The Case of Fitness Centres* (Doctoral dissertation). University of Hull.

Yrjölä, S., Ahokangas, P., & Matinmikko, M. (2015). Evaluation of recent spectrum sharing concepts from business model scalability point of view. *Dynamic Spectrum Access Networks (DySPAN), 2015 IEEE International Symposium*, 241-250. doi:10.1109/DySPAN.2015.7343907

Yrjölä, S., Ahokangas, P., & Matinmikko-Blue, M. (2019a). *Novel Platform-based Ecosystemic Business Models in the Future Mobile Operator Business.* Paper presented at the 3rd Business Model Conference, New York, NY.

Yrjölä, S., Ahokangas, P., & Matinmikko-Blue, M. (2019b). *Novel platform ecosystem business models for future wireless communications services and networks.* Paper presented at NFF 2019 Conference, Vaasa, Finland.

Yu, J., Li, Y., & Zhao, C. (2011). Analysis on structure and complexity characteristics of electronic business ecosystem. *Procedia Engineering*, *15*, 1400–1404. doi:10.1016/j.proeng.2011.08.259

Yu, K. H., Beam, A. L., & Kohane, I. S. (2018). Artificial intelligence in healthcare. *Nature Biomedical Engineering*, *2*(10), 719–731. doi:10.103841551-018-0305-z PMID:31015651

Zadeh, A. H., Zolfagharian, M., & Hofacker, C. F. (2019). Customer–customer value co-creation in social media: Conceptualization and antecedents. *Journal of Strategic Marketing*, *27*(4), 283–302. doi:10.1080/0965254X.2017.1344289

Zahra, S. A., & Nambisan, S. (2011). Entrepreneurship in global innovation ecosystems. *AMS Review*, *1*(1), 4–17. doi:10.100713162-011-0004-3

Zahra, S. A., & Nambisan, S. (2012). Entrepreneurship and strategic thinking in business ecosystems. *Business Horizons*, *55*(3), 219–229.

Zare, S., Bettiga, D., & Lamberti, L. (2018). Does one design fit them all? Study of drivers of co-creation interest along different consumer segments. *Journal of Strategic Marketing*, 1–21. doi:10.1080/0965254X.2018.1464051

Zhang, J. (2014, June). Customer resource integration: Antecedents and its impact on intent to co-create value. In *2014 11th International Conference on Service Systems and Service Management (ICSSSM)* (pp. 1-5). IEEE.

Zhang, M., Guo, L., Hu, M., & Liu, W. (2017). Influence of customer engagement with company social networks on stickiness: Mediating effect of customer value creation. *International Journal of Information Management*, *37*(3), 229–240. doi:10.1016/j.ijinfomgt.2016.04.010

Zhao, J., Gomez-Perez, J. M., Belhajjame, K., & Klyne, G. (2012). Why workflows break — Understanding and combating decay in Taverna workflows. *2012 IEEE 8th International Conference on E-Science*. 10.1109/eScience.2012.6404482

Zhao, J., Wang, T., & Fan, X. (2015). Patient value co-creation in online health communities: Social identity effects on customer knowledge contributions and membership continuance intentions in online health communities. *Journal of Service Management*, *26*(1), 72–96. doi:10.1108/JOSM-12-2013-0344

Ziouvelou, X., & McGroarty, F. (2017). Business Models for Crowd-driven IoT Ecosystems: A Review. *International Journal of Computer & Software Engineering*, *2*(2), 121. doi:10.15344/2456-4451/2017/121

Zittoun, T. (2007). Symbolic resources and responsibility in transitions. *Young*, *15*(2), 193–211. doi:10.1177/110330880701500205

Zott, C., & Amit, R. (2010). Designing your future business model: An activity system perspective. *Long Range Planning*, *43*(2–3), 216–226.

Zott, C., Amit, R., & Massa, L. (2011). The business model: Recent developments and future research. *Journal of Management*, *37*(4), 1019–1042.

Zott, C., Amit, R., & Massa, L. (2011). The Business Model: Recent Developments and Future Research. *Journal of Management*, *37*(4), 1019–1042. doi:10.1177/0149206311406265

Related References

To continue our tradition of advancing information science and technology research, we have compiled a list of recommended IGI Global readings. These references will provide additional information and guidance to further enrich your knowledge and assist you with your own research and future publications.

Abtahi, M. S., Behboudi, L., & Hasanabad, H. M. (2017). Factors Affecting Internet Advertising Adoption in Ad Agencies. *International Journal of Innovation in the Digital Economy*, *8*(4), 18–29. doi:10.4018/IJIDE.2017100102

Agrawal, S. (2017). The Impact of Emerging Technologies and Social Media on Different Business(es): Marketing and Management. In O. Rishi & A. Sharma (Eds.), *Maximizing Business Performance and Efficiency Through Intelligent Systems* (pp. 37–49). Hershey, PA: IGI Global. doi:10.4018/978-1-5225-2234-8.ch002

Alnoukari, M., Razouk, R., & Hanano, A. (2016). BSC-SI: A Framework for Integrating Strategic Intelligence in Corporate Strategic Management. *International Journal of Social and Organizational Dynamics in IT*, *5*(2), 1–14. doi:10.4018/IJSODIT.2016070101

Alnoukari, M., Razouk, R., & Hanano, A. (2016). BSC-SI, A Framework for Integrating Strategic Intelligence in Corporate Strategic Management. *International Journal of Strategic Information Technology and Applications*, *7*(1), 32–44. doi:10.4018/IJSITA.2016010103

Altındağ, E. (2016). Current Approaches in Change Management. In A. Goksoy (Ed.), *Organizational Change Management Strategies in Modern Business* (pp. 24–51). Hershey, PA: IGI Global. doi:10.4018/978-1-4666-9533-7.ch002

Related References

Alvarez-Dionisi, L. E., Turner, R., & Mittra, M. (2016). Global Project Management Trends. *International Journal of Information Technology Project Management, 7*(3), 54–73. doi:10.4018/IJITPM.2016070104

Anantharaman, R. N., Rajeswari, K. S., Angusamy, A., & Kuppusamy, J. (2017). Role of Self-Efficacy and Collective Efficacy as Moderators of Occupational Stress Among Software Development Professionals. *International Journal of Human Capital and Information Technology Professionals, 8*(2), 45–58. doi:10.4018/IJHCITP.2017040103

Aninze, F., El-Gohary, H., & Hussain, J. (2018). The Role of Microfinance to Empower Women: The Case of Developing Countries. *International Journal of Customer Relationship Marketing and Management, 9*(1), 54–78. doi:10.4018/IJCRMM.2018010104

Arsenijević, O. M., Orčić, D., & Kastratović, E. (2017). Development of an Optimization Tool for Intangibles in SMEs: A Case Study from Serbia with a Pilot Research in the Prestige by Milka Company. In M. Vemić (Ed.), *Optimal Management Strategies in Small and Medium Enterprises* (pp. 320–347). Hershey, PA: IGI Global. doi:10.4018/978-1-5225-1949-2.ch015

Aryanto, V. D., Wismantoro, Y., & Widyatmoko, K. (2018). Implementing Eco-Innovation by Utilizing the Internet to Enhance Firm's Marketing Performance: Study of Green Batik Small and Medium Enterprises in Indonesia. *International Journal of E-Business Research, 14*(1), 21–36. doi:10.4018/IJEBR.2018010102

Atiku, S. O., & Fields, Z. (2017). Multicultural Orientations for 21st Century Global Leadership. In N. Baporikar (Ed.), *Management Education for Global Leadership* (pp. 28–51). Hershey, PA: IGI Global. doi:10.4018/978-1-5225-1013-0.ch002

Atiku, S. O., & Fields, Z. (2018). Organisational Learning Dimensions and Talent Retention Strategies for the Service Industries. In N. Baporikar (Ed.), *Global Practices in Knowledge Management for Societal and Organizational Development* (pp. 358–381). Hershey, PA: IGI Global. doi:10.4018/978-1-5225-3009-1.ch017

Ávila, L., & Teixeira, L. (2018). The Main Concepts Behind the Dematerialization of Business Processes. In M. Khosrow-Pour, D.B.A. (Ed.), Encyclopedia of Information Science and Technology, Fourth Edition (pp. 888-898). Hershey, PA: IGI Global. doi:10.4018/978-1-5225-2255-3.ch076

Bartens, Y., Chunpir, H. I., Schulte, F., & Voß, S. (2017). Business/IT Alignment in Two-Sided Markets: A COBIT 5 Analysis for Media Streaming Business Models. In S. De Haes & W. Van Grembergen (Eds.), *Strategic IT Governance and Alignment in Business Settings* (pp. 82–111). Hershey, PA: IGI Global. doi:10.4018/978-1-5225-0861-8.ch004

Bashayreh, A. M. (2018). Organizational Culture and Organizational Performance. In W. Lee & F. Sabetzadeh (Eds.), *Contemporary Knowledge and Systems Science* (pp. 50–69). Hershey, PA: IGI Global. doi:10.4018/978-1-5225-5655-8.ch003

Bedford, D. A. (2018). Sustainable Knowledge Management Strategies: Aligning Business Capabilities and Knowledge Management Goals. In N. Baporikar (Ed.), *Global Practices in Knowledge Management for Societal and Organizational Development* (pp. 46–73). Hershey, PA: IGI Global. doi:10.4018/978-1-5225-3009-1.ch003

Benmoussa, F., Nakara, W. A., & Jaouen, A. (2016). The Use of Social Media by SMEs in the Tourism Industry. In I. Lee (Ed.), *Encyclopedia of E-Commerce Development, Implementation, and Management* (pp. 2159–2170). Hershey, PA: IGI Global. doi:10.4018/978-1-4666-9787-4.ch155

Berger, R. (2016). Indigenous Management and Bottom of Pyramid Countries: The Role of National Institutions. In U. Aung & P. Ordoñez de Pablos (Eds.), *Managerial Strategies and Practice in the Asian Business Sector* (pp. 107–123). Hershey, PA: IGI Global. doi:10.4018/978-1-4666-9758-4.ch007

Bharwani, S., & Musunuri, D. (2018). Reflection as a Process From Theory to Practice. In M. Khosrow-Pour, D.B.A. (Ed.), Encyclopedia of Information Science and Technology, Fourth Edition (pp. 1529-1539). Hershey, PA: IGI Global. doi:10.4018/978-1-5225-2255-3.ch132

Bhatt, G. D., Wang, Z., & Rodger, J. A. (2017). Information Systems Capabilities and Their Effects on Competitive Advantages: A Study of Chinese Companies. *Information Resources Management Journal, 30*(3), 41–57. doi:10.4018/IRMJ.2017070103

Bhushan, M., & Yadav, A. (2017). Concept of Cloud Computing in ESB. In R. Bhadoria, N. Chaudhari, G. Tomar, & S. Singh (Eds.), *Exploring Enterprise Service Bus in the Service-Oriented Architecture Paradigm* (pp. 116–127). Hershey, PA: IGI Global. doi:10.4018/978-1-5225-2157-0.ch008

Bhushan, S. (2017). System Dynamics Base-Model of Humanitarian Supply Chain (HSCM) in Disaster Prone Eco-Communities of India: A Discussion on Simulation and Scenario Results. *International Journal of System Dynamics Applications, 6*(3), 20–37. doi:10.4018/IJSDA.2017070102

Biswas, A., & De, A. K. (2017). On Development of a Fuzzy Stochastic Programming Model with Its Application to Business Management. In S. Trivedi, S. Dey, A. Kumar, & T. Panda (Eds.), *Handbook of Research on Advanced Data Mining Techniques and Applications for Business Intelligence* (pp. 353–378). Hershey, PA: IGI Global. doi:10.4018/978-1-5225-2031-3.ch021

Bücker, J., & Ernste, K. (2018). Use of Brand Heroes in Strategic Reputation Management: The Case of Bacardi, Adidas, and Daimler. In A. Erdemir (Ed.), *Reputation Management Techniques in Public Relations* (pp. 126–150). Hershey, PA: IGI Global. doi:10.4018/978-1-5225-3619-2.ch007

Bureš, V. (2018). Industry 4.0 From the Systems Engineering Perspective: Alternative Holistic Framework Development. In R. Brunet-Thornton & F. Martinez (Eds.), *Analyzing the Impacts of Industry 4.0 in Modern Business Environments* (pp. 199–223). Hershey, PA: IGI Global. doi:10.4018/978-1-5225-3468-6.ch011

Buzady, Z. (2017). Resolving the Magic Cube of Effective Case Teaching: Benchmarking Case Teaching Practices in Emerging Markets – Insights from the Central European University Business School, Hungary. In D. Latusek (Ed.), *Case Studies as a Teaching Tool in Management Education* (pp. 79–103). Hershey, PA: IGI Global. doi:10.4018/978-1-5225-0770-3.ch005

Campatelli, G., Richter, A., & Stocker, A. (2016). Participative Knowledge Management to Empower Manufacturing Workers. *International Journal of Knowledge Management, 12*(4), 37–50. doi:10.4018/IJKM.2016100103

Căpusneanu, S., & Topor, D. I. (2018). Business Ethics and Cost Management in SMEs: Theories of Business Ethics and Cost Management Ethos. In I. Oncioiu (Ed.), *Ethics and Decision-Making for Sustainable Business Practices* (pp. 109–127). Hershey, PA: IGI Global. doi:10.4018/978-1-5225-3773-1.ch007

Carneiro, A. (2016). Maturity in Health Organization Information Systems: Metrics and Privacy Perspectives. *International Journal of Privacy and Health Information Management, 4*(2), 1–18. doi:10.4018/IJPHIM.2016070101

Chan, R. L., Mo, P. L., & Moon, K. K. (2018). Strategic and Tactical Measures in Managing Enterprise Risks: A Study of the Textile and Apparel Industry. In K. Strang, M. Korstanje, & N. Vajjhala (Eds.), *Research, Practices, and Innovations in Global Risk and Contingency Management* (pp. 1–19). Hershey, PA: IGI Global. doi:10.4018/978-1-5225-4754-9.ch001

Chandan, H. C. (2016). Motivations and Challenges of Female Entrepreneurship in Developed and Developing Economies. In N. Baporikar (Ed.), *Handbook of Research on Entrepreneurship in the Contemporary Knowledge-Based Global Economy* (pp. 260–286). Hershey, PA: IGI Global. doi:10.4018/978-1-4666-8798-1.ch012

Charlier, S. D., Burke-Smalley, L. A., & Fisher, S. L. (2018). Undergraduate Programs in the U.S: A Contextual and Content-Based Analysis. In J. Mendy (Ed.), *Teaching Human Resources and Organizational Behavior at the College Level* (pp. 26–57). Hershey, PA: IGI Global. doi:10.4018/978-1-5225-2820-3.ch002

Chaudhuri, S. (2016). Application of Web-Based Geographical Information System (GIS) in E-Business. In U. Panwar, R. Kumar, & N. Ray (Eds.), *Handbook of Research on Promotional Strategies and Consumer Influence in the Service Sector* (pp. 389–405). Hershey, PA: IGI Global. doi:10.4018/978-1-5225-0143-5.ch023

Choudhuri, P. S. (2016). An Empirical Study on the Quality of Services Offered by the Private Life Insurers in Burdwan. In U. Panwar, R. Kumar, & N. Ray (Eds.), *Handbook of Research on Promotional Strategies and Consumer Influence in the Service Sector* (pp. 31–55). Hershey, PA: IGI Global. doi:10.4018/978-1-5225-0143-5.ch002

Dahlberg, T., Kivijärvi, H., & Saarinen, T. (2017). IT Investment Consistency and Other Factors Influencing the Success of IT Performance. In S. De Haes & W. Van Grembergen (Eds.), *Strategic IT Governance and Alignment in Business Settings* (pp. 176–208). Hershey, PA: IGI Global. doi:10.4018/978-1-5225-0861-8.ch007

Damnjanović, A. M. (2017). Knowledge Management Optimization through IT and E-Business Utilization: A Qualitative Study on Serbian SMEs. In M. Vemić (Ed.), *Optimal Management Strategies in Small and Medium Enterprises* (pp. 249–267). Hershey, PA: IGI Global. doi:10.4018/978-1-5225-1949-2.ch012

Daneshpour, H. (2017). Integrating Sustainable Development into Project Portfolio Management through Application of Open Innovation. In M. Vemić (Ed.), *Optimal Management Strategies in Small and Medium Enterprises* (pp. 370–387). Hershey, PA: IGI Global. doi:10.4018/978-1-5225-1949-2.ch017

Daniel, A. D., & Reis de Castro, V. (2018). Entrepreneurship Education: How to Measure the Impact on Nascent Entrepreneurs. In A. Carrizo Moreira, J. Guilherme Leitão Dantas, & F. Manuel Valente (Eds.), *Nascent Entrepreneurship and Successful New Venture Creation* (pp. 85–110). Hershey, PA: IGI Global. doi:10.4018/978-1-5225-2936-1.ch004

David, F., van der Sijde, P., & van den Besselaar, P. (2016). Enterpreneurial Incentives, Obstacles, and Management in University-Business Co-Operation: The Case of Indonesia. In J. Saiz-Álvarez (Ed.), *Handbook of Research on Social Entrepreneurship and Solidarity Economics* (pp. 499–518). Hershey, PA: IGI Global. doi:10.4018/978-1-5225-0097-1.ch024

David, R., Swami, B. N., & Tangirala, S. (2018). Ethics Impact on Knowledge Management in Organizational Development: A Case Study. In N. Baporikar (Ed.), *Global Practices in Knowledge Management for Societal and Organizational Development* (pp. 19–45). Hershey, PA: IGI Global. doi:10.4018/978-1-5225-3009-1.ch002

Delias, P., & Lakiotaki, K. (2018). Discovering Process Horizontal Boundaries to Facilitate Process Comprehension. *International Journal of Operations Research and Information Systems*, *9*(2), 1–31. doi:10.4018/IJORIS.2018040101

Denholm, J., & Lee-Davies, L. (2018). Success Factors for Games in Business and Project Management. In *Enhancing Education and Training Initiatives Through Serious Games* (pp. 34–68). Hershey, PA: IGI Global. doi:10.4018/978-1-5225-3689-5.ch002

Deshpande, M. (2017). Best Practices in Management Institutions for Global Leadership: Policy Aspects. In N. Baporikar (Ed.), *Management Education for Global Leadership* (pp. 1–27). Hershey, PA: IGI Global. doi:10.4018/978-1-5225-1013-0.ch001

Deshpande, M. (2018). Policy Perspectives for SMEs Knowledge Management. In N. Baporikar (Ed.), *Knowledge Integration Strategies for Entrepreneurship and Sustainability* (pp. 23–46). Hershey, PA: IGI Global. doi:10.4018/978-1-5225-5115-7.ch002

Dezdar, S. (2017). ERP Implementation Projects in Asian Countries: A Comparative Study on Iran and China. *International Journal of Information Technology Project Management*, *8*(3), 52–68. doi:10.4018/IJITPM.2017070104

Domingos, D., Martinho, R., & Varajão, J. (2016). Controlled Flexibility in Healthcare Processes: A BPMN-Extension Approach. In M. Cruz-Cunha, I. Miranda, R. Martinho, & R. Rijo (Eds.), *Encyclopedia of E-Health and Telemedicine* (pp. 521–535). Hershey, PA: IGI Global. doi:10.4018/978-1-4666-9978-6.ch040

Domingos, D., Respício, A., & Martinho, R. (2017). Reliability of IoT-Aware BPMN Healthcare Processes. In C. Reis & M. Maximiano (Eds.), *Internet of Things and Advanced Application in Healthcare* (pp. 214–248). Hershey, PA: IGI Global. doi:10.4018/978-1-5225-1820-4.ch008

Dosumu, O., Hussain, J., & El-Gohary, H. (2017). An Exploratory Study of the Impact of Government Policies on the Development of Small and Medium Enterprises in Developing Countries: The Case of Nigeria. *International Journal of Customer Relationship Marketing and Management*, *8*(4), 51–62. doi:10.4018/IJCRMM.2017100104

Durst, S., Bruns, G., & Edvardsson, I. R. (2017). Retaining Knowledge in Smaller Building and Construction Firms. *International Journal of Knowledge and Systems Science*, *8*(3), 1–12. doi:10.4018/IJKSS.2017070101

Edvardsson, I. R., & Durst, S. (2017). Outsourcing, Knowledge, and Learning: A Critical Review. *International Journal of Knowledge-Based Organizations*, *7*(2), 13–26. doi:10.4018/IJKBO.2017040102

Edwards, J. S. (2018). Integrating Knowledge Management and Business Processes. In M. Khosrow-Pour, D.B.A. (Ed.), Encyclopedia of Information Science and Technology, Fourth Edition (pp. 5046-5055). Hershey, PA: IGI Global. doi:10.4018/978-1-5225-2255-3.ch437

Ejiogu, A. O. (2018). Economics of Farm Management. In *Agricultural Finance and Opportunities for Investment and Expansion* (pp. 56–72). Hershey, PA: IGI Global. doi:10.4018/978-1-5225-3059-6.ch003

Ekanem, I., & Abiade, G. E. (2018). Factors Influencing the Use of E-Commerce by Small Enterprises in Nigeria. *International Journal of ICT Research in Africa and the Middle East*, *7*(1), 37–53. doi:10.4018/IJICTRAME.2018010103

Ekanem, I., & Alrossais, L. A. (2017). Succession Challenges Facing Family Businesses in Saudi Arabia. In P. Zgheib (Ed.), *Entrepreneurship and Business Innovation in the Middle East* (pp. 122–146). Hershey, PA: IGI Global. doi:10.4018/978-1-5225-2066-5.ch007

El Faquih, L., & Fredj, M. (2017). Ontology-Based Framework for Quality in Configurable Process Models. *Journal of Electronic Commerce in Organizations*, *15*(2), 48–60. doi:10.4018/JECO.2017040104

El-Gohary, H., & El-Gohary, Z. (2016). An Attempt to Explore Electronic Marketing Adoption and Implementation Aspects in Developing Countries: The Case of Egypt. *International Journal of Customer Relationship Marketing and Management*, *7*(4), 1–26. doi:10.4018/IJCRMM.2016100101

Entico, G. J. (2016). Knowledge Management and the Medical Health Librarians: A Perception Study. In J. Yap, M. Perez, M. Ayson, & G. Entico (Eds.), *Special Library Administration, Standardization and Technological Integration* (pp. 52–77). Hershey, PA: IGI Global. doi:10.4018/978-1-4666-9542-9.ch003

Faisal, M. N., & Talib, F. (2017). Building Ambidextrous Supply Chains in SMEs: How to Tackle the Barriers? *International Journal of Information Systems and Supply Chain Management, 10*(4), 80–100. doi:10.4018/IJISSCM.2017100105

Fernandes, T. M., Gomes, J., & Romão, M. (2017). Investments in E-Government: A Benefit Management Case Study. *International Journal of Electronic Government Research, 13*(3), 1–17. doi:10.4018/IJEGR.2017070101

Fouda, F. A. (2016). A Suggested Curriculum in Career Education to Develop Business Secondary Schools Students' Career Knowledge Management Domains and Professional Thinking. *International Journal of Technology Diffusion, 7*(2), 42–62. doi:10.4018/IJTD.2016040103

Gallardo-Vázquez, D., & Pajuelo-Moreno, M. L. (2016). How Spanish Universities are Promoting Entrepreneurship through Your Own Lines of Teaching and Research? In L. Carvalho (Ed.), *Handbook of Research on Entrepreneurial Success and its Impact on Regional Development* (pp. 431–454). Hershey, PA: IGI Global. doi:10.4018/978-1-4666-9567-2.ch019

Gao, S. S., Oreal, S., & Zhang, J. (2018). Contemporary Financial Risk Management Perceptions and Practices of Small-Sized Chinese Businesses. In I. Management Association (Ed.), Global Business Expansion: Concepts, Methodologies, Tools, and Applications (pp. 917-931). Hershey, PA: IGI Global. doi:10.4018/978-1-5225-5481-3.ch041

Garg, R., & Berning, S. C. (2017). Indigenous Chinese Management Philosophies: Key Concepts and Relevance for Modern Chinese Firms. In B. Christiansen & G. Koc (Eds.), *Transcontinental Strategies for Industrial Development and Economic Growth* (pp. 43–57). Hershey, PA: IGI Global. doi:10.4018/978-1-5225-2160-0.ch003

Gencer, Y. G. (2017). Supply Chain Management in Retailing Business. In U. Akkucuk (Ed.), *Ethics and Sustainability in Global Supply Chain Management* (pp. 197–210). Hershey, PA: IGI Global. doi:10.4018/978-1-5225-2036-8.ch011

Giacosa, E. (2016). Innovation in Luxury Fashion Businesses as a Means for the Regional Development. In L. Carvalho (Ed.), *Handbook of Research on Entrepreneurial Success and its Impact on Regional Development* (pp. 206–222). Hershey, PA: IGI Global. doi:10.4018/978-1-4666-9567-2.ch010

Giacosa, E. (2018). The Increasing of the Regional Development Thanks to the Luxury Business Innovation. In L. Carvalho (Ed.), *Handbook of Research on Entrepreneurial Ecosystems and Social Dynamics in a Globalized World* (pp. 260–273). Hershey, PA: IGI Global. doi:10.4018/978-1-5225-3525-6.ch011

Gianni, M., & Gotzamani, K. (2016). Integrated Management Systems and Information Management Systems: Common Threads. In P. Papajorgji, F. Pinet, A. Guimarães, & J. Papathanasiou (Eds.), *Automated Enterprise Systems for Maximizing Business Performance* (pp. 195–214). Hershey, PA: IGI Global. doi:10.4018/978-1-4666-8841-4.ch011

Gianni, M., Gotzamani, K., & Linden, I. (2016). How a BI-wise Responsible Integrated Management System May Support Food Traceability. *International Journal of Decision Support System Technology*, *8*(2), 1–17. doi:10.4018/IJDSST.2016040101

Glykas, M., & George, J. (2017). Quality and Process Management Systems in the UAE Maritime Industry. *International Journal of Productivity Management and Assessment Technologies*, *5*(1), 20–39. doi:10.4018/IJPMAT.2017010102

Glykas, M., Valiris, G., Kokkinaki, A., & Koutsoukou, Z. (2018). Banking Business Process Management Implementation. *International Journal of Productivity Management and Assessment Technologies*, *6*(1), 50–69. doi:10.4018/IJPMAT.2018010104

Gomes, J., & Romão, M. (2017). The Balanced Scorecard: Keeping Updated and Aligned with Today's Business Trends. *International Journal of Productivity Management and Assessment Technologies*, *5*(2), 1–15. doi:10.4018/IJPMAT.2017070101

Gomes, J., & Romão, M. (2017). Aligning Information Systems and Technology with Benefit Management and Balanced Scorecard. In S. De Haes & W. Van Grembergen (Eds.), *Strategic IT Governance and Alignment in Business Settings* (pp. 112–131). Hershey, PA: IGI Global. doi:10.4018/978-1-5225-0861-8.ch005

Grefen, P., & Turetken, O. (2017). Advanced Business Process Management in Networked E-Business Scenarios. *International Journal of E-Business Research*, *13*(4), 70–104. doi:10.4018/IJEBR.2017100105

Haider, A., & Saetang, S. (2017). Strategic IT Alignment in Service Sector. In S. Rozenes & Y. Cohen (Eds.), *Handbook of Research on Strategic Alliances and Value Co-Creation in the Service Industry* (pp. 231–258). Hershey, PA: IGI Global. doi:10.4018/978-1-5225-2084-9.ch012

Haider, A., & Tang, S. S. (2016). Maximising Value Through IT and Business Alignment: A Case of IT Governance Institutionalisation at a Thai Bank. *International Journal of Technology Diffusion*, *7*(3), 33–58. doi:10.4018/IJTD.2016070104

Hajilari, A. B., Ghadaksaz, M., & Fasghandis, G. S. (2017). Assessing Organizational Readiness for Implementing ERP System Using Fuzzy Expert System Approach. *International Journal of Enterprise Information Systems*, *13*(1), 67–85. doi:10.4018/IJEIS.2017010105

Haldorai, A., Ramu, A., & Murugan, S. (2018). Social Aware Cognitive Radio Networks: Effectiveness of Social Networks as a Strategic Tool for Organizational Business Management. In H. Bansal, G. Shrivastava, G. Nguyen, & L. Stanciu (Eds.), *Social Network Analytics for Contemporary Business Organizations* (pp. 188–202). Hershey, PA: IGI Global. doi:10.4018/978-1-5225-5097-6.ch010

Hall, O. P. Jr. (2017). Social Media Driven Management Education. *International Journal of Knowledge-Based Organizations*, *7*(2), 43–59. doi:10.4018/IJKBO.2017040104

Hanifah, H., Halim, H. A., Ahmad, N. H., & Vafaei-Zadeh, A. (2017). Innovation Culture as a Mediator Between Specific Human Capital and Innovation Performance Among Bumiputera SMEs in Malaysia. In N. Ahmad, T. Ramayah, H. Halim, & S. Rahman (Eds.), *Handbook of Research on Small and Medium Enterprises in Developing Countries* (pp. 261–279). Hershey, PA: IGI Global. doi:10.4018/978-1-5225-2165-5.ch012

Hartlieb, S., & Silvius, G. (2017). Handling Uncertainty in Project Management and Business Development: Similarities and Differences. In Y. Raydugin (Ed.), *Handbook of Research on Leveraging Risk and Uncertainties for Effective Project Management* (pp. 337–362). Hershey, PA: IGI Global. doi:10.4018/978-1-5225-1790-0.ch016

Hass, K. B. (2017). Living on the Edge: Managing Project Complexity. In Y. Raydugin (Ed.), *Handbook of Research on Leveraging Risk and Uncertainties for Effective Project Management* (pp. 177–201). Hershey, PA: IGI Global. doi:10.4018/978-1-5225-1790-0.ch009

Hassan, A., & Privitera, D. S. (2016). Google AdSense as a Mobile Technology in Education. In J. Holland (Ed.), *Wearable Technology and Mobile Innovations for Next-Generation Education* (pp. 200–223). Hershey, PA: IGI Global. doi:10.4018/978-1-5225-0069-8.ch011

Hassan, A., & Rahimi, R. (2016). Consuming "Innovation" in Tourism: Augmented Reality as an Innovation Tool in Digital Tourism Marketing. In N. Pappas & I. Bregoli (Eds.), *Global Dynamics in Travel, Tourism, and Hospitality* (pp. 130–147). Hershey, PA: IGI Global. doi:10.4018/978-1-5225-0201-2.ch008

Hawking, P., & Carmine Sellitto, C. (2017). Developing an Effective Strategy for Organizational Business Intelligence. In M. Tavana (Ed.), *Enterprise Information Systems and the Digitalization of Business Functions* (pp. 222–237). Hershey, PA: IGI Global. doi:10.4018/978-1-5225-2382-6.ch010

Hawking, P., & Sellitto, C. (2017). A Fast-Moving Consumer Goods Company and Business Intelligence Strategy Development. *International Journal of Enterprise Information Systems*, *13*(2), 22–33. doi:10.4018/IJEIS.2017040102

Hawking, P., & Sellitto, C. (2017). Business Intelligence Strategy: Two Case Studies. *International Journal of Business Intelligence Research*, *8*(2), 17–30. doi:10.4018/IJBIR.2017070102

Haynes, J. D., Arockiasamy, S., Al Rashdi, M., & Al Rashdi, S. (2016). Business and E Business Strategies for Coopetition and Thematic Management as a Sustained Basis for Ethics and Social Responsibility in Emerging Markets. In M. Al-Shammari & H. Masri (Eds.), *Ethical and Social Perspectives on Global Business Interaction in Emerging Markets* (pp. 25–39). Hershey, PA: IGI Global. doi:10.4018/978-1-4666-9864-2.ch002

Hee, W. J., Jalleh, G., Lai, H., & Lin, C. (2017). E-Commerce and IT Projects: Evaluation and Management Issues in Australian and Taiwanese Hospitals. *International Journal of Public Health Management and Ethics*, *2*(1), 69–90. doi:10.4018/IJPHME.2017010104

Hernandez, A. A. (2018). Exploring the Factors to Green IT Adoption of SMEs in the Philippines. *Journal of Cases on Information Technology*, *20*(2), 49–66. doi:10.4018/JCIT.2018040104

Hernandez, A. A., & Ona, S. E. (2016). Green IT Adoption: Lessons from the Philippines Business Process Outsourcing Industry. *International Journal of Social Ecology and Sustainable Development*, *7*(1), 1–34. doi:10.4018/IJSESD.2016010101

Hollman, A., Bickford, S., & Hollman, T. (2017). Cyber InSecurity: A Post-Mortem Attempt to Assess Cyber Problems from IT and Business Management Perspectives. *Journal of Cases on Information Technology*, *19*(3), 42–70. doi:10.4018/JCIT.2017070104

Igbinakhase, I. (2017). Responsible and Sustainable Management Practices in Developing and Developed Business Environments. In Z. Fields (Ed.), *Collective Creativity for Responsible and Sustainable Business Practice* (pp. 180–207). Hershey, PA: IGI Global. doi:10.4018/978-1-5225-1823-5.ch010

Ilahi, L., Ghannouchi, S. A., & Martinho, R. (2016). A Business Process Management Approach to Home Healthcare Processes: On the Gap between Intention and Reality. In M. Cruz-Cunha, I. Miranda, R. Martinho, & R. Rijo (Eds.), *Encyclopedia of E-Health and Telemedicine* (pp. 439–457). Hershey, PA: IGI Global. doi:10.4018/978-1-4666-9978-6.ch035

Iwata, J. J., & Hoskins, R. G. (2017). Managing Indigenous Knowledge in Tanzania: A Business Perspective. In P. Jain & N. Mnjama (Eds.), *Managing Knowledge Resources and Records in Modern Organizations* (pp. 198–214). Hershey, PA: IGI Global. doi:10.4018/978-1-5225-1965-2.ch012

Jabeen, F., Ahmad, S. Z., & Alkaabi, S. (2016). The Internationalization Decision-Making of United Arab Emirates Family Businesses. In N. Zakaria, A. Abdul-Talib, & N. Osman (Eds.), *Handbook of Research on Impacts of International Business and Political Affairs on the Global Economy* (pp. 1–22). Hershey, PA: IGI Global. doi:10.4018/978-1-4666-9806-2.ch001

Jain, P. (2017). Ethical and Legal Issues in Knowledge Management Life-Cycle in Business. In P. Jain & N. Mnjama (Eds.), *Managing Knowledge Resources and Records in Modern Organizations* (pp. 82–101). Hershey, PA: IGI Global. doi:10.4018/978-1-5225-1965-2.ch006

Jamali, D., Abdallah, H., & Matar, F. (2016). Opportunities and Challenges for CSR Mainstreaming in Business Schools. *International Journal of Technology and Educational Marketing*, *6*(2), 1–29. doi:10.4018/IJTEM.2016070101

James, S., & Hauli, E. (2017). Holistic Management Education at Tanzanian Rural Development Planning Institute. In N. Baporikar (Ed.), *Management Education for Global Leadership* (pp. 112–136). Hershey, PA: IGI Global. doi:10.4018/978-1-5225-1013-0.ch006

Janošková, M., Csikósová, A., & Čulková, K. (2018). Measurement of Company Performance as Part of Its Strategic Management. In R. Leon (Ed.), *Managerial Strategies for Business Sustainability During Turbulent Times* (pp. 309–335). Hershey, PA: IGI Global. doi:10.4018/978-1-5225-2716-9.ch017

Jean-Vasile, A., & Alecu, A. (2017). Theoretical and Practical Approaches in Understanding the Influences of Cost-Productivity-Profit Trinomial in Contemporary Enterprises. In A. Jean Vasile & D. Nicolò (Eds.), *Sustainable Entrepreneurship and Investments in the Green Economy* (pp. 28–62). Hershey, PA: IGI Global. doi:10.4018/978-1-5225-2075-7.ch002

Jha, D. G. (2016). Preparing for Information Technology Driven Changes. In S. Tiwari & L. Nafees (Eds.), *Innovative Management Education Pedagogies for Preparing Next-Generation Leaders* (pp. 258–274). Hershey, PA: IGI Global. doi:10.4018/978-1-4666-9691-4.ch015

Joia, L. A., & Correia, J. C. (2018). CIO Competencies From the IT Professional Perspective: Insights From Brazil. *Journal of Global Information Management*, *26*(2), 74–103. doi:10.4018/JGIM.2018040104

Juma, A., & Mzera, N. (2017). Knowledge Management and Records Management and Competitive Advantage in Business. In P. Jain & N. Mnjama (Eds.), *Managing Knowledge Resources and Records in Modern Organizations* (pp. 15–28). Hershey, PA: IGI Global. doi:10.4018/978-1-5225-1965-2.ch002

K., I., & A, V. (2018). Monitoring and Auditing in the Cloud. In K. Munir (Ed.), *Cloud Computing Technologies for Green Enterprises* (pp. 318-350). Hershey, PA: IGI Global. doi:10.4018/978-1-5225-3038-1.ch013

Kabra, G., Ghosh, V., & Ramesh, A. (2018). Enterprise Integrated Business Process Management and Business Intelligence Framework for Business Process Sustainability. In A. Paul, D. Bhattacharyya, & S. Anand (Eds.), *Green Initiatives for Business Sustainability and Value Creation* (pp. 228–238). Hershey, PA: IGI Global. doi:10.4018/978-1-5225-2662-9.ch010

Kaoud, M. (2017). Investigation of Customer Knowledge Management: A Case Study Research. *International Journal of Service Science, Management, Engineering, and Technology*, *8*(2), 12–22. doi:10.4018/IJSSMET.2017040102

Kara, M. E., & Fırat, S. Ü. (2016). Sustainability, Risk, and Business Intelligence in Supply Chains. In M. Erdoğdu, T. Arun, & I. Ahmad (Eds.), *Handbook of Research on Green Economic Development Initiatives and Strategies* (pp. 501–538). Hershey, PA: IGI Global. doi:10.4018/978-1-5225-0440-5.ch022

Katuu, S. (2018). A Comparative Assessment of Enterprise Content Management Maturity Models. In N. Gwangwava & M. Mutingi (Eds.), *E-Manufacturing and E-Service Strategies in Contemporary Organizations* (pp. 93–118). Hershey, PA: IGI Global. doi:10.4018/978-1-5225-3628-4.ch005

Khan, M. A. (2016). MNEs Management Strategies in Developing Countries: Establishing the Context. In M. Khan (Ed.), *Multinational Enterprise Management Strategies in Developing Countries* (pp. 1–33). Hershey, PA: IGI Global. doi:10.4018/978-1-5225-0276-0.ch001

Khan, M. A. (2016). Operational Approaches in Organizational Structure: A Case for MNEs in Developing Countries. In M. Khan (Ed.), *Multinational Enterprise Management Strategies in Developing Countries* (pp. 129–151). Hershey, PA: IGI Global. doi:10.4018/978-1-5225-0276-0.ch007

Kinnunen, S., Ylä-Kujala, A., Marttonen-Arola, S., Kärri, T., & Baglee, D. (2018). Internet of Things in Asset Management: Insights from Industrial Professionals and Academia. *International Journal of Service Science, Management, Engineering, and Technology*, *9*(2), 104–119. doi:10.4018/IJSSMET.2018040105

Klein, A. Z., Sabino de Freitas, A., Machado, L., Freitas, J. C. Jr, Graziola, P. G. Jr, & Schlemmer, E. (2017). Virtual Worlds Applications for Management Education. In L. Tomei (Ed.), *Exploring the New Era of Technology-Infused Education* (pp. 279–299). Hershey, PA: IGI Global. doi:10.4018/978-1-5225-1709-2.ch017

Kożuch, B., & Jabłoński, A. (2017). Adopting the Concept of Business Models in Public Management. In M. Lewandowski & B. Kożuch (Eds.), *Public Sector Entrepreneurship and the Integration of Innovative Business Models* (pp. 10–46). Hershey, PA: IGI Global. doi:10.4018/978-1-5225-2215-7.ch002

Kumar, J., Adhikary, A., & Jha, A. (2017). Small Active Investors' Perceptions and Preferences Towards Tax Saving Mutual Fund Schemes in Eastern India: An Empirical Note. *International Journal of Asian Business and Information Management*, *8*(2), 35–45. doi:10.4018/IJABIM.2017040103

Lassoued, Y., Bouzguenda, L., & Mahmoud, T. (2016). Context-Aware Business Process Versions Management. *International Journal of e-Collaboration*, *12*(3), 7–33. doi:10.4018/IJeC.2016070102

Lavassani, K. M., & Movahedi, B. (2017). Applications Driven Information Systems: Beyond Networks toward Business Ecosystems. *International Journal of Innovation in the Digital Economy*, *8*(1), 61–75. doi:10.4018/IJIDE.2017010104

Lazzareschi, V. H., & Brito, M. S. (2017). Strategic Information Management: Proposal of Business Project Model. In G. Jamil, A. Soares, & C. Pessoa (Eds.), *Handbook of Research on Information Management for Effective Logistics and Supply Chains* (pp. 59–88). Hershey, PA: IGI Global. doi:10.4018/978-1-5225-0973-8.ch004

Lederer, M., Kurz, M., & Lazarov, P. (2017). Usage and Suitability of Methods for Strategic Business Process Initiatives: A Multi Case Study Research. *International Journal of Productivity Management and Assessment Technologies*, *5*(1), 40–51. doi:10.4018/IJPMAT.2017010103

Lee, I. (2017). A Social Enterprise Business Model and a Case Study of Pacific Community Ventures (PCV). In V. Potocan, M. Üngan, & Z. Nedelko (Eds.), *Handbook of Research on Managerial Solutions in Non-Profit Organizations* (pp. 182–204). Hershey, PA: IGI Global. doi:10.4018/978-1-5225-0731-4.ch009

Lee, L. J., & Leu, J. (2016). Exploring the Effectiveness of IT Application and Value Method in the Innovation Performance of Enterprise. *International Journal of Enterprise Information Systems*, *12*(2), 47–65. doi:10.4018/IJEIS.2016040104

Lee, Y. (2016). Alignment Effect of Entrepreneurial Orientation and Marketing Orientation on Firm Performance. *International Journal of Customer Relationship Marketing and Management*, *7*(4), 58–69. doi:10.4018/IJCRMM.2016100104

Leon, L. A., Seal, K. C., Przasnyski, Z. H., & Wiedenman, I. (2017). Skills and Competencies Required for Jobs in Business Analytics: A Content Analysis of Job Advertisements Using Text Mining. *International Journal of Business Intelligence Research*, *8*(1), 1–25. doi:10.4018/IJBIR.2017010101

Leu, J., Lee, L. J., & Krischke, A. (2016). Value Engineering-Based Method for Implementing the ISO14001 System in the Green Supply Chains. *International Journal of Strategic Decision Sciences*, *7*(4), 1–20. doi:10.4018/IJSDS.2016100101

Levy, C. L., & Elias, N. I. (2017). SOHO Users' Perceptions of Reliability and Continuity of Cloud-Based Services. In M. Moore (Ed.), *Cybersecurity Breaches and Issues Surrounding Online Threat Protection* (pp. 248–287). Hershey, PA: IGI Global. doi:10.4018/978-1-5225-1941-6.ch011

Levy, M. (2018). Change Management Serving Knowledge Management and Organizational Development: Reflections and Review. In N. Baporikar (Ed.), *Global Practices in Knowledge Management for Societal and Organizational Development* (pp. 256–270). Hershey, PA: IGI Global. doi:10.4018/978-1-5225-3009-1.ch012

Lewandowski, M. (2017). Public Organizations and Business Model Innovation: The Role of Public Service Design. In M. Lewandowski & B. Kożuch (Eds.), *Public Sector Entrepreneurship and the Integration of Innovative Business Models* (pp. 47–72). Hershey, PA: IGI Global. doi:10.4018/978-1-5225-2215-7.ch003

Lhannaoui, H., Kabbaj, M. I., & Bakkoury, Z. (2017). A Survey of Risk-Aware Business Process Modelling. *International Journal of Risk and Contingency Management*, *6*(3), 14–26. doi:10.4018/IJRCM.2017070102

Li, J., Sun, W., Jiang, W., Yang, H., & Zhang, L. (2017). How the Nature of Exogenous Shocks and Crises Impact Company Performance?: The Effects of Industry Characteristics. *International Journal of Risk and Contingency Management*, *6*(4), 40–55. doi:10.4018/IJRCM.2017100103

Lu, C., & Liu, S. (2016). Cultural Tourism O2O Business Model Innovation-A Case Study of CTrip. *Journal of Electronic Commerce in Organizations*, *14*(2), 16–31. doi:10.4018/JECO.2016040102

Machen, B., Hosseini, M. R., Wood, A., & Bakhshi, J. (2016). An Investigation into using SAP-PS as a Multidimensional Project Control System (MPCS). *International Journal of Enterprise Information Systems*, *12*(2), 66–81. doi:10.4018/IJEIS.2016040105

Malega, P. (2017). Small and Medium Enterprises in the Slovak Republic: Status and Competitiveness of SMEs in the Global Markets and Possibilities of Optimization. In M. Vemić (Ed.), *Optimal Management Strategies in Small and Medium Enterprises* (pp. 102–124). Hershey, PA: IGI Global. doi:10.4018/978-1-5225-1949-2.ch006

Malewska, K. M. (2017). Intuition in Decision-Making on the Example of a Non-Profit Organization. In V. Potocan, M. Üngan, & Z. Nedelko (Eds.), *Handbook of Research on Managerial Solutions in Non-Profit Organizations* (pp. 378–399). Hershey, PA: IGI Global. doi:10.4018/978-1-5225-0731-4.ch018

Maroofi, F. (2017). Entrepreneurial Orientation and Organizational Learning Ability Analysis for Innovation and Firm Performance. In N. Baporikar (Ed.), *Innovation and Shifting Perspectives in Management Education* (pp. 144–165). Hershey, PA: IGI Global. doi:10.4018/978-1-5225-1019-2.ch007

Martins, P. V., & Zacarias, M. (2017). A Web-based Tool for Business Process Improvement. *International Journal of Web Portals*, *9*(2), 68–84. doi:10.4018/IJWP.2017070104

Matthies, B., & Coners, A. (2017). Exploring the Conceptual Nature of e-Business Projects. *Journal of Electronic Commerce in Organizations*, *15*(3), 33–63. doi:10.4018/JECO.2017070103

McKee, J. (2018). Architecture as a Tool to Solve Business Planning Problems. In M. Khosrow-Pour, D.B.A. (Ed.), Encyclopedia of Information Science and Technology, Fourth Edition (pp. 573-586). Hershey, PA: IGI Global. doi:10.4018/978-1-5225-2255-3.ch050

McMurray, A. J., Cross, J., & Caponecchia, C. (2018). The Risk Management Profession in Australia: Business Continuity Plan Practices. In N. Bajgoric (Ed.), *Always-On Enterprise Information Systems for Modern Organizations* (pp. 112–129). Hershey, PA: IGI Global. doi:10.4018/978-1-5225-3704-5.ch006

Meddah, I. H., & Belkadi, K. (2018). Mining Patterns Using Business Process Management. In R. Hamou (Ed.), *Handbook of Research on Biomimicry in Information Retrieval and Knowledge Management* (pp. 78–89). Hershey, PA: IGI Global. doi:10.4018/978-1-5225-3004-6.ch005

Mendes, L. (2017). TQM and Knowledge Management: An Integrated Approach Towards Tacit Knowledge Management. In D. Jaziri-Bouagina & G. Jamil (Eds.), *Handbook of Research on Tacit Knowledge Management for Organizational Success* (pp. 236–263). Hershey, PA: IGI Global. doi:10.4018/978-1-5225-2394-9.ch009

Mnjama, N. M. (2017). Preservation of Recorded Information in Public and Private Sector Organizations. In P. Jain & N. Mnjama (Eds.), *Managing Knowledge Resources and Records in Modern Organizations* (pp. 149–167). Hershey, PA: IGI Global. doi:10.4018/978-1-5225-1965-2.ch009

Mokoqama, M., & Fields, Z. (2017). Principles of Responsible Management Education (PRME): Call for Responsible Management Education. In Z. Fields (Ed.), *Collective Creativity for Responsible and Sustainable Business Practice* (pp. 229–241). Hershey, PA: IGI Global. doi:10.4018/978-1-5225-1823-5.ch012

Muniapan, B. (2017). Philosophy and Management: The Relevance of Vedanta in Management. In P. Ordóñez de Pablos (Ed.), *Managerial Strategies and Solutions for Business Success in Asia* (pp. 124–139). Hershey, PA: IGI Global. doi:10.4018/978-1-5225-1886-0.ch007

Muniapan, B., Gregory, M. L., & Ling, L. A. (2016). Marketing Education in Sarawak: Looking at It from the Employers' Viewpoint. In B. Smith & A. Porath (Eds.), *Global Perspectives on Contemporary Marketing Education* (pp. 112–130). Hershey, PA: IGI Global. doi:10.4018/978-1-4666-9784-3.ch008

Murad, S. E., & Dowaji, S. (2017). Using Value-Based Approach for Managing Cloud-Based Services. In A. Turuk, B. Sahoo, & S. Addya (Eds.), *Resource Management and Efficiency in Cloud Computing Environments* (pp. 33–60). Hershey, PA: IGI Global. doi:10.4018/978-1-5225-1721-4.ch002

Mutahar, A. M., Daud, N. M., Thurasamy, R., Isaac, O., & Abdulsalam, R. (2018). The Mediating of Perceived Usefulness and Perceived Ease of Use: The Case of Mobile Banking in Yemen. *International Journal of Technology Diffusion*, *9*(2), 21–40. doi:10.4018/IJTD.2018040102

Naidoo, V. (2017). E-Learning and Management Education at African Universities. In N. Baporikar (Ed.), *Management Education for Global Leadership* (pp. 181–201). Hershey, PA: IGI Global. doi:10.4018/978-1-5225-1013-0.ch009

Naidoo, V., & Igbinakhase, I. (2018). Opportunities and Challenges of Knowledge Retention in SMEs. In N. Baporikar (Ed.), *Knowledge Integration Strategies for Entrepreneurship and Sustainability* (pp. 70–94). Hershey, PA: IGI Global. doi:10.4018/978-1-5225-5115-7.ch004

Nayak, S., & Prabhu, N. (2017). Paradigm Shift in Management Education: Need for a Cross Functional Perspective. In N. Baporikar (Ed.), *Management Education for Global Leadership* (pp. 241–255). Hershey, PA: IGI Global. doi:10.4018/978-1-5225-1013-0.ch012

Ndede-Amadi, A. A. (2016). Student Interest in the IS Specialization as Predictor of the Success Potential of New Information Systems Programmes within the Schools of Business in Kenyan Public Universities. *International Journal of Information Systems and Social Change*, *7*(2), 63–79. doi:10.4018/IJISSC.2016040104

Nedelko, Z., & Potocan, V. (2016). Management Practices for Processes Optimization: Case of Slovenia. In G. Alor-Hernández, C. Sánchez-Ramírez, & J. García-Alcaraz (Eds.), *Handbook of Research on Managerial Strategies for Achieving Optimal Performance in Industrial Processes* (pp. 545–561). Hershey, PA: IGI Global. doi:10.4018/978-1-5225-0130-5.ch025

Nedelko, Z., & Potocan, V. (2017). Management Solutions in Non-Profit Organizations: Case of Slovenia. In V. Potocan, M. Üngan, & Z. Nedelko (Eds.), *Handbook of Research on Managerial Solutions in Non-Profit Organizations* (pp. 1–22). Hershey, PA: IGI Global. doi:10.4018/978-1-5225-0731-4.ch001

Nedelko, Z., & Potocan, V. (2017). Priority of Management Tools Utilization among Managers: International Comparison. In V. Wang (Ed.), *Encyclopedia of Strategic Leadership and Management* (pp. 1083–1094). Hershey, PA: IGI Global. doi:10.4018/978-1-5225-1049-9.ch075

Nedelko, Z., Raudeliūnienė, J., & Črešnar, R. (2018). Knowledge Dynamics in Supply Chain Management. In N. Baporikar (Ed.), *Knowledge Integration Strategies for Entrepreneurship and Sustainability* (pp. 150–166). Hershey, PA: IGI Global. doi:10.4018/978-1-5225-5115-7.ch008

Nguyen, H. T., & Hipsher, S. A. (2018). Innovation and Creativity Used by Private Sector Firms in a Resources-Constrained Environment. In S. Hipsher (Ed.), *Examining the Private Sector's Role in Wealth Creation and Poverty Reduction* (pp. 219–238). Hershey, PA: IGI Global. doi:10.4018/978-1-5225-3117-3.ch010

Nycz, M., & Półkowski, Z. (2016). Business Intelligence as a Modern IT Supporting Management of Local Government Units in Poland. *International Journal of Knowledge and Systems Science, 7*(4), 1–18. doi:10.4018/IJKSS.2016100101

Obaji, N. O., Senin, A. A., & Olugu, M. U. (2016). Supportive Government Policy as a Mechanism for Business Incubation Performance in Nigeria. *International Journal of Information Systems and Social Change, 7*(4), 52–66. doi:10.4018/IJISSC.2016100103

Obicci, P. A. (2017). Risk Sharing in a Partnership. In *Risk Management Strategies in Public-Private Partnerships* (pp. 115–152). Hershey, PA: IGI Global. doi:10.4018/978-1-5225-2503-5.ch004

Obidallah, W. J., & Raahemi, B. (2017). Managing Changes in Service Oriented Virtual Organizations: A Structural and Procedural Framework to Facilitate the Process of Change. *Journal of Electronic Commerce in Organizations, 15*(1), 59–83. doi:10.4018/JECO.2017010104

Ojasalo, J., & Ojasalo, K. (2016). Service Logic Business Model Canvas for Lean Development of SMEs and Start-Ups. In N. Baporikar (Ed.), *Handbook of Research on Entrepreneurship in the Contemporary Knowledge-Based Global Economy* (pp. 217–243). Hershey, PA: IGI Global. doi:10.4018/978-1-4666-8798-1.ch010

Ojo, O. (2017). Impact of Innovation on the Entrepreneurial Success in Selected Business Enterprises in South-West Nigeria. *International Journal of Innovation in the Digital Economy, 8*(2), 29–38. doi:10.4018/IJIDE.2017040103

Okdinawati, L., Simatupang, T. M., & Sunitiyoso, Y. (2017). Multi-Agent Reinforcement Learning for Value Co-Creation of Collaborative Transportation Management (CTM). *International Journal of Information Systems and Supply Chain Management, 10*(3), 84–95. doi:10.4018/IJISSCM.2017070105

Ortner, E., Mevius, M., Wiedmann, P., & Kurz, F. (2016). Design of Interactional Decision Support Applications for E-Participation in Smart Cities. *International Journal of Electronic Government Research, 12*(2), 18–38. doi:10.4018/IJEGR.2016040102

Pal, K. (2018). Building High Quality Big Data-Based Applications in Supply Chains. In A. Kumar & S. Saurav (Eds.), *Supply Chain Management Strategies and Risk Assessment in Retail Environments* (pp. 1–24). Hershey, PA: IGI Global. doi:10.4018/978-1-5225-3056-5.ch001

Palos-Sanchez, P. R., & Correia, M. B. (2018). Perspectives of the Adoption of Cloud Computing in the Tourism Sector. In J. Rodrigues, C. Ramos, P. Cardoso, & C. Henriques (Eds.), *Handbook of Research on Technological Developments for Cultural Heritage and eTourism Applications* (pp. 377–400). Hershey, PA: IGI Global. doi:10.4018/978-1-5225-2927-9.ch018

Parry, V. K., & Lind, M. L. (2016). Alignment of Business Strategy and Information Technology Considering Information Technology Governance, Project Portfolio Control, and Risk Management. *International Journal of Information Technology Project Management, 7*(4), 21–37. doi:10.4018/IJITPM.2016100102

Pashkova, N., Trujillo-Barrera, A., Apostolakis, G., Van Dijk, G., Drakos, P. D., & Baourakis, G. (2016). Business Management Models of Microfinance Institutions (MFIs) in Africa: A Study into Their Enabling Environments. *International Journal of Food and Beverage Manufacturing and Business Models, 1*(2), 63–82. doi:10.4018/IJFBMBM.2016070105

Patiño, B. E. (2017). New Generation Management by Convergence and Individual Identity: A Systemic and Human-Oriented Approach. In N. Baporikar (Ed.), *Innovation and Shifting Perspectives in Management Education* (pp. 119–143). Hershey, PA: IGI Global. doi:10.4018/978-1-5225-1019-2.ch006

Pawliczek, A., & Rössler, M. (2017). Knowledge of Management Tools and Systems in SMEs: Knowledge Transfer in Management. In A. Bencsik (Ed.), *Knowledge Management Initiatives and Strategies in Small and Medium Enterprises* (pp. 180–203). Hershey, PA: IGI Global. doi:10.4018/978-1-5225-1642-2.ch009

Pejic-Bach, M., Omazic, M. A., Aleksic, A., & Zoroja, J. (2018). Knowledge-Based Decision Making: A Multi-Case Analysis. In R. Leon (Ed.), *Managerial Strategies for Business Sustainability During Turbulent Times* (pp. 160–184). Hershey, PA: IGI Global. doi:10.4018/978-1-5225-2716-9.ch009

Perano, M., Hysa, X., & Calabrese, M. (2018). Strategic Planning, Cultural Context, and Business Continuity Management: Business Cases in the City of Shkoder. In A. Presenza & L. Sheehan (Eds.), *Geopolitics and Strategic Management in the Global Economy* (pp. 57–77). Hershey, PA: IGI Global. doi:10.4018/978-1-5225-2673-5.ch004

Pereira, R., Mira da Silva, M., & Lapão, L. V. (2017). IT Governance Maturity Patterns in Portuguese Healthcare. In S. De Haes & W. Van Grembergen (Eds.), *Strategic IT Governance and Alignment in Business Settings* (pp. 24–52). Hershey, PA: IGI Global. doi:10.4018/978-1-5225-0861-8.ch002

Perez-Uribe, R., & Ocampo-Guzman, D. (2016). Conflict within Colombian Family Owned SMEs: An Explosive Blend between Feelings and Business. In J. Saiz-Álvarez (Ed.), *Handbook of Research on Social Entrepreneurship and Solidarity Economics* (pp. 329–354). Hershey, PA: IGI Global. doi:10.4018/978-1-5225-0097-1.ch017

Pérez-Uribe, R. I., Torres, D. A., Jurado, S. P., & Prada, D. M. (2018). Cloud Tools for the Development of Project Management in SMEs. In R. Perez-Uribe, C. Salcedo-Perez, & D. Ocampo-Guzman (Eds.), *Handbook of Research on Intrapreneurship and Organizational Sustainability in SMEs* (pp. 95–120). Hershey, PA: IGI Global. doi:10.4018/978-1-5225-3543-0.ch005

Petrisor, I., & Cozmiuc, D. (2017). Global Supply Chain Management Organization at Siemens in the Advent of Industry 4.0. In L. Saglietto & C. Cezanne (Eds.), *Global Intermediation and Logistics Service Providers* (pp. 123–142). Hershey, PA: IGI Global. doi:10.4018/978-1-5225-2133-4.ch007

Pierce, J. M., Velliaris, D. M., & Edwards, J. (2017). A Living Case Study: A Journey Not a Destination. In N. Silton (Ed.), *Exploring the Benefits of Creativity in Education, Media, and the Arts* (pp. 158–178). Hershey, PA: IGI Global. doi:10.4018/978-1-5225-0504-4.ch008

Radosavljevic, M., & Andjelkovic, A. (2017). Multi-Criteria Decision Making Approach for Choosing Business Process for the Improvement: Upgrading of the Six Sigma Methodology. In J. Stanković, P. Delias, S. Marinković, & S. Rochhia (Eds.), *Tools and Techniques for Economic Decision Analysis* (pp. 225–247). Hershey, PA: IGI Global. doi:10.4018/978-1-5225-0959-2.ch011

Radovic, V. M. (2017). Corporate Sustainability and Responsibility and Disaster Risk Reduction: A Serbian Overview. In M. Camilleri (Ed.), *CSR 2.0 and the New Era of Corporate Citizenship* (pp. 147–164). Hershey, PA: IGI Global. doi:10.4018/978-1-5225-1842-6.ch008

Raghunath, K. M., Devi, S. L., & Patro, C. S. (2018). Impact of Risk Assessment Models on Risk Factors: A Holistic Outlook. In K. Strang, M. Korstanje, & N. Vajjhala (Eds.), *Research, Practices, and Innovations in Global Risk and Contingency Management* (pp. 134–153). Hershey, PA: IGI Global. doi:10.4018/978-1-5225-4754-9.ch008

Raman, A., & Goyal, D. P. (2017). Extending IMPLEMENT Framework for Enterprise Information Systems Implementation to Information System Innovation. In M. Tavana (Ed.), *Enterprise Information Systems and the Digitalization of Business Functions* (pp. 137–177). Hershey, PA: IGI Global. doi:10.4018/978-1-5225-2382-6.ch007

Rao, Y., & Zhang, Y. (2017). The Construction and Development of Academic Library Digital Special Subject Databases. In L. Ruan, Q. Zhu, & Y. Ye (Eds.), *Academic Library Development and Administration in China* (pp. 163–183). Hershey, PA: IGI Global. doi:10.4018/978-1-5225-0550-1.ch010

Ravasan, A. Z., Mohammadi, M. M., & Hamidi, H. (2018). An Investigation Into the Critical Success Factors of Implementing Information Technology Service Management Frameworks. In K. Jakobs (Ed.), *Corporate and Global Standardization Initiatives in Contemporary Society* (pp. 200–218). Hershey, PA: IGI Global. doi:10.4018/978-1-5225-5320-5.ch009

Renna, P., Izzo, C., & Romaniello, T. (2016). The Business Process Management Systems to Support Continuous Improvements. In W. Nuninger & J. Châtelet (Eds.), *Handbook of Research on Quality Assurance and Value Management in Higher Education* (pp. 237–256). Hershey, PA: IGI Global. doi:10.4018/978-1-5225-0024-7.ch009

Rezaie, S., Mirabedini, S. J., & Abtahi, A. (2018). Designing a Model for Implementation of Business Intelligence in the Banking Industry. *International Journal of Enterprise Information Systems, 14*(1), 77–103. doi:10.4018/IJEIS.2018010105

Riccò, R. (2016). Diversity Management: Bringing Equality, Equity, and Inclusion in the Workplace. In J. Prescott (Ed.), *Handbook of Research on Race, Gender, and the Fight for Equality* (pp. 335–359). Hershey, PA: IGI Global. doi:10.4018/978-1-5225-0047-6.ch015

Romano, L., Grimaldi, R., & Colasuonno, F. S. (2017). Demand Management as a Success Factor in Project Portfolio Management. In L. Romano (Ed.), *Project Portfolio Management Strategies for Effective Organizational Operations* (pp. 202–219). Hershey, PA: IGI Global. doi:10.4018/978-1-5225-2151-8.ch008

Rostek, K. B. (2016). Risk Management: Role and Importance in Business Organization. In D. Jakóbczak (Ed.), *Analyzing Risk through Probabilistic Modeling in Operations Research* (pp. 149–178). Hershey, PA: IGI Global. doi:10.4018/978-1-4666-9458-3.ch007

Rouhani, S., & Savoji, S. R. (2016). A Success Assessment Model for BI Tools Implementation: An Empirical Study of Banking Industry. *International Journal of Business Intelligence Research, 7*(1), 25–44. doi:10.4018/IJBIR.2016010103

Ruan, Z. (2016). A Corpus-Based Functional Analysis of Complex Nominal Groups in Written Business Discourse: The Case of "Business". *International Journal of Computer-Assisted Language Learning and Teaching*, *6*(2), 74–90. doi:10.4018/IJCALLT.2016040105

Ruhi, U. (2018). Towards an Interdisciplinary Socio-Technical Definition of Virtual Communities. In M. Khosrow-Pour, D.B.A. (Ed.), Encyclopedia of Information Science and Technology, Fourth Edition (pp. 4278-4295). Hershey, PA: IGI Global. doi:10.4018/978-1-5225-2255-3.ch371

Ryan, J., Doster, B., Daily, S., & Lewis, C. (2016). A Case Study Perspective for Balanced Perioperative Workflow Achievement through Data-Driven Process Improvement. *International Journal of Healthcare Information Systems and Informatics*, *11*(3), 19–41. doi:10.4018/IJHISI.2016070102

Safari, M. R., & Jiang, Q. (2018). The Theory and Practice of IT Governance Maturity and Strategies Alignment: Evidence From Banking Industry. *Journal of Global Information Management*, *26*(2), 127–146. doi:10.4018/JGIM.2018040106

Sahoo, J., Pati, B., & Mohanty, B. (2017). Knowledge Management as an Academic Discipline: An Assessment. In B. Gunjal (Ed.), *Managing Knowledge and Scholarly Assets in Academic Libraries* (pp. 99–126). Hershey, PA: IGI Global. doi:10.4018/978-1-5225-1741-2.ch005

Saini, D. (2017). Relevance of Teaching Values and Ethics in Management Education. In N. Baporikar (Ed.), *Management Education for Global Leadership* (pp. 90–111). Hershey, PA: IGI Global. doi:10.4018/978-1-5225-1013-0.ch005

Sambhanthan, A. (2017). Assessing and Benchmarking Sustainability in Organisations: An Integrated Conceptual Model. *International Journal of Systems and Service-Oriented Engineering*, *7*(4), 22–43. doi:10.4018/IJSSOE.2017100102

Sambhanthan, A., & Potdar, V. (2017). A Study of the Parameters Impacting Sustainability in Information Technology Organizations. *International Journal of Knowledge-Based Organizations*, *7*(3), 27–39. doi:10.4018/IJKBO.2017070103

Sánchez-Fernández, M. D., & Manríquez, M. R. (2018). The Entrepreneurial Spirit Based on Social Values: The Digital Generation. In P. Isaias & L. Carvalho (Eds.), *User Innovation and the Entrepreneurship Phenomenon in the Digital Economy* (pp. 173–193). Hershey, PA: IGI Global. doi:10.4018/978-1-5225-2826-5.ch009

Sanchez-Ruiz, L., & Blanco, B. (2017). Process Management for SMEs: Barriers, Enablers, and Benefits. In M. Vemić (Ed.), *Optimal Management Strategies in Small and Medium Enterprises* (pp. 293–319). Hershey, PA: IGI Global. doi:10.4018/978-1-5225-1949-2.ch014

Sanz, L. F., Gómez-Pérez, J., & Castillo-Martinez, A. (2018). Analysis of the European ICT Competence Frameworks. In V. Ahuja & S. Rathore (Eds.), *Multidisciplinary Perspectives on Human Capital and Information Technology Professionals* (pp. 225–245). Hershey, PA: IGI Global. doi:10.4018/978-1-5225-5297-0.ch012

Sarvepalli, A., & Godin, J. (2017). Business Process Management in the Classroom. *Journal of Cases on Information Technology, 19*(2), 17–28. doi:10.4018/JCIT.2017040102

Satpathy, B., & Muniapan, B. (2016). Ancient Wisdom for Transformational Leadership and Its Insights from the Bhagavad-Gita. In U. Aung & P. Ordoñez de Pablos (Eds.), *Managerial Strategies and Practice in the Asian Business Sector* (pp. 1–10). Hershey, PA: IGI Global. doi:10.4018/978-1-4666-9758-4.ch001

Saygili, E. E., Ozturkoglu, Y., & Kocakulah, M. C. (2017). End Users' Perceptions of Critical Success Factors in ERP Applications. *International Journal of Enterprise Information Systems, 13*(4), 58–75. doi:10.4018/IJEIS.2017100104

Saygili, E. E., & Saygili, A. T. (2017). Contemporary Issues in Enterprise Information Systems: A Critical Review of CSFs in ERP Implementations. In M. Tavana (Ed.), *Enterprise Information Systems and the Digitalization of Business Functions* (pp. 120–136). Hershey, PA: IGI Global. doi:10.4018/978-1-5225-2382-6.ch006

Seidenstricker, S., & Antonino, A. (2018). Business Model Innovation-Oriented Technology Management for Emergent Technologies. In M. Khosrow-Pour, D.B.A. (Ed.), Encyclopedia of Information Science and Technology, Fourth Edition (pp. 4560-4569). Hershey, PA: IGI Global. doi:10.4018/978-1-5225-2255-3.ch396

Senaratne, S., & Gunarathne, A. D. (2017). Excellence Perspective for Management Education from a Global Accountants' Hub in Asia. In N. Baporikar (Ed.), *Management Education for Global Leadership* (pp. 158–180). Hershey, PA: IGI Global. doi:10.4018/978-1-5225-1013-0.ch008

Sensuse, D. I., & Cahyaningsih, E. (2018). Knowledge Management Models: A Summative Review. *International Journal of Information Systems in the Service Sector, 10*(1), 71–100. doi:10.4018/IJISSS.2018010105

Sensuse, D. I., Wibowo, W. C., & Cahyaningsih, E. (2016). Indonesian Government Knowledge Management Model: A Theoretical Model. *Information Resources Management Journal, 29*(1), 91–108. doi:10.4018/irmj.2016010106

Seth, M., Goyal, D., & Kiran, R. (2017). Diminution of Impediments in Implementation of Supply Chain Management Information System for Enhancing its Effectiveness in Indian Automobile Industry. *Journal of Global Information Management, 25*(3), 1–20. doi:10.4018/JGIM.2017070101

Seyal, A. H., & Rahman, M. N. (2017). Investigating Impact of Inter-Organizational Factors in Measuring ERP Systems Success: Bruneian Perspectives. In M. Tavana (Ed.), *Enterprise Information Systems and the Digitalization of Business Functions* (pp. 178–204). Hershey, PA: IGI Global. doi:10.4018/978-1-5225-2382-6.ch008

Shaikh, A. A., & Karjaluoto, H. (2016). On Some Misconceptions Concerning Digital Banking and Alternative Delivery Channels. *International Journal of E-Business Research, 12*(3), 1–16. doi:10.4018/IJEBR.2016070101

Shams, S. M. (2016). Stakeholder Relationship Management in Online Business and Competitive Value Propositions: Evidence from the Sports Industry. *International Journal of Online Marketing, 6*(2), 1–17. doi:10.4018/IJOM.2016040101

Shamsuzzoha, A. (2016). Management of Risk and Resilience within Collaborative Business Network. In R. Addo-Tenkorang, J. Kantola, P. Helo, & A. Shamsuzzoha (Eds.), *Supply Chain Strategies and the Engineer-to-Order Approach* (pp. 143–159). Hershey, PA: IGI Global. doi:10.4018/978-1-5225-0021-6.ch008

Shaqrah, A. A. (2018). Analyzing Business Intelligence Systems Based on 7s Model of McKinsey. *International Journal of Business Intelligence Research, 9*(1), 53–63. doi:10.4018/IJBIR.2018010104

Sharma, A. J. (2017). Enhancing Sustainability through Experiential Learning in Management Education. In N. Baporikar (Ed.), *Management Education for Global Leadership* (pp. 256–274). Hershey, PA: IGI Global. doi:10.4018/978-1-5225-1013-0.ch013

Shetty, K. P. (2017). Responsible Global Leadership: Ethical Challenges in Management Education. In N. Baporikar (Ed.), *Innovation and Shifting Perspectives in Management Education* (pp. 194–223). Hershey, PA: IGI Global. doi:10.4018/978-1-5225-1019-2.ch009

Sinthupundaja, J., & Kohda, Y. (2017). Effects of Corporate Social Responsibility and Creating Shared Value on Sustainability. *International Journal of Sustainable Entrepreneurship and Corporate Social Responsibility*, *2*(1), 27–38. doi:10.4018/IJSECSR.2017010103

Škarica, I., & Hrgović, A. V. (2018). Implementation of Total Quality Management Principles in Public Health Institutes in the Republic of Croatia. *International Journal of Productivity Management and Assessment Technologies*, *6*(1), 1–16. doi:10.4018/IJPMAT.2018010101

Smuts, H., Kotzé, P., Van der Merwe, A., & Loock, M. (2017). Framework for Managing Shared Knowledge in an Information Systems Outsourcing Context. *International Journal of Knowledge Management*, *13*(4), 1–30. doi:10.4018/IJKM.2017100101

Soares, E. R., & Zaidan, F. H. (2016). Information Architecture and Business Modeling in Modern Organizations of Information Technology: Professional Career Plan in Organizations IT. In G. Jamil, J. Poças Rascão, F. Ribeiro, & A. Malheiro da Silva (Eds.), *Handbook of Research on Information Architecture and Management in Modern Organizations* (pp. 439–457). Hershey, PA: IGI Global. doi:10.4018/978-1-4666-8637-3.ch020

Sousa, M. J., Cruz, R., Dias, I., & Caracol, C. (2017). Information Management Systems in the Supply Chain. In G. Jamil, A. Soares, & C. Pessoa (Eds.), *Handbook of Research on Information Management for Effective Logistics and Supply Chains* (pp. 469–485). Hershey, PA: IGI Global. doi:10.4018/978-1-5225-0973-8.ch025

Spremic, M., Turulja, L., & Bajgoric, N. (2018). Two Approaches in Assessing Business Continuity Management Attitudes in the Organizational Context. In N. Bajgoric (Ed.), *Always-On Enterprise Information Systems for Modern Organizations* (pp. 159–183). Hershey, PA: IGI Global. doi:10.4018/978-1-5225-3704-5.ch008

Steenkamp, A. L. (2018). Some Insights in Computer Science and Information Technology. In *Examining the Changing Role of Supervision in Doctoral Research Projects: Emerging Research and Opportunities* (pp. 113–133). Hershey, PA: IGI Global. doi:10.4018/978-1-5225-2610-0.ch005

Studdard, N., Dawson, M., Burton, S. L., Jackson, N., Leonard, B., Quisenberry, W., & Rahim, E. (2016). Nurturing Social Entrepreneurship and Building Social Entrepreneurial Self-Efficacy: Focusing on Primary and Secondary Schooling to Develop Future Social Entrepreneurs. In Z. Fields (Ed.), *Incorporating Business Models and Strategies into Social Entrepreneurship* (pp. 154–175). Hershey, PA: IGI Global. doi:10.4018/978-1-4666-8748-6.ch010

Sun, Z. (2016). A Framework for Developing Management Intelligent Systems. *International Journal of Systems and Service-Oriented Engineering*, *6*(1), 37–53. doi:10.4018/IJSSOE.2016010103

Swami, B., & Mphele, G. T. (2016). Problems Preventing Growth of Small Entrepreneurs: A Case Study of a Few Small Entrepreneurs in Botswana Sub-Urban Areas. In N. Baporikar (Ed.), *Handbook of Research on Entrepreneurship in the Contemporary Knowledge-Based Global Economy* (pp. 479–508). Hershey, PA: IGI Global. doi:10.4018/978-1-4666-8798-1.ch020

Tabach, A., & Croteau, A. (2017). Configurations of Information Technology Governance Practices and Business Unit Performance. *International Journal of IT/Business Alignment and Governance*, *8*(2), 1–27. doi:10.4018/IJITBAG.2017070101

Talaue, G. M., & Iqbal, T. (2017). Assessment of e-Business Mode of Selected Private Universities in the Philippines and Pakistan. *International Journal of Online Marketing*, *7*(4), 63–77. doi:10.4018/IJOM.2017100105

Tam, G. C. (2017). Project Manager Sustainability Competence. In *Managerial Strategies and Green Solutions for Project Sustainability* (pp. 178–207). Hershey, PA: IGI Global. doi:10.4018/978-1-5225-2371-0.ch008

Tambo, T. (2018). Fashion Retail Innovation: About Context, Antecedents, and Outcome in Technological Change Projects. In I. Management Association (Ed.), Fashion and Textiles: Breakthroughs in Research and Practice (pp. 233-260). Hershey, PA: IGI Global. doi:10.4018/978-1-5225-3432-7.ch010

Tambo, T., & Mikkelsen, O. E. (2016). Fashion Supply Chain Optimization: Linking Make-to-Order Purchasing and B2B E-Commerce. In S. Joshi & R. Joshi (Eds.), *Designing and Implementing Global Supply Chain Management* (pp. 1–21). Hershey, PA: IGI Global. doi:10.4018/978-1-4666-9720-1.ch001

Tandon, K. (2016). Innovative Andragogy: The Paradigm Shift to Heutagogy. In S. Tiwari & L. Nafees (Eds.), *Innovative Management Education Pedagogies for Preparing Next-Generation Leaders* (pp. 238–257). Hershey, PA: IGI Global. doi:10.4018/978-1-4666-9691-4.ch014

Tantau, A. D., & Frăţilă, L. C. (2018). Information and Management System for Renewable Energy Business. In *Entrepreneurship and Business Development in the Renewable Energy Sector* (pp. 200–244). Hershey, PA: IGI Global. doi:10.4018/978-1-5225-3625-3.ch006

Teixeira, N., Pardal, P. N., & Rafael, B. G. (2018). Internationalization, Financial Performance, and Organizational Challenges: A Success Case in Portugal. In L. Carvalho (Ed.), *Handbook of Research on Entrepreneurial Ecosystems and Social Dynamics in a Globalized World* (pp. 379–423). Hershey, PA: IGI Global. doi:10.4018/978-1-5225-3525-6.ch017

Trad, A., & Kalpić, D. (2016). The E-Business Transformation Framework for E-Commerce Architecture-Modeling Projects. In I. Lee (Ed.), *Encyclopedia of E-Commerce Development, Implementation, and Management* (pp. 733–753). Hershey, PA: IGI Global. doi:10.4018/978-1-4666-9787-4.ch052

Trad, A., & Kalpić, D. (2016). The E-Business Transformation Framework for E-Commerce Control and Monitoring Pattern. In I. Lee (Ed.), *Encyclopedia of E-Commerce Development, Implementation, and Management* (pp. 754–777). Hershey, PA: IGI Global. doi:10.4018/978-1-4666-9787-4.ch053

Trad, A., & Kalpić, D. (2018). The Business Transformation Framework, Agile Project and Change Management. In M. Khosrow-Pour, D.B.A. (Ed.), Encyclopedia of Information Science and Technology, Fourth Edition (pp. 620-635). Hershey, PA: IGI Global. doi:10.4018/978-1-5225-2255-3.ch054

Trad, A., & Kalpić, D. (2018). The Business Transformation and Enterprise Architecture Framework: The Financial Engineering E-Risk Management and E-Law Integration. In B. Sergi, F. Fidanoski, M. Ziolo, & V. Naumovski (Eds.), *Regaining Global Stability After the Financial Crisis* (pp. 46–65). Hershey, PA: IGI Global. doi:10.4018/978-1-5225-4026-7.ch003

Turulja, L., & Bajgoric, N. (2018). Business Continuity and Information Systems: A Systematic Literature Review. In N. Bajgoric (Ed.), *Always-On Enterprise Information Systems for Modern Organizations* (pp. 60–87). Hershey, PA: IGI Global. doi:10.4018/978-1-5225-3704-5.ch004

van Wessel, R. M., de Vries, H. J., & Ribbers, P. M. (2016). Business Benefits through Company IT Standardization. In K. Jakobs (Ed.), *Effective Standardization Management in Corporate Settings* (pp. 34–53). Hershey, PA: IGI Global. doi:10.4018/978-1-4666-9737-9.ch003

Vargas-Hernández, J. G. (2017). Professional Integrity in Business Management Education. In N. Baporikar (Ed.), *Management Education for Global Leadership* (pp. 70–89). Hershey, PA: IGI Global. doi:10.4018/978-1-5225-1013-0.ch004

Vasista, T. G., & AlAbdullatif, A. M. (2017). Role of Electronic Customer Relationship Management in Demand Chain Management: A Predictive Analytic Approach. *International Journal of Information Systems and Supply Chain Management, 10*(1), 53–67. doi:10.4018/IJISSCM.2017010104

Vergidis, K. (2016). Rediscovering Business Processes: Definitions, Patterns, and Modelling Approaches. In P. Papajorgji, F. Pinet, A. Guimarães, & J. Papathanasiou (Eds.), *Automated Enterprise Systems for Maximizing Business Performance* (pp. 97–122). Hershey, PA: IGI Global. doi:10.4018/978-1-4666-8841-4.ch007

Vieru, D., & Bourdeau, S. (2017). Survival in the Digital Era: A Digital Competence-Based Multi-Case Study in the Canadian SME Clothing Industry. *International Journal of Social and Organizational Dynamics in IT, 6*(1), 17–34. doi:10.4018/IJSODIT.2017010102

Vijayan, G., & Kamarulzaman, N. H. (2017). An Introduction to Sustainable Supply Chain Management and Business Implications. In M. Khan, M. Hussain, & M. Ajmal (Eds.), *Green Supply Chain Management for Sustainable Business Practice* (pp. 27–50). Hershey, PA: IGI Global. doi:10.4018/978-1-5225-0635-5.ch002

Vlachvei, A., & Notta, O. (2017). Firm Competitiveness: Theories, Evidence, and Measurement. In A. Vlachvei, O. Notta, K. Karantininis, & N. Tsounis (Eds.), *Factors Affecting Firm Competitiveness and Performance in the Modern Business World* (pp. 1–42). Hershey, PA: IGI Global. doi:10.4018/978-1-5225-0843-4.ch001

von Rosing, M., Fullington, N., & Walker, J. (2016). Using the Business Ontology and Enterprise Standards to Transform Three Leading Organizations. *International Journal of Conceptual Structures and Smart Applications, 4*(1), 71–99. doi:10.4018/IJCSSA.2016010104

von Rosing, M., & von Scheel, H. (2016). Using the Business Ontology to Develop Enterprise Standards. *International Journal of Conceptual Structures and Smart Applications, 4*(1), 48–70. doi:10.4018/IJCSSA.2016010103

Walczak, S. (2016). Artificial Neural Networks and other AI Applications for Business Management Decision Support. *International Journal of Sociotechnology and Knowledge Development, 8*(4), 1–20. doi:10.4018/IJSKD.2016100101

Wamba, S. F., Akter, S., Kang, H., Bhattacharya, M., & Upal, M. (2016). The Primer of Social Media Analytics. *Journal of Organizational and End User Computing, 28*(2), 1–12. doi:10.4018/JOEUC.2016040101

Wang, C., Schofield, M., Li, X., & Ou, X. (2017). Do Chinese Students in Public and Private Higher Education Institutes Perform at Different Level in One of the Leadership Skills: Critical Thinking?: An Exploratory Comparison. In V. Wang (Ed.), *Encyclopedia of Strategic Leadership and Management* (pp. 160–181). Hershey, PA: IGI Global. doi:10.4018/978-1-5225-1049-9.ch013

Wang, F., Raisinghani, M. S., Mora, M., & Wang, X. (2016). Strategic E-Business Management through a Balanced Scored Card Approach. In I. Lee (Ed.), *Encyclopedia of E-Commerce Development, Implementation, and Management* (pp. 361–386). Hershey, PA: IGI Global. doi:10.4018/978-1-4666-9787-4.ch027

Wang, J. (2017). Multi-Agent based Production Management Decision System Modelling for the Textile Enterprise. *Journal of Global Information Management*, *25*(4), 1–15. doi:10.4018/JGIM.2017100101

Wiedemann, A., & Gewald, H. (2017). Examining Cross-Domain Alignment: The Correlation of Business Strategy, IT Management, and IT Business Value. *International Journal of IT/Business Alignment and Governance*, *8*(1), 17–31. doi:10.4018/IJITBAG.2017010102

Wolf, R., & Thiel, M. (2018). Advancing Global Business Ethics in China: Reducing Poverty Through Human and Social Welfare. In S. Hipsher (Ed.), *Examining the Private Sector's Role in Wealth Creation and Poverty Reduction* (pp. 67–84). Hershey, PA: IGI Global. doi:10.4018/978-1-5225-3117-3.ch004

Wu, J., Ding, F., Xu, M., Mo, Z., & Jin, A. (2016). Investigating the Determinants of Decision-Making on Adoption of Public Cloud Computing in E-government. *Journal of Global Information Management*, *24*(3), 71–89. doi:10.4018/JGIM.2016070104

Xu, L., & de Vrieze, P. (2016). Building Situational Applications for Virtual Enterprises. In I. Lee (Ed.), *Encyclopedia of E-Commerce Development, Implementation, and Management* (pp. 715–724). Hershey, PA: IGI Global. doi:10.4018/978-1-4666-9787-4.ch050

Yablonsky, S. (2018). Innovation Platforms: Data and Analytics Platforms. In *Multi-Sided Platforms (MSPs) and Sharing Strategies in the Digital Economy: Emerging Research and Opportunities* (pp. 72–95). Hershey, PA: IGI Global. doi:10.4018/978-1-5225-5457-8.ch003

Yusoff, A., Ahmad, N. H., & Halim, H. A. (2017). Agropreneurship among Gen Y in Malaysia: The Role of Academic Institutions. In N. Ahmad, T. Ramayah, H. Halim, & S. Rahman (Eds.), *Handbook of Research on Small and Medium Enterprises in Developing Countries* (pp. 23–47). Hershey, PA: IGI Global. doi:10.4018/978-1-5225-2165-5.ch002

Zanin, F., Comuzzi, E., & Costantini, A. (2018). The Effect of Business Strategy and Stock Market Listing on the Use of Risk Assessment Tools. In *Management Control Systems in Complex Settings: Emerging Research and Opportunities* (pp. 145–168). Hershey, PA: IGI Global. doi:10.4018/978-1-5225-3987-2.ch007

Zgheib, P. W. (2017). Corporate Innovation and Intrapreneurship in the Middle East. In P. Zgheib (Ed.), *Entrepreneurship and Business Innovation in the Middle East* (pp. 37–56). Hershey, PA: IGI Global. doi:10.4018/978-1-5225-2066-5.ch003

About the Contributors

Xenia Ziouvelou is an innovation officer and researcher at the Software and Knowledge Engineering Lab of the Institute of the Institute of Informatics and Telecommunications (IIT) of NCSR "Demokritos" (NCSRD). She is a visiting academic at the Business School of the University of Southampton (UK) and acts as an external innovation expert for the European Commission. Xenia is a Sectorial Committee Member on Data and AI (Artificial Intelligence) Policy, at the National Council for Research, Technology & Innovation in Greece. Her principal research interests are in innovation, strategy and technological transformation and the way that they revolutionise business, law and policy.

Frank McGroarty is Professor of Computational Finance and Investment Analytics, and Director of the Centre for Digital Finance at the University of Southampton, UK. His research mainly resides in the intersection of Business and Computer Science and is primarily motivated by real world commercial and policy issues. Prior to joining the University of Southampton, Frank spent 13 years working as a fund manager in London.

* * *

Petri Ahokangas is a senior research fellow and leader of FUTURALIS research group at Martti Ahtisaari Institute, Oulu Business School, University of Oulu, Finland. FUTURALIS focuses on future digital business models and ecosystems. He is also an adjunct professor of international software entrepreneurship at the University of Oulu. His research interests are in how innovation and technological change affect the international business creation, transformation, and strategies in highly technology-intensive or software-intensive business domains. He is co-editor-in-chief of Journal or Business Models, and he has over 170 publications in scientific journals, books, conference proceedings, and other reports. He is actively working in several ICT-focused research consortia leading the business research activities.

Prior to his academic career, he worked in the telecommunications software industry. He is also a serial entrepreneur and active consultant in the field on digitalization, strategy and internationalization.

Charilaos Akasiadis holds a PhD degree at Electrical and Computer Engineering (Technical University of Crete, 2017). He also received an M.Sc. in Electrical and Computer Engineering at the same institution (2013), and completed his undergraduate studies as a Computer Engineer in the Computer Engineering and Informatics Department at the University of Patras in 2011. He currently works as a postdoctoral researcher at N.C.S.R. "Demokritos". His research topics include Mechanism Design, Multiagent Learning methods, Internet of Things, Blockchain technology, and Artificial Intelligence with applications to the Smart Grid. Member of the Hellenic Artificial Intelligence Society (EETN) and of the Technical Chamber of Greece (TEE).

Hj Mohammad Nabil Almunawar is currently an associate professor at the School of Business and Economics, Universiti of Brunei Darussalam (UBDSBE), Brunei Darussalam. He received his bachelor's degree in 1983 from Bogor Agricultural University, Indonesia, master's degree (MSc) from the Department of Computer Science, University of Western Ontario, London, Canada in 1991, and Ph.D. from the University of New South Wales in 1998. Dr. Almunawar has published more than 100 papers in refereed journals, books, book chapters, and international conference proceedings. He has more than 30 years of teaching experience in the area of information systems. His overall research interests include applications of IT in management, e-business/commerce, digital marketplace/platform, digital business ecosystem, health informatics, information security, and cloud computing. Currently, he focuses his research on digital platform and digital business ecosystem.

Amritesh is presently working as Assistant Professor (Services Marketing Area) at IIT Ropar. Prior to that, he has held positions as Assistant Professor (Marketing Management) at BITS Pilani Dubai Campus and Senior Researcher in a European research project OPAALS. He has completed his Ph.D. from IIT Kanpur, India. His research articles have appeared in reputed international journals and his top three areas of research interest include Transformative Services, Consumer Research, and Online Marketing.

Muhammad Anshari is researcher and academic staff at School of Business & Economics, Universiti Brunei Darussalam. His professional experience started when he was IT Business Analyst at Astra International. Research Fellowship from The Government Republic of China (Taiwan) at National Taiwan University (Jan-Dec,

2014). Research Fellowship from King Saud University - the Kingdom of Saudi Arabia 2009. Senior Associate Researcher of Informatics Department, Universitas Islam Negeri Yogyakarta, Indonesia.

Marcos de Sousa works as a bioinformatics researcher at the Laboratory of Molecular Biology at Museu Paraense Emílio Goeldi (MPEG), and professor at the University Center of the State of Pará (CESUPA). His contributions include works that highlight research in biological database modeling, software development for bioinformatics and computational reproducibility. Your research interests include: Database of Biodiversity, Bioinformatics and Computational Reproducibility. ORCID: 0000-0002-3379-4754.

Helio Aisenberg Ferenhof Doctor in Production Engineering from Federal University of Santa Catarina, UFSC. He has a Master's degree in Knowledge Management from UFSC. MBA in E-Business from FGV / RJ; Specialist in Didactics for Higher Education from SENAC/SC; Bachelor's degree in Computer Science from UNESA; Bachelor's degree in Business Administration from Faculdade UniBF. Was a Visiting Professor at Post Graduation Program of Communication and Information Technology (PPGTIC) at the Federal University of Santa Catarina (UFSC) Campus Araranguá. Actually, he is contributing as Project Manager at Secretaria de Admnistração do Estado de Santa Catarina. Also, is an associate member of the research group Knowledge and Innovation Management (KIM) at the School of Business at University of Skövde and Product, Process and Service Engineering Group (GEPPS) / UFSC. His research areas include knowledge management, innovation, intellectual capital, project management, service management, product development and computer science. Before joining academia, he worked as system developer, system analyst, project manager and consultant in different industries. In 2010 received a prize of innovation from Nancy-Université -INPL, "Prix d`innovation - à l'évenément international - 48H pour faire émerger des idées". https://orcid.org/0000-0001-5167-0838

Marika Iivari (Econ. & Bus. Admin) has been a Postdoctoral Researcher within Martti Ahtisaari Institute at Oulu Business School, and is member of the FUTURALIS (Future Digital Business) research group. She defended her doctoral dissertation on business models, open innovation and ecosystems in 2016, and is one of the first researchers to study the concept of ecosystemic business models. She has been involved in several R&D&I projects within various industrial domains, such as healthcare, industrial internet and the ICT industry. In addition to business models and ecosystems, her research interests include digitalization, demand-driven co-creation, innovation collaboration, knowledge management and data-driven decision making. She worked as a business model expert for the European Union Digital Transition Partnership in 2017-2018.

Faidon Komisopoulos is a lecturer at University of West Attica in Greece. He has studied Business Administration and Computer Science. Obtained his MBA from "Haute Ecole Groupe ICHEC - ISC St Louis". His PHD thesis was on "Creation of a Model for Estimating and Managing an Organisation's Capability to Innovate, using the Innovation Management Techniques" (University of Piraeus 2011). Right now, he is lecturing on "Strategic management" and "Innovation and Entrepreneurship". He has published more than 10 Papers and Publications over the 4 past years. A lot of research activities, consulting, and adult training programmes. Former commercial director in multinational company with adequate managerial experience.

Masairol Haji Masri earned his Ph.D. in Business Administration from Manchester Business School, University of Manchester, UK. He did his Master in Business Administration in 2002 at International Islamic University, Malaysia. At the moment, he is the Deputy Dean of Academic and Administration at the School of Business and Economics, Universiti Brunei Darussalam. He is currently a member of the Brunei Darussalam Public Accountant Oversight committee (PAOC) under Ministry of Finance.

Marja Matinmikko-Blue received the Dr.Sc. (Tech.) degree in telecommunications engineering from the University of Oulu on cognitive radio techniques and the Ph.D. degree in industrial engineering and management on stakeholder analysis for spectrum sharing. She was with the VTT Technical Research Centre of Finland, Ltd., from 2001 to 2015. She is a Senior Research Fellow with the Centre for Wireless Communications, University of Oulu. From 2016 to 2018, she managed uO5G project that proposed a new micro operator concept. She is currently a Research Coordinator 6G Flagship – Finnish Wireless Flagship from 2018 to 2026. She conducts interdisciplinary research on future mobile communication networks from business, technical, and regulatory perspective in close collaboration with industry, academia, and regulators. She has published over 120 scientific papers and prepared 100 contributions to spectrum regulatory forums in Europe (CEPT) and globally (ITU).

Sumit Saxena is a Research Scholar in the dept. of Humanities & Social Sciences, IIT Ropar (India) specifically working in Healthcare Service Management. Prior to joining the doctoral program, he has worked in the Pharmaceutical Industry for a few years and has been associated with Multinational firms like Johnson & Johnson

(Consumer Division). He also served as a Marketing Faculty in ICFAI Business School Dehradun, India. His core areas of interest include Services Marketing, Value co-creation, Service Innovation, Role of ICT in healthcare, and Consumer research in healthcare.

Seppo Yrjölä is Principal Engineer at Nokia Enterprise and have been with Nokia for 30 years. He incubates and steers opportunities externally with customers, partners and governments with the purpose of driving growth by innovating holistically from technology to business models. Previously as head of wireless technology for the Networks division, his role required to look beyond the product roadmap and identify what new trends, technologies and tools were on the horizon, and determine and validate how those future opportunities fit into the Nokia pipeline. Seppo holds a Doctoral degree in telecommunications from the University of Oulu and is Professor of Practice at the Faculty of Information Technology and Electrical Engineering, University of Oulu in the field of techno-economics of future wireless communications services and networks. His current research is focused on to explore how and why platform-based ecosystemic business models can emerge in the future wireless systems context.

Index

www.ingramcontent.com/pod-product-compliance
Lightning Source LLC
LaVergne TN
LVHW061535290926
849162LV00004B/803